PADI®
Open Water
Diver Manual

PADI®

PADI®
Open Water
Diver Manual

Published by PADI, P.O. Box 25011
Santa Ana, CA 92799-5011
ISBN 1-878 663-16-X

Printed in the United States of America

Version 1.0

PRODUCT NO. 70009N
With Recreational Dive Planner — The Wheel

PRODUCT NO. 70011N
With Recreational Dive Planner (table version)

PADI®
Open Water Diver Manual

Acknowledgments

Development, Consultation and Review
Al Hornsby, Drew Richardson, CK Stewart

Editor In Chief
Drew Richardson

Technical Writers
Karl Shreeves, Bob Wohlers

Instructional Designer
Bob Wohlers

Associate Editors
Mary Ellen Hurrell, Beth Kneeland, Tonya Talley

Contributing Writers
Alex Brylske, Ralph Erickson

Design and Production
Greg Beatty, Jean Kester, Joy Zuehls

Illustrations
Harry Averill, Greg Beatty, Joe De La Torre

Photography
Frank Palazzi

Additional Photography
Greg Beatty, Al Hornsby, Jeff Mondle, Drew Richardson,
Karl Shreeves, Bob Wohlers

Typography
Jeanne Jenkins, Dail Schroeder

Cover Design
Joe De La Torre

Contents

One

1   Introduction
6   The Underwater World
21   Diving Equipment
35   Scuba Systems
47   The Buddy System
49   Confined-Water Training Preview

Knowledge Review

Two

69   Adapting to the Underwater World
75   Respiration
78   Diving Equipment
101   Diving Communications
105   Buddy System Procedures
107   Confined-Water Training Preview

Knowledge Review

Three

119   The Diving Environment
141   Dive Planning
144   Boat-Diving Procedures
148   Problem Management
158   Confined-Water Training Preview
167   General Open-Water Skills
174   Open-Water Training Preview — Dives 1-3

Knowledge Review

Four

177	Accessory Diving Equipment
185	Health for Diving
187	Breathing Air at Depth
195	Dive Tables Introduction
200	Using the Recreational Dive Planner (table version)
214	Confined-Water Training Preview
	Knowledge Review

Five

223	Recreational Dive Planner Special Circumstances
229	Finding Minimum Surface Interval on the Recreational Dive Planner (table version)
233	Dive Tables Definitions Review
235	Basic Compass Navigation
239	Confined-Water Training Preview
245	Open-Water Training Preview — Dives 4-5
247	Continuing Education
254	Epilogue
255	Summary of Diving Safety Practices
	Knowledge Review
259	Appendix
269	Index

The Wheel

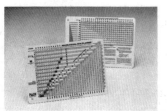

The Recreational Dive Planner, table version

About the Recreational Dive Planner

This book comes packaged with the Recreational Diver Planner in either The Wheel or table version. Your instructor will tell you which version you'll be learning to use as part of this course.

In Modules Four and Five, this manual contains the information and procedures to be followed when using either version. If you're learning to use the table version, you'll find specific instructions for using it in this manual. If you're learning to use The Wheel, you'll be using the "Instructions For Use" booklet included with The Wheel, or watching PADI's wheel training video "Diving With The Wheel."

Use of This Book

The Open Water Diver course is divided into five modules. This book is divided into one chapter for each module. Each chapter elaborates on the knowledge and skills you'll be developing as you progress through the course.

Within each chapter, knowledge and skill objectives are stated at the head of each topic. These objectives tell you exactly what you need to know and be able to do to successfully complete the module.

As you read each knowledge objective, try to rephrase it into a question. For example, if the objective reads: "By the end of this section, you will be able to name the two pieces of equipment a diver commonly uses to control his buoyancy," ask yourself, "What are the two pieces of equipment a diver uses to control his buoyancy?" Making questions out of each of the objectives helps you learn quickly and easily.

After reading the objectives, study the material within each section. Special exercises have been placed throughout the book, allowing you to assess your comprehension of the material. The exercises require an immediate response that is to be marked directly in your book. Once an answer or answers has been chosen, compare it with the correct answer(s) provided. Reviewing the correct answer will provide you with immediate feedback on your performance. If your answer was incorrect, reread the related material.

Knowledge Reviews are placed at the end of each module. You are expected to read the appropriate chapter for each module and complete the Knowledge Review before attending that module's academic training session. Be prepared to hand the Knowledge Review in to your instructor before class begins.

During the academic training sessions, your instructor will review and discuss the key points in each module. If you still have any questions, be sure to have your instructor answer them. Your instructor will be glad to work with you until you understand the material.

About This Book And The Open Water Diver Course

The PADI *Open Water Diver Manual* is an easy book to use and read. By reading the book and completing your course, you will learn everything you need to know to become a safe Open Water Diver. In fact, by using the PADI *Open Water Diver Manual* during an Open Water Diver course, your instructor may offer you the opportunity to receive college credit upon completion of your course. The American Council on Education (ACE) has determined that PADI's Open Water Diver course meets the educational standards and requirements for credit at the college level.

As complete as the PADI *Open Water Diver Manual* is, you may want to further explore topics that interest you. To guide you in your effort, look for the "open book" symbol. This symbol will direct you to further reading.

One

☐ **Introduction**
☐ **The Underwater World**
☐ **Diving Equipment**
☐ **The Buddy System**
☐ **Confined-Water Training Preview**

Introduction

Welcome to the course! You're about to experience the excitement and adventure of inner space — the underwater realm. As a scuba diver, you will come to know diverse wildlife in astounding abundance and discover a world of rapturous beauty. Oceans, rivers, seas, lakes and quarries hold submerged habitats that will capture your interest and imagination for a lifetime.

This course, the PADI Open Water Diver course, will provide you with the knowledge and skills you'll need to safely visit the underwater world. You'll have fun as your instructor prepares you for the excitement of entry-level diving activities in your local area. As you gain experience and your interests grow, your instructor can help you with additional training for special diving activities. Your instructor will also tell you how you can get the necessary orientation to diving in new areas. As a PADI Open Water Diver,

your fun has just begun.

Although you may have seen films or photos of the underwater world, you are about to discover that it is quite impossible for a nondiver to fully understand what diving is like. Besides seeing beautiful and fascinating aquatic creatures firsthand, you'll experience sensations unique to diving, like the thrill of breathing under water for the first time and the feeling of floating weightless, like an astronaut in space. As you gain diving experience, the mystery diving holds for you now will be replaced by curiosity, excitement and adventure.

With the proper equipment, knowledge and skills, diving is both safe and easy. You can explore some aquatic environments with little more than a mask, snorkel and a pair of fins as a skin diver (also called a "free diver"), or you can make deeper, longer visits with the use of scuba (**s**elf-**c**ontained **u**nderwater **b**reathing **a**pparatus) equipment.

Figure 1-1
As you gain diving experience, the mystery diving holds for you now will be replaced by curiosity, excitement and adventure.

Figure 1-2
Left to right: skin diver and scuba diver.

This course will make you comfortable with the equipment you need and will ensure that you develop the knowledge and skills necessary for safe and enjoyable diving. Most people easily meet the prerequisites for this course. Physically, you should be a reasonably proficient swimmer who is comfortable and relaxed in the water. Mentally, you need a mature attitude, good judgment and self-discipline. Your overall health should be good, particularly your circulatory and respiratory systems.

This course is only the beginning of what diving offers. You will want to continue your diving education after you complete this course as you discover new opportunities for fun in advanced experiences and specialized diving skills. Through the progressive PADI System of continuing diver education, you will find that courses on topics, such as underwater photography, wreck diving, deep diving and night diving open the doors to broader enjoyment and adventure.

Certification

Upon successful completion of this course, you will be awarded either the PADI Open Water Diver certification card (minimum age 15 years) or the PADI Junior Open Water Diver certification card (minimum age 12 years). Either credential attests to your completion of training and your ability to meet the standard requirements established by PADI. Professional dive store personnel, boat operators and other professionals in diving will ask to see your certification card before they will allow you to rent or buy scuba equipment, obtain air for your scuba tanks or participate in diving activities.

Figure 1-3
Your PADI certification card and emblem show you've completed your training. You'll need your C-card when you rent or buy scuba equipment, obtain air for your tank or participate in diving activities.

What is PADI?

PADI (Professional Association of Diving Instructors) is the world's largest diver-training organization. PADI establishes standards for diver training, trains and certifies instructors, provides support materials and services to its members, and maintains training activity records. Because PADI has the most complete and widely recognized diver-training programs, you can be confident that you are earning the finest and most respected diver credentials available.

Course Overview

The PADI Open Water Diver course is divided into three segments: Academic training, confined-water training and open-water training. Academic training gives you the basic principles and knowledge you need for safe and enjoyable diving. Academic training takes place as you use this text and attend the classroom sessions. Confined-water training

Figure 1-4
The PADI Open Water Diver
course is divided into three
segments: Academic training,...

Figure 1-5
...confined-water training and...

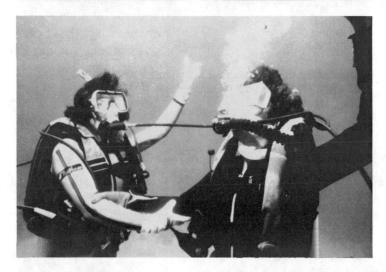

Figure 1-6
...open-water training.

takes place in a pool or confined-water environment (*confined water* is any body of water offering conditions similar to a swimming pool) and will teach you the basic skills of diving. The open-water training allows you to demonstrate your mastery of these skills and practice them in a typical diving situation.

These segments will be taught to you in five modules; each module has both an academic training and a confined-water session. For each module there are specific knowledge objectives and skill performance requirements that need to be learned and completed before participating in the next module. This course has been structured so you may progress according to your individual ability — individual modules may be repeated as needed. This structure assures that you understand each step before you continue to the next level in developing your knowledge and skills.

The open-water dives allow you to apply what you have learned during the knowledge development and skills development segments at an actual dive site. During the open-water dives, you will be given an orientation to some of the local conditions and environments you will be diving in once you complete the course. You will participate in four scuba dives and possibly a skin dive, at the discretion of your instructor.

This text clearly outlines the academic, confined-water and open-water training objectives you need to meet to successfully complete this course. It's up to you, with your instructor's help, to achieve these objectives. Your instructor is a highly trained professional who is able and willing to help you become a capable diver. Ask questions and expect individual attention. It is your instructor's goal to help you fulfill your desire to become a diver.

Note: Units of measurement are expressed in U.S. increments throughout this book. A table for conversion to metric units is included in the Appendix. A metric-measurement version of this text is also available.

The PADI Open Water Diver Certification

Successfully earning the PADI Open Water Diver certification means you are qualified to:

• Buy air fills, equipment and other diving services.

• Engage in recreational open-water diving without the direct or indirect supervision of an instructor.

• Plan, conduct and log open-water, no-decompression dives in conditions generally comparable to, or better than, those you were trained in. You must be properly equipped and accompanied by another certified diver.

• Participate in the PADI Advanced Open Water Diver program and PADI Specialty courses such as Night Diver, Equipment Specialist, Research Diver, Underwater Hunter, Underwater Navigator, Underwater Photographer, Altitude Diver, Boat Diver, Drift Diver, Dry Suit Diver, Multilevel Diver, Underwater Naturalist and Peak Performance Buoyancy.

Objectives

After reading this section on the underwater world, you will be able to:

1. Determine the buoyancy (positive, neutral or negative) of an object if it displaces an amount of water:

   a. more than its own weight

   b. less than its own weight

   c. equal to its own weight

2. Name two items used to control a diver's buoyancy.

3. Explain why buoyancy control, both at the surface and under water, is one of the most important skills a diver can master.

4. Compare the buoyancy of an object in fresh and salt water.

5. Explain the effect of lung volume on buoyancy.

The Underwater World

Shortly, you will enter the underwater world — inner space — for the first time. Immediately, you'll notice new and different sensations as you venture into a realm where everything looks, sounds and feels different than it does above the water. These sensations are part of what makes diving so special, and as you become accustomed to them, you'll find they add to your enjoyment of diving.

Understanding why the underwater world is different helps you adapt and become accustomed to the changes. In this module, you will learn about two factors that greatly affect you as a diver under water: buoyancy and pressure.

Figure 1-7
As you enter the underwater world for the first time, you'll notice new and different sensations that add to your enjoyment of diving.

Have you ever wondered why a large steel ocean liner floats, but a small steel nail sinks? The answer is surprisingly simple: The steel hull of the ship is formed in a shape that displaces much water. If the steel used to manufacture the ocean liner were placed in the sea without being shaped into a large hull, it would sink like the nail. The ocean liner demonstrates that whether an object floats depends not only on its weight, but on how much water it displaces.

The principle of buoyancy can be stated this way: An object placed in water is buoyed up by a force equal to the weight of the quantity of water it displaces.

The principle of buoyancy is that if an object displaces an amount of water weighing *more* than its own weight, it will *float.* If an object displaces an amount of water weighing *less* than its own weight, it will *sink.* If an object displaces an amount of water *equal* to its own weight, it will neither float nor sink, but remain suspended. If an object floats, it is said to be *positively buoyant;* if it sinks, it is *nega-*

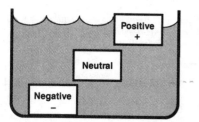

Figure 1-8
Positive, neutral and negative buoyancy.

Figure 1-9
Under water, you'll want to be neutrally buoyant so that you're weightless and can stay off the bottom, avoiding delicate corals and other aquatic life.

Weight of
Water displaced
> = < Weight of
Object

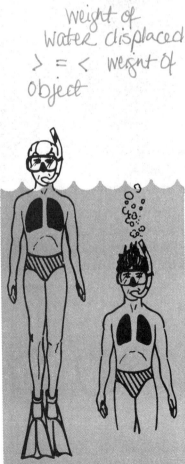

Figure 1-10
Exhaling results in less buoyancy.

tively buoyant; and if it neither floats nor sinks, it is *neutrally buoyant.*

It is important for you to learn to use the principles of buoyancy so you can effortlessly maintain your position under water. You must control your buoyancy carefully. When you are at the surface, you will want to be positively buoyant so you can conserve energy while resting or swimming. Under water, you will want to be neutrally buoyant so that you're weightless and can stay off the bottom and avoid crushing or damaging delicate corals and other aquatic life. Neutral buoyancy permits you to move freely in all directions.

Buoyancy control is one of the most important skills you will master, but it's also one of the easiest. It takes only a little instruction and practice. As a diver, you control your buoyancy using lead weight and a *buoyancy control device* (BCD). The lead weight, which is incorporated into a weight system, such as a weight belt, is negatively buoyant. The BCD is a device that can be partially inflated or deflated to change buoyancy. You will learn more about BCDs and weight systems later.

Another factor that affects the buoyancy of an object is the density of the water. The denser the water, the greater the buoyancy. Salt water (due to its dissolved salts) is more dense than fresh water, so you'll be more buoyant in salt water than in fresh water. Most people are positively buoyant in either fresh or salt water — in fact, when floating motionless at the surface, most divers need to exhale air from their lungs to sink. By exhaling, the volume of the lungs is decreased, and less water is displaced, resulting in less buoyancy.

We can see, then, that changing the volume of an object changes its buoyancy. Divers primarily control buoyancy by changing the volume of air in their BCDs.

Exercise 1-1

The Underwater World

1. Place a check next to the letter that best describes an object that is positively buoyant.
   - ☐ a. The object displaces an amount of water weighing less than its own weight.
   - ☒ b. The object displaces an amount of water weighing more than its own weight.

2. Check the two articles of equipment used to control your buoyancy.
   - ☒ a. BCD   ☐ b. Fins   ☒ c. Lead weight

3. Buoyancy control is one of the most important skills you can master because it allows you to maintain your position under water and conserve energy at the surface.
   - ☒ True   ☐ False

4. The same object would be more buoyant in _____ than it would be in _____.
   - ☐ a. fresh water, salt water   ☒ b. salt water, fresh water

5. When you exhale, your lung volume decreases, meaning your lungs displace less water. The result is _____ buoyancy.   ☐ a. more   ☒ b. less

How did you do?   *1. b   2. a, c   3. True   4. b   5. b.*

Objectives

By the end of the section on body air spaces and water pressure, you will be able to:

1. **Explain why changing pressure is usually only felt in the air spaces of the body.**

2. **Explain why pressure changes under water occur faster than pressure changes on the surface.**

Body Air Spaces and Water Pressure 📖

Although you don't usually notice it, air is constantly exerting pressure on you. If you have ever walked against a strong wind, however, you've felt its force pushing against your body. This demonstrates that air can exert pressure, or

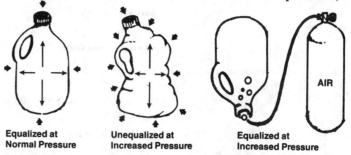

Equalized at Normal Pressure   Unequalized at Increased Pressure   Equalized at Increased Pressure

Figure 1-11
Water exerts pressure, as shown by a submerged, sealed plastic jug filled with air. At the surface, the pressure inside and outside the jug are the same. As the jug is taken deeper, water pressure pushes in on the lesser pressure in the jug, crushing it. If the jug is taken under water unsealed and filled with air at depth, the pressure is in balance inside and outside, and it is not crushed.

📖 See *The Encyclopedia of Recreational Diving*

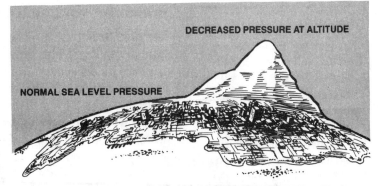

DECREASED PRESSURE AT ALTITUDE

NORMAL SEA LEVEL PRESSURE

Figure 1-12
Surrounding air pressure changes
when you change altitude.

weight. You don't usually feel the air's pressure, though, because your body is primarily liquid, which distributes the pressure equally throughout your entire body. The few air spaces your body does have — in your ears, sinuses and lungs — are filled with air *equal* in pressure to the external air. However, when the surrounding air pressure changes, such as when you change altitude by flying or driving through mountains, you can feel the change as a popping sensation in your ears.

Just as air exerts pressure on you at the surface, water exerts pressure on you when you are submerged. But because water is much denser than air, pressure changes under water occur more rapidly, making you more aware of them.

As with air pressure, you don't feel water pressure on most of your body, but you can feel it in your body's air spaces. When water pressure changes corresponding with a change in depth, it creates a pressure sensation you can feel. Through training and experience you will learn to avoid the problems associated with water pressure and the air spaces in your body.

Now that you understand the basic concepts of buoyancy and pressure, let's look at the relationships between pressure, volume and density; their effects on you while diving; and how you can deal with these effects.

Exercise 1-2

Body Air Spaces and Water Pressure

1. You don't usually feel pressure because your body is primarily _____, which distributes the pressure _____ throughout your entire body. ☑ a. liquid, equally   ☐ b. solid, equally

2. Because water is much denser than air, pressure changes under water occur rapidly. ☑ True   ☐ False

How did you do?   *1. a   2. True.*

Objectives

After reading this section on pressure, volume and density relationships, you will be able to:

1. State the relationship between increasing and decreasing depth and water pressure.

2. Calculate the absolute pressure, in atmospheres, for a depth of 33 feet, 66 feet, 99 feet and 132 feet.

3. Describe the relationship between volume and density when pressure increases and decreases around an air space.

Pressure/Volume/Density Relationships 📖

The pressure of the atmosphere around us is relatively constant at sea level. This pressure is a standard reference for pressure measurement, referred to as one atmosphere of pressure. In seawater, pressure increases by one atmosphere for each 33 feet. This means that at a depth of 33 feet, the total pressure exerted on a diver is two atmospheres: one atmosphere of water pressure and one atmosphere of air pressure.

Pressure increases at a rate of one atmosphere (ATM) for each additional 33 feet of depth under water, as shown in Figure 1-13. Notice that the total pressure is twice as great at 33 feet than at the surface, three times as great at 66 feet, and so on. This pressure pushes in on flexible air spaces, compressing them and reducing their volume. The reduction of the volume of the air space is in proportion to the amount of pressure, as shown by an inverted bell full of air lowered into water (Figure 1-14).

DEPTH	PRESSURE
0'	1 ATM
33'	2 ATM
66'	3 ATM
99'	4 ATM

Figure 1-13
Pressure increases at a rate of one atmosphere (ATM) for each additional 33 feet of depth under water.

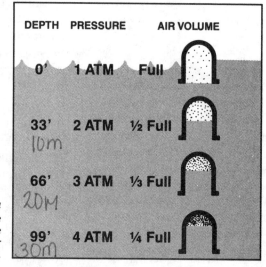

DEPTH	PRESSURE	AIR VOLUME
0'	1 ATM	Full
33'	2 ATM	½ Full
66'	3 ATM	⅓ Full
99'	4 ATM	¼ Full

Figure 1-14
As water pressure increases, the volume of air within an air space decreases.

When the total pressure doubles, the air volume is halved. When the pressure triples, the volume is reduced to one third, and so on.

The density of air in the air space is also affected by pressure. As the volume of the air space is reduced due to compression, the density of the air increases as it is squeezed into a smaller space. No air is lost; it is simply compressed. Air density is also proportional to pressure, so that when the total pressure is doubled, the air density is doubled. When the pressure is tripled, the air density triples, and so on, as shown in Figure 1-16.

📖 See *The Encyclopedia of Recreational Diving.*

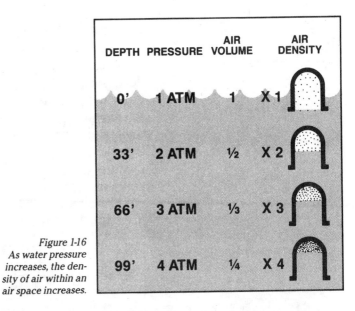

Figure 1-16
As water pressure increases, the density of air within an air space increases.

Shallow

*Figure 1-15
The reduction of the balloon's volume is proportionate to the amount of pressure.*

Deeper

To maintain an air space at its original volume when pressure is increased, more air must be added to the space. This is the concept of pressure equalization, and the amount of air that must be added is proportional to the pressure increase, as shown in Figure 1-17.

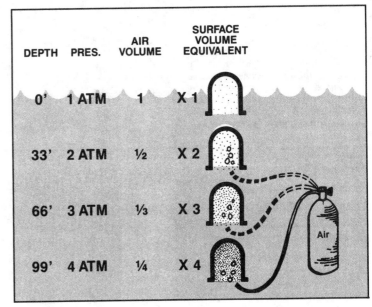

*Figure 1-17
To maintain an air space at its original volume when pressure is increased, more air must be added to the space.*

Air within an air space expands as pressure is reduced. If no air has been added to the air space, the air will simply expand to fill the original volume of the air space upon reaching the surface. As shown in Figure 1-14, the air compressed in the bell during descent will expand on ascent in proportion to the pressure.

If air has been added to an air space to equalize the pressure, this air will also expand as pressure is reduced during ascent. The amount of expansion is again proportional to the pressure. In an open container, such as the bell, the expanding air will simply bubble out the opening, maintaining its original volume during ascent. In a closed, flexible container, however, the volume will increase as the pressure is reduced. If the volume exceeds the capacity of the container, the container may be ruptured by the expanding air. This effect can be noted on a plastic bag filled with air at a depth of 99 feet and released (Figure 1-18).

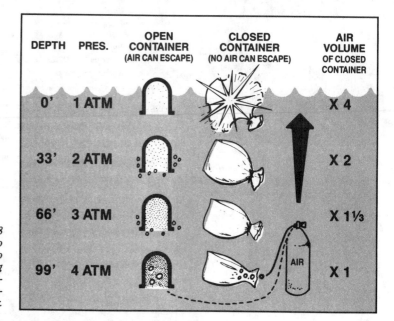

Figure 1-18
If air has been added to an air space to equalize the pressure, this air will also expand as pressure is reduced during ascent. In an open container, the air simply bubbles out. A closed, flexible container can be ruptured by expanding air.

Exercise 1-3

Pressure/Volume/Density Relationships

Complete the following chart for a sealed flexible bag, full of air at the surface.

Depth	Pressure	Volume	Density
0'	1 ATM	x 1	x 1
33'	2 ATM	x 1/2	x 2
99'	4 ATM	1/4	x 4
132'	5 ATM	x 1/5	x 5

How did you do? *0' Depth:* **1 ATM**, *x 1, x 1. 33' Depth: 2 ATM,* **1/2, x 2**. *99' Depth:* **4 ATM**, *1/4,* **x 4**. *132' Depth: 5 ATM,* **1/5**, *x 5 (Answers for Exercise 1-3 appear in bold face type.)*

Objectives

After reading this section on the effects of increasing pressure, you will be able to:

1. List the three major air spaces affected by pressure.

2. Define *squeeze*, as it relates to air spaces and descending under water.

3. Define *equalization* as it relates to air spaces in a diver's body.

Effects of Increasing Pressure 📖

Now let's look at how the relationships between pressure, volume and density affect you while diving. As you have seen, air spaces are affected by changes in pressure. The air spaces you will be concerned with as a diver are both the natural ones in your body and those artificially created by wearing diving equipment.

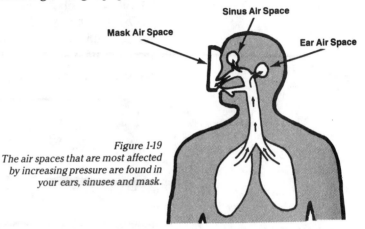

Figure 1-19
The air spaces that are most affected by increasing pressure are found in your ears, sinuses and mask.

The air spaces within your body that are most obviously affected by increasing pressure are found in your *ears* and *sinuses*. The artificial air space most affected by increasing pressure is the one created by your *mask*.

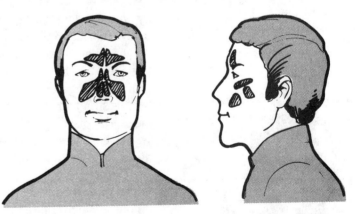

Figure 1-20
Location of sinus air spaces.

During descent, water pressure increases and pushes in on your body's air spaces, compressing them. If pressure within these air spaces is not kept in balance with this increasing water pressure, the sensation of pressure builds, becoming uncomfortable and possibly even painful as you continue to descend. This sensation is the result of a *squeeze* on the air space. You may have felt a squeeze in your ears when diving to the bottom of a swimming pool. A squeeze, then, is a pressure imbalance resulting in pain or discomfort in a body air space. In this situation, the imbalance is such that the pressure outside the air space is greater than the pressure inside (Figure 1-21).

Squeezes are possible in several places: ears, sinuses, teeth, lungs and your mask. Fortunately, divers can easily avoid all these squeezes.

To avoid discomfort, pressure inside an air space must always equal the water pressure outside the air space. This is accomplished by adding air to the air spaces during descent, before discomfort occurs. This action is called *equalization*.

Figure 1-21 (left)
Ear squeeze — occurs when external pressure is greater than internal pressure.

Figure 1-22 (right)
Equalization — to avoid discomfort, pressure inside an air space must always equal the water pressure outside the air space. This is accomplished by adding air to the air spaces during descent.

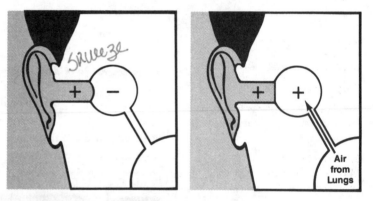

As shown in Figure 1-22, the ear and the sinus air spaces are connected to the throat, allowing each to be easily equalized with air from the lungs. The air space created by the mask can be equalized because it encloses the nose.

Air spaces rarely exist in your teeth, but may occur in filled teeth, where the tooth or filling has continued to erode. During descent, the increasing pressure pushing in on this small air space causes a tooth squeeze. In most cases, the discomfort prevents further descent. There is no way to equalize an air space under a tooth filling, but annual dental checkups help avoid the problem altogether.

Compared to the ear and sinus air spaces, your lungs are large and flexible. As a scuba diver, you automatically equalize the pressure in your lungs as you breathe continuously from your scuba equipment. When you skin dive, holding your breath, the lungs can be compressed with no consequence as long as they are filled with air when you begin your descent. They will be reduced in volume during descent and will re-expand during ascent to nearly the original volume when you reach the surface (you will use some of the air from your lungs to equalize your other body air spaces).

Figure 1-23
Air spaces rarely exist in your teeth, but may occur under fillings that have continued to erode. The small air space may cause a tooth squeeze.

Exercise 1-4

Effects of Increasing Pressure

1. The three major air spaces affected by pressure during descent are:

   ☐ a. sinuses, lungs and stomach.   ☒ b. ears, sinuses and mask.

2. The best definition of a *squeeze* is:

   ☐ a. A condition that causes pain and discomfort when the pressure outside an air space of your body is less than the pressure inside an air space.

   ☒ b. A condition that causes pain and discomfort when the pressure outside an air space of your body is greater than the pressure inside an air space.

3. To avoid the discomfort of a squeeze, pressure inside an air space must always equal the water pressure outside the air space.   ☒ True   ☐ False

How did you do?   *1. b   2. b   3. True.*

Objectives

After reading this section on equalization techniques, you will be able to:

1. Describe the three techniques used to equalize air spaces during descent.

2. State how often a diver should equalize his air spaces during descent.

3. Outline the three steps that should be followed when discomfort is felt in an air space while descending.

Equalization Techniques 📖

As mentioned previously, it's important to equalize your body's air spaces to prevent squeezes. The air spaces in your ears are the most sensitive to increasing pressure, but they are easily equalized.

Figure 1-24
Blocking the nose and attempting to gently blow through it, with the mouth closed, will equalize the ear and sinus air spaces.

— Equalize often every few feet

In a healthy diver, blocking the nose and attempting to gently blow through it with the mouth closed will direct air into the ear and sinus air spaces. Swallowing and wiggling the jaw from side to side may also be an effective equalization technique. For some individuals, swallowing and wiggling the jaw from side to side *while* attempting to blow through a blocked nose is the most successful way to equalize.

📖 See *The Encyclopedia of Recreational Diving*

Figure 1-25
Equalize pressure every few feet while descending, before *you feel discomfort.*

Equalize pressure every few feet while descending, *before* you feel discomfort. If discomfort occurs, continued efforts to equalize may be ineffective because the water pressure actually holds the air passages shut. Continuing to descend with an unequalized air space may result in injury. If discomfort in an air space occurs, 1) ascend until the discomfort is gone, 2) attempt to equalize once more, and 3) continue a slow descent. *If equalization cannot be*

Figure 1-26
If you can't equalize, discontinue the dive. Never continue your descent with an unequalized air space.

achieved, the dive must be discontinued. Equalization of the ears and sinuses usually becomes easier with experience.

Congestion (due to colds or allergies) can plug air passages, making equalization difficult or impossible. The use of medications, such as sprays and decongestants, to clear the openings and permit diving is *not* advised. Medication used to clear congestion often has undesirable side effects and may wear off under water, creating problems (discussed under The Effects of Decreasing Pressure).

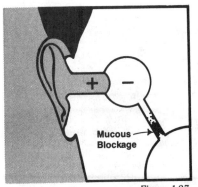

Figure 1-27
A cold or congestion can swell or plug air passages, making equalization difficult or impossible.

Mucous Blockage

The ear can also be affected if an air space that cannot be equalized is created in the ear canal. This could occur from wearing a too-tight wet-suit hood or from wearing ear plugs. To prevent this, pull your hood away from your ears momentarily to allow any air to escape. Ear plugs should never be worn while diving, under any circumstances, because they create air spaces that cannot be equalized.

You can equalize the air space in your mask by simply exhaling into it through your nose. If you forget to equalize your mask, you'll feel a mask squeeze as a pulling sensation on your face and eyes. Mask equalization will become automatic with experience.

Exercise 1-5

Equalization Techniques

1. Check each statement that describes a technique used to equalize air spaces during descent:
   - ☑ a. Block your nose and attempt to gently blow through it.
   - ☑ b. Swallow and wiggle the jaw from side to side.
   - ☐ c. Close your eyes and exhale through your regulator.

2. You should equalize your air spaces:
   - ☐ a. only when you feel discomfort.   ☑ b. every few feet while descending, *before* you feel discomfort.

3. If you feel discomfort in your ear while descending, ascend until discomfort is gone, attempt to equalize once again and continue a slow descent.   ☑ True ☐ False

How did you do?   *1.* a, b *2.* b *3.* True.

The Effects of Decreasing Pressure 📖

Objectives

After reading this section on the effects of decreasing pressure, you will be able to:

1. State the most important rule in scuba diving.

2. Define the term *reverse block*.

3. Describe the action a diver should take if he feels discomfort during ascent due to air expansion in his ears, sinuses, stomach, intestines or teeth.

As you read in the discussion on squeezes, your lungs experience no harmful effects from changes in pressure when you're holding your breath while skin diving. At the start of the skin dive, you take a breath and descend; the increasing water pressure compresses the air in your lungs. During ascent, this air re-expands so that when you reach the surface, your lungs return to approximately their original volume (see Figure 1-28 next page).

When you scuba dive, however, the situation is different. Scuba equipment allows you to breathe under water by automatically delivering air at a pressure equal to the surrounding water pressure. This means your lungs will be at their normal volume while at depth, full of air that will expand upon ascent.

If you breathe normally, keeping the airway to your

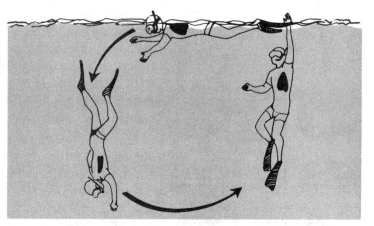

Figure 1-28
When you skin dive, the increasing pressure compresses the air in your lungs. During ascent, this air re-expands, so your lungs return to approximately their original volume when you reach the surface.

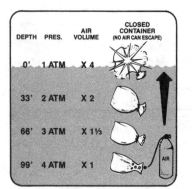

DEPTH	PRES.	AIR VOLUME	CLOSED CONTAINER (NO AIR CAN ESCAPE)
0'	1 ATM	X 4	
33'	2 ATM	X 2	
66'	3 ATM	X 1⅓	
99'	4 ATM	X 1	

Figure 1-29
If you hold your breath, blocking the airway to your lungs while you ascend, your lungs will overexpand much like the sealed bag.

lungs open, the expanding air escapes during ascent and your lungs remain at their normal volume. But, if you were to hold your breath, blocking your airway while ascending, your lungs would overexpand, much like the sealed bag in Figure 1-29. Expanding air can cause lung overpressurization (lung rupture), the most serious injury that can occur to a diver. *The most important rule in scuba diving is to breathe continuously and never, never hold your breath.* Lung overpressurization will occur unless pressure is continuously equalized by breathing normally at all times.

Some people find they have a natural tendency to hold their breath when they first begin learning to use scuba, but this tendency must be changed. The lungs can be injured by even slight pressure changes if you hold your breath, so it is important to *always* breathe continuously when using scuba, even in water only two or three feet deep.

Although lung overexpansion injuries are among the most difficult diving injuries to treat, they are also the easiest to avoid: **Simply breathe at all times and do not hold your breath when using scuba.**

Figure 1-30
Always breathe continuously and never, never hold your breath.

Other air spaces generally pose no problems during ascent. Normally, expanding air releases from these air spaces without effort. It is possible, though, to feel pain and discomfort in your ear and sinus air spaces while ascending due to a condition called a *reverse block.* A reverse block is the condition that occurs when expanding air cannot escape from a body air space during ascent.

Reverse blocks are uncommon and are generally caused by diving with congestion or by having a decongestant medication wear off while at depth. To avoid a reverse block, never dive with a cold and avoid using decongestants before diving.

Gas formed in the stomach or intestines during diving can also expand during ascent, causing discomfort. This situation is uncommon and can be prevented by avoiding gas-producing foods prior to diving. Air swallowed at depth can also cause discomfort during ascent, so avoid swallowing air while diving.

Most important Rule! always breathe continuously

It is possible, though very rare, for a reverse block to occur in an air space under an inadequate tooth filling or a tooth filling with secondary erosion. This reverse block, like tooth squeeze, can be avoided through regular dental checkups.

If you feel discomfort during ascent due to air expansion — whether in your ears, sinuses, stomach, intestines or teeth — slow or stop your ascent, descend a few feet and allow the trapped air to work its way out. If you experience severe or frequent reverse blocks, see a physician knowledgeable about diving medicine.

Exercise 1-6

The Effects of Decreasing Pressure

1. The most important rule in scuba diving is: *Breathe continuously and never hold your breath.*
   ☐ True ☐ False

2. The best definition for a *reverse block* is:
   ☐ a. A condition that occurs when expanding air cannot escape from a body air space during ascent, causing pain and discomfort.
   ☐ b. A condition that occurs when expanding air escapes from a body air space during ascent, causing pain and discomfort.

3. If you feel discomfort during ascent due to air expansion in any body air space during ascent:
   ☐ a. slow or stop your ascent, descend a few feet and allow the trapped air to work its way out.
   ☐ b. ignore the discomfort and continue ascending.

How did you do? *1. True 2. a 3. a.*

Objectives

After reading this section on the effects of increased air density, you will be able to:

1. **Explain the relationship between increasing depth and air supply when scuba diving.**

2. **Describe the most efficient method of breathing dense air under water.**

Effects of Increased Air Density 📖

If you've told friends and acquaintances that you're learning to scuba dive, they've probably asked you how long you can stay under water with a scuba tank. As you will see, the answer depends, in part, on how deep you dive.

From Figure 1-17, it's easy to determine that more air is required to fill an air space as pressure increases. Applying this concept to breathing, it is easy to understand that a given quantity of air in a scuba tank will be used more quickly the deeper you go. For example, three times more air is needed to fill your lungs at 66 feet than at the surface. Therefore, your air supply lasts only one third as long at 66 feet as it does at the surface.

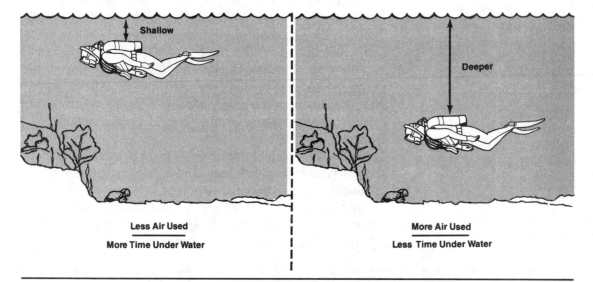

Shallow

Deeper

Less Air Used

More Time Under Water

More Air Used

Less Time Under Water

Figure 1-31
A given quantity of air in a scuba tank will be used more quickly the deeper you go.

Additionally, the deeper you descend, the denser the air becomes. This affects breathing because dense air is harder to inhale and exhale than air at normal surface pressure and density. Deep, slow breathing is the most efficient method for breathing dense air while diving. For maximum air conservation, relax and don't overextend yourself. Pace yourself so that you breathe normally through your entire dive. You should never be out of breath while diving — recreational diving is relaxed diving.

📖 See *The Encyclopedia of Recreational Diving*

Exercise 1-7

Effects of Increased Air Density

1. As depth increases, your use of air _____ ☐ a. decreases. ☐ b. increases.

2. The most efficient method for breathing dense air under water is rapid, shallow breathing. ☐ True ☐ False

How did you do? *1.* b *2. False. The most efficient method of respiration when breathing dense air under water is deep, slow breathing.*

Summary

In this section, you learned about buoyancy and how buoyancy control, through proper use of lead weight and a BCD, helps you conserve energy and experience the joy and freedom of being weightless under water. Furthermore, you learned how buoyancy is affected by changes in volume (as with your lungs and BCD) and the density of the water (fresh or salt) you dive in.

You should now be familiar with the relationships between pressure, volume and density, and how, as a diver, you will be affected by these relationships. You learned that although your body is primarily made up of liquid and is unaffected by pressure, there are several air spaces in your body that may be affected. You now know that air pressure in these air spaces, primarily in the ears, sinuses and mask, can easily be equalized to avoid the potential discomfort of a squeeze. Lung overexpansion is potentially hazardous, but you learned how easy it is to avoid this problem: **Breathe continuously and never, never hold your breath while scuba diving.**

Finally, this section introduced you to concepts relative to the effects of increased air density at depth. You learned that as depth increases, your air supply is used more quickly, and that because the air you breathe at depth is denser, you need to breathe slowly and deeply.

air becomes more dense the deeper you dive and becomes harder to inhale

Diving Equipment

Diving is possible thanks to specialized modern equipment that adapts you to the aquatic environment. Diving equipment is available in a wide variety of colors and designs that make it not only functional, but comfortable and stylish as well.

In this section you will learn about masks, snorkels, fins, buoyancy control devices (BCDs), scuba tanks, tank valves, backpacks, regulators and submersible pressure gauges. Become familiar with this equipment now, because you will be using these items during confined-water training.

When you're selecting your equipment, you will find that your PADI Instructor or Training Facility will be glad to assist you in choosing suitable equipment for your particular needs.

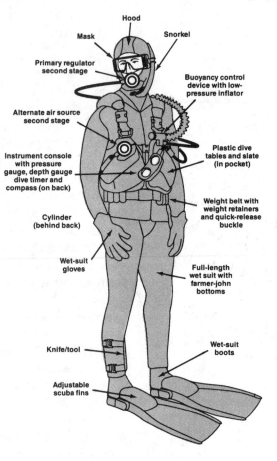

Hood

Mask

Snorkel

Primary regulator
second stage

Buoyancy control
device with low-
pressure inflator

Alternate air source
second stage

Instrument console
with pressure
gauge, depth gauge
dive timer and
compass (on back)

Plastic dive
tables and slate
(in pocket)

Weight belt with
weight retainers
and quick-release
buckle

Cylinder
(behind back)

Wet-suit
gloves

Full-length
wet suit with
farmer-john
bottoms

Wet-suit
boots

Knife/tool

Adjustable
scuba fins

Figure 1-32
Diving is possible thanks to specialized
modern equipment that adapts you to
the aquatic environment.

Objectives

After reading this section on masks, you will be able to:

1. **State the purpose of a mask.**

2. **Explain why the nose must be enclosed in a mask when scuba diving.**

3. **List six features a scuba diving mask should have.**

4. **State the two most important factors in the selection of a mask.**

5. **Prepare a new mask for use.**

6. **List three general maintenance procedures used to care for a mask.**

Mask 📖

Purpose — The mask is your window to the underwater world. It allows you to see clearly by creating an air space in front of your eyes. As you have just learned, this air space must be equalized during descent to prevent mask squeeze. For this reason, your nose must be enclosed in the mask so you can exhale into it and equalize. Goggles, which cover only the eyes and do not enclose the nose, can't be equalized and aren't acceptable for diving. Be certain to purchase a mask specifically designed for scuba diving.

A mask consists of a faceplate (also called the lens), a comfortable skirt and a head strap. Masks come in a variety of styles and shapes, may incorporate several possible features and are made from at least two different materials.

Figure 1-33
Wraparound Mask (top),
Low-Profile Mask (bottom).

3MM VS
5MM less fogging

Diving is largely a visual activity, and the importance of having the proper mask cannot be overemphasized.

Styles — Mask styles range from simple round- or oval-shaped models to more modern styles with lower internal volumes and wider fields of vision. *Wraparound* masks feature two additional panes of glass along the sides to improve peripheral vision. *Low-profile* masks have a notched faceplate and a nose pocket to allow your nose to protrude past the plane of the lens. This design allows the lens to be closer to your face, resulting in a lower internal volume and a wider field of vision. Many of the newer wraparound type masks incorporate the low-profile design, as well as the additional glass panes.

Features — When choosing a mask, consider the following features.

1. Tempered-glass lens plate. If broken, tempered glass is less likely to shatter into fine, hazardous slivers.

2. Comfortable skirt with a close fit against your face and a good seal.

3. Nose or finger pockets. To make equalizing your ears easier, a mask should have some way of letting you conveniently block off your nose.

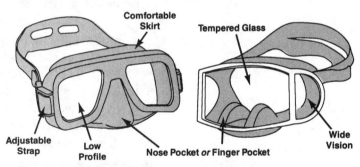

Figure 1-34
When choosing a mask, consider the six desirable features.

4. Low-profile. The lower the profile of the mask, the easier it is to equalize and the easier it is to clear if it floods. (You'll learn more about mask clearing during the confined-water portion of this module.)

5. Adjustable strap that can be locked in place.

6. Wide field of vision. This is accomplished through the low profile and/or through side windows.

An optional feature found in a few masks is a purge valve. A purge valve is a one-way valve used for clearing a mask of water. Today, few modern masks have purge valves, because with only a little practice, it is easy to clear water from a mask without a purge valve. For this reason, the purge valve is optional.

Vision Correction Under Water

For people with less-than-perfect vision, lens correction is available. Prescription lenses can be bonded to the mask's face plate or ground directly into it. Some people also find they have no problem wearing soft contact lenses while diving.

If you need visual correction while diving, see your instructor or dive store and your eye specialist to determine the best option for you.

Materials — Masks (and other pieces of diving equipment) are most often made from either neoprene rubber or silicone. Neoprene masks are typically black, while silicone masks are usually translucent (though coloring agents are sometimes added to both types). Masks made from silicone usually cost more than comparable neoprene masks, but they offer several advantages that offset the price difference. These advantages include the fact that silicone lasts three to four times longer than neoprene; is generally softer and more comfortable; is usually more attractive; is less likely to irritate sensitive skin; and lets light in through the sides of the mask, which allows some peripheral vision.

Selection — The two most important factors in selecting all diving equipment are *fit* and *comfort.* This is particularly true of the mask, which must fit precisely to make a good seal.

To test for a proper fit, place the mask gently against your face without using the strap and inhale through your nose. A properly fitting mask should be pulled into place by the suction and stay in place as long as you continue to inhale. If you have to push the mask on your face to make it seal, it does not fit. Try other masks until a proper fit can be achieved. Next, be sure you can seal your nostrils easily

Figure 1-35
The two most important factors in selecting all diving equipment are fit *and comfort.* This is particularly true of the mask.

from outside the mask.

Choose a mask that fits properly and has the six desirable features. Other features, such as color, shape and style are a matter of personal preference. If you need visual correction, be sure to take it into account when you select your mask. One way to be sure you're getting the best mask for your needs is to select it with the assistance of your PADI Dive Center or Instructor.

Preparation for Use — New masks have an oily film on the faceplate (a protective coating for silicone or rubber, left from the manufacturing process) that must be scrubbed off. If you don't remove this film, condensation (fog) will form on the faceplate while you're diving, obscuring your vision. To remove the film, use a soft cloth to gently scour the glass inside and out with a non-gel toothpaste. Most non-gel toothpastes contain fine grit that will remove the film without scratching the glass. Be sure to do this *before* the first confined-water training session.

You also need to adjust the mask strap for a comfortable fit across the back of your head. The strap should be snug, but not tight. Be sure the strap is properly secured with the mask-strap locking device after adjustment.

Maintenance — There are three general maintenance procedures used in caring for all diving equipment, including masks: 1) rinse thoroughly with fresh water after each use, 2) keep out of direct sunlight and 3) store in a cool, dry place.

A freshwater rinse after each use will eliminate contaminants and corrosion. After you've used your equipment in salt water, it should also be soaked for several minutes in warm, fresh water to prevent the buildup of damaging salt crystals.

Because the sun's rays can damage neoprene and silicone products, avoid leaving your equipment in direct sunlight. Dry your equipment thoroughly before storing it.

In addition, masks and other diving equipment composed of silicone should be stored away from black rubber products to prevent staining of the silicone.

Exercise 1-8

Mask

1. A mask allows you to see clearly under water by:

☐ a. maintaining an air space in front of your eyes.

☐ b. filtering available light through a glass faceplate.

2. Goggles can't be used for diving because:
   □ a. they have a limited field of view.
   □ b. they don't enclose your nose and therefore can't be equalized.

3. Of the six desirable features of a mask, check those listed here.
   □ a. Low profile □ b. High-profile □ c. Nose or finger pockets □ d. Wide field of vision

4. The two most important factors in selecting all diving equipment, including the mask, are:
   □ a. style and color. □ b. fit and comfort.

5. Of the three general maintenance procedures used in caring for all diving equipment, including masks, check the one listed here:
   □ a. Store in a cool, dry place. □ b. Dry in the sun.

How did you do? *1.* a **2.** b **3.** a, c, d **4.** b **5.** a.

Objectives

After reading this section on snorkels, you will be able to:

1. State the purpose of the snorkel.

2. Identify three features of an easy-breathing snorkel.

3. Explain how to select a snorkel by checking for fit, comfort and minimum breathing resistance.

4. Prepare a snorkel for use.

Figure 1-36
A snorkel allows you to breathe at the surface without having to lift your head from the water.

Snorkel 📖

Purpose — The snorkel is a standard piece of diving equipment that allows you to breathe at the surface without having to lift your head from the water. When you're skin diving, the snorkel permits you to view the underwater

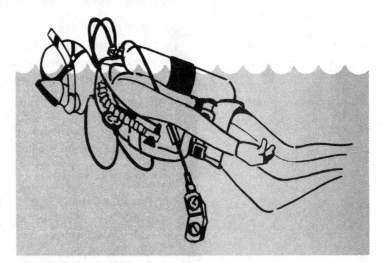

world continuously, without the interruption of having to lift your head for a breath. Scuba divers use snorkels while swimming or resting at the surface to conserve the air in their tanks.

Styles — All snorkels suitable for scuba diving are simple devices, being little more than a mouthpiece and tube that fits comfortably in your mouth and extends above the surface. They are available with a variety of features.

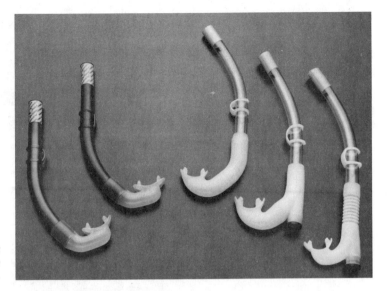

Figure 1-37
Snorkels are available with a variety
of features to choose from.

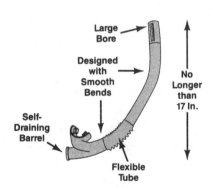

Figure 1-38
These features/options are common
among today's more popular snorkels.

comfortable
fit

Features — Snorkels used for scuba diving must allow unrestricted, easy breathing. The snorkel's tube diameter (*bore*), length and shape all affect breathing resistance. The proper snorkel for scuba diving should have these three features:

1. A large bore.
2. Be no longer than 17 inches.
3. Be designed with smooth, rounded bends. Avoid snorkels with sharply angled curves.

Today's most popular snorkels are designed to fit closely to the contours of your head to minimize drag as you move through the water. Many snorkels have an optional self-draining feature. This feature is popular because it allows water to be drained from the snorkel with minimal effort. Some snorkels have a flexible lower portion that allows the mouthpiece to comfortably drop away from the mouth area when not in use.

As you will discover when you learn about snorkel clearing in Module Two, it is quite easy to rid your snorkel of any water that enters it. For this reason, a means of preventing water from entering the snorkel is not required.

Materials — Most snorkels sold today are made from a combination of silicone or neoprene and plastic. The upper portion of the snorkel (the *barrel*) is usually constructed of semirigid plastic tubing. The lower portion and mouthpiece is usually made from silicone or neoprene rubber. Like

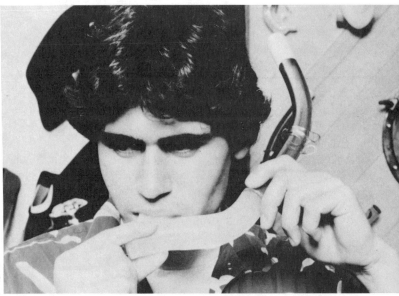

Figure 1-39
*The top of the snorkel should be at
the top of the back of your head.*

masks, snorkels may be found in a variety of colors.

Selection — The important considerations are comfort, fit and minimal breathing resistance. To check for these, place the snorkel in your mouth with the mouthpiece flange between your lips and teeth, and the barrel of the snorkel against the front of your left ear. The mouthpiece should fit comfortably, without chaffing or causing jaw fatigue, and be straight in your mouth. Next, take deep breaths through the snorkel to test ease of breathing. Compare various snorkels for comfort and breathing ease. Your PADI Instructor or Dive Center will be glad to help you make the best selection for your needs.

Preparation for Use — Attach the snorkel to the left side of your mask with the small rubber snorkel keeper that comes with the snorkel. As shown in Figure 1-40, first put one loop of the snorkel keeper on the snorkel barrel. Now pass the straight part of the keeper (the part that connects the loops) around the mask strap. Next, put the other loop on the barrel. Finally, adjust the snorkel and snorkel keeper so the mouthpiece is in reach of your mouth when the mask is in place.

Put on your mask and position the snorkel near the front of your left ear. Adjust the snorkel height and rotate it until the snorkel remains in your mouth even when your mouth is wide open. The top of the snorkel should be at the top of the back of your head. When properly positioned, the muscles of your mouth should not have to hold the snorkel in place when you use it.

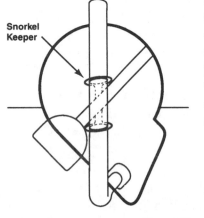

Snorkel
Keeper

Figure 1-40
*Attach the snorkel to the left side of
your mask with the small rubber snorkel
keeper that comes with the snorkel.*

Maintenance — As with the mask, the snorkel should be rinsed in fresh water after each use, stored in a cool, dry place and kept out of direct sunlight. Store it away from neoprene rubber to prevent staining of silicone parts.

Exercise 1-9

Snorkel

1. A snorkel allows you to breathe at the surface without having to lift your head from the water.
   ☐ True ☐ False

2. Of the three features of an easy-breathing snorkel, check those listed here:
   ☐ a. Large bore ☐ b. Flexible plastic ☐ c. Smooth, rounded bends

3. When selecting a snorkel, you should:
   ☐ a. Place it in your mouth to check for chaffing, jaw fatigue and ease of breathing.
   ☐ b. Never place the snorkel in your mouth.

How did you do? *1. True* **2.** *a, c* **3.** *a.*

Objectives

After reading this section on fins, you will be able to:

1. **State the purpose of fins.**

2. **Identify the two basic styles of fins.**

3. **List three blade design features used to enhance a fin's performance.**

4. **Prepare fins for use.**

5. **State three considerations when selecting a specific type of fin.**

Fins

Purpose — Fins allow you to move through the water with far less effort and far greater efficiency than swimming with only your hands. By providing a large surface area that your powerful leg muscles can use for swimming, you have more effective propulsion than your arms can provide, and your hands are freed for other activities. All fins, regardless of style or features, have two aspects in common: 1) pockets for your feet and 2) blades for propulsion.

Styles — Modern fins come in two basic styles: 1) adjustable strap and 2) full-foot. Adjustable fins have foot pockets that are open at the back and equipped with adjustable heel straps. Full-foot fins have foot pockets that enclose the heel. Adjustable fins are the style most commonly worn by scuba divers because they can be worn with wet-suit boots

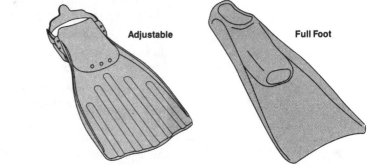

Adjustable   *Full Foot*

Figure 1-41
Modern fins come in two basic styles:
1) adjustable-strap and 2) full-foot.

📖 See *The Encyclopedia of Recreational Diving*

and because most of the high-power models of fins are the adjustable fin variety. Full-foot fins are the preferred choice of many warm-water skin and scuba divers who do not require wet-suit boots.

Features — Fins, particularly the adjustable strap style, have several features to choose from. Fin straps should be capable of being adjusted quickly and with minimal effort, and are available with quick-release and easy-to-adjust

Figure 1-42
Blade design features are incorporated
to enhance a fin's performance.

mechanisms. Blade design features are incorporated to enhance fin performance. These include: 1) *ribs,* which add rigidity to the blade and act as vertical stabilizers, 2) *vents,* which reduce resistance to fin movement and increase efficiency and 3) *channels,* which increase efficiency by guiding water smoothly over the fin.

Materials — Most modern fins use what is known as *composite construction.* This means that the fins are made from a combination of materials. Foot pockets and heel straps are usually made from neoprene rubber or a similar materi-

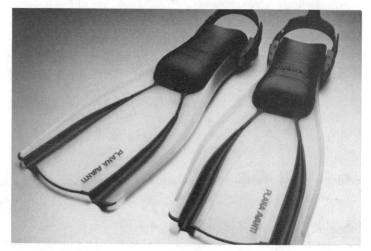

Figure 1-43
Most modern fins use what is known
as composite construction. *Foot*
pockets and straps are made from
neoprene rubber, and the blade is made
from thermoplastics.

al, and the blade is made from one of a variety of what is referred to as *thermoplastics.* Noncomposite, all-neoprene fins are also available.

Thermoplastic blades are the most popular because of: 1) lighter weight, 2) greater propulsion efficiency and 3) a variety of colors.

Selection — The type of fin you select will be determined by your 1) size, 2) physical ability and 3) the geographic area in which you dive. The shape of the fin is relatively unimportant compared to blade size and rigidity. The larger and stiffer the blade, the more leg strength required to use the fin. If protective wet-suit boots are commonly used in your local area, you should purchase them when you buy your fins so that the fins can be fitted with the boots on. Boots are not normally worn with full-foot fins. As has been mentioned regarding all equipment, fit and comfort are the most important considerations in choosing the right fins. The fins and boots should not bind, cramp or pinch. Your PADI Instructor or Dive Center will be able to assist you in selecting your fins.

Preparation for Use — Full-foot fins generally require no preparation, but adjustable-strap fins should be adjusted for a snug, comfortable fit, then locked in place. As mentioned previously, the adjustment should be made with your wet-suit boots on. New fin straps are often coated with a slick preservative that should be rinsed and wiped off, otherwise the straps may slip out of adjustment.

Maintenance — As with the mask and snorkel, fins should be rinsed in fresh water after use, stored in a cool, dry place and kept out of direct sunlight.

Exercise 1-10

Fins

1. Fins allow you to move through the water with less effort and greater efficiency than swimming with only your hands. ☐ True ☐ False

2. This illustration depicts a: ☐ a. full-foot fin. ☐ b. adjustable-strap fin.

3. Of the choices given, check the blade designs that enhance a fin's performance.
   ☐ a. Vents ☐ b. Ribs ☐ c. Channels

4. Check the factors that influence the type of fin you select:
   ☐ a. Your size ☐ b. Geographical area ☐ c. Physical ability

How did you do? *1.* True *2.* a *3.* a, b, c *4.* a, b, c.

Objectives

After reading this section on buoyancy control devices, you will be able to:

1. State the purpose of a BCD.

2. Identify the three basic styles of BCDs.

3. Name five features of a BCD.

4. Prepare a BCD for use.

5. List two special maintenance procedures used in caring for a BCD.

The Buoyancy Control Device (BCD) 📖

Purpose — As mentioned in the discussion on buoyancy, the buoyancy control device, or *BCD,* is an expandable bladder that can be inflated or deflated to regulate your buoyancy. The modern BCD can be orally inflated or mechanically inflated with air from your tank to increase buoyancy. To decrease buoyancy, the BCD is deflated through special air-dump valves or hoses.

The BCD is a mandatory piece of equipment for all diving. It is used to provide positive buoyancy for resting, swimming or lending assistance to others. Under water, the BCD allows you to maintain neutral buoyancy at any depth simply by adding or releasing air.

Styles — The three basic styles of BCDs are: 1) front-mounted, 2) back-mounted and 3) jacket-style. The front-

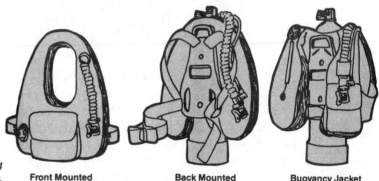

Figure 1-44
Three basic styles of BCDs.

Front Mounted   **Back Mounted**   **Buoyancy Jacket**

mounted BCD is similar in appearance to a life vest and is worn over the head. The back-mounted BCD rests behind the diver, and the jacket-style BCD is worn like a sleeveless coat, with part of the BCD in front and part in back of the diver. Today, the jacket-style BCD is by far the most popular.

Figure 1-45
Jacket-Style BCD.

📖 See *The Encyclopedia of Recreational Diving*

Features — Regardless of the style, a BCD has five features that are necessary for scuba diving:

1. It must hold enough air to give you and your equipment ample buoyancy at the surface.

2. It must have a large-diameter inflation/deflation hose, so air can be released easily.

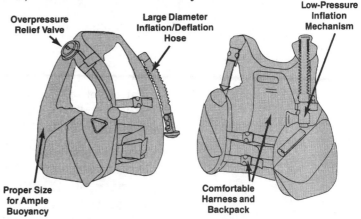

Figure 1-46
Necessary BCD features.

Overpressure Relief Valve

Large Diameter Inflation/Deflation Hose

Low-Pressure Inflation Mechanism

Proper Size for Ample Buoyancy

Comfortable Harness and Backpack

3. It should have a low-pressure inflation system to make it possible to slowly fill your BCD with air directly from your tank. (*Note: The BCD you use during confined-water training will have a low-pressure inflation system.*) The low-pressure inflation system should be easy to locate and operate.

4. It must have an overpressure relief valve to prevent the BCD from rupturing if it is accidentally overfilled.

5. It should have a configuration and harness that makes wearing the BCD comfortable and keeps it from riding up around your neck when inflated.

Figure 1-47
BCD Low-Pressure Inflator.

The BCD should fit as streamlined as possible against your body. Other desirable BCD features include a utility pocket, a whistle for surface communication, hose retainers and utility rings for attaching accessory equipment.

Materials — Modern BCDs are constructed in either double-bladder (or "bag") or single-bladder designs. Double-bladder BCDs consist of an inner bladder (usually made of urethane plastic), which holds the air, and the outer bag — a nylon shell that protects the inner bladder from cuts, punctures and abrasions. The single-bladder design is usually made from a rubber-coated fabric that serves to hold both air and resist cuts, punctures and abrasions. BCDs of both types are popular, and (provided the materials used are durable and scuff-resistant) neither design has a clear, definite advantage over the other.

Preparation for Use — BCDs require careful adjustment for a proper fit. When a BCD is too loose, it can rotate uncomfortably on your body. If a BCD is too tight, it will also be uncomfortable, particularly when fully inflated.

If the BCD is the jacket or back-mounted style, attach it to your tank before you adjust the fit. With the BCD deflated, estimate the adjustment of the straps, lengthening or shortening them as needed. Next, have someone help you put the BCD on and fine-tune the adjustments until the BCD fits snugly, yet allows you to move side to side and lean forward comfortably. Finally, inflate the BCD. Even when fully inflated, your BCD should not feel restrictive. Your PADI Instructor will assist you in preparing your BCD for use during the confined-water training of this module.

Maintenance — In addition to rinsing, drying and storing out of sunlight, your BCD has two additional maintenance considerations: 1) The inside, not just the outside, of the BCD must be rinsed with fresh water. (To rinse the inside, fill it about one third with water through the inflator hose, then inflate it the rest of the way with air. Swish the water around the inside, then drain completely through the hose.) 2) Store your BCD *partially inflated*.

Some BCDs may have special maintenance requirements for their mechanisms. Follow the recommendations in the owner's manual provided by the manufacturer.

Exercise 1-11

The Buoyancy Control Device (BCD)

1. The purpose of a BCD is to: ☐ a. insulate the chest area from cold. ☐ b. regulate buoyancy.

2. The illustration depicts a: ☐ a. jacket-style BCD. ☐ b. back-mounted BCD. ☐ c. front-mounted BCD.

3. Of the five desirable BCD features, check those listed here:
   ☐ a. Large-diameter inflation/deflation hose
   ☐ b. Overpressure relief valve
   ☐ c. Knife pocket

4. Besides rinsing, drying and storing out of the sunlight, which of the following are additional maintenance considerations for a BCD?
   ☐ a. Rinse inside with fresh water and drain.
   ☐ b. Store deflated.
   ☐ c. Store partially inflated.

How did you do? *1.* b *2.* a *3.* a, b *4.* a, c

Scuba Systems

As a skin diver, your excursion beneath the surface is limited to the length of time you can comfortably hold your breath. Scuba equipment, however, allows you to spend an extended time under water by providing you with a portable air supply. Scuba equipment is reliable and simple to operate. It consists of a tank (a high-pressure cylinder that stores compressed air — *never* oxygen), a valve (to turn the flow of air on and off), a backpack (to secure the tank to your back), a regulator (to deliver a controlled amount of air when you inhale) and a submersible pressure gauge (so you can monitor your air supply).

Let's begin by looking at scuba tanks.

Scuba Tanks

Purpose — A scuba tank is a cylindrical metal container used to safely store high-pressure air for breathing.

Figure 1-48
Tanks come in a variety of air capacities, depending upon their pressure rating and size.

Styles and Features — Tanks come in a variety of air capacities, depending upon their pressure rating and size. The tank capacity is expressed in the number of cubic feet of surface-volume air it can contain. By compressing this air, a small scuba tank can hold quite a lot of air. The three most common tank sizes are 50, 71.2 and 80 cubic feet, although other sizes are available. For some diving situations, two tanks can be combined to form double tanks to provide additional air.

The standard 71.2- or 80-cubic-foot tanks contain an amount of air approximately equal to the volume of a walk-in closet compressed into a space about two feet long and half a foot in diameter. As this air is compressed into the tank, its pressure increases. The pressure in scuba tanks may be higher than 4000 pounds per square inch (psi), but typical pressure ratings are 1800, 2250 and 3000 psi.

Materials — Scuba tanks are either made of aluminum or steel. Both types are subject to regulations established by the U.S. Department of Transportation (DOT) and similar agencies in other countries. Among these regulations, scuba tanks must pass periodic pressure tests (discussed under Handling and Maintenance of Tanks and Valves) mandated by these agencies. Both steel and aluminum are equally acceptable materials.

The regulating agency requires specific information to be stamped onto the neck of high-pressure cylinders. These markings indicate the type of material the tank is made of and the maximum pressure permitted in the tank (working pressure). Additional markings include a serial number identifying the tank, dates of all pressure tests, and a manufacturer or distributor symbol (Figure 1-49).

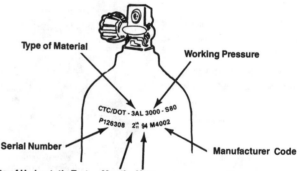

Figure 1-49
Regulating agencies require specific infor-mation to be stamped onto a scuba tank.

Selection — Selection of the appropriate tank will depend, among other factors, on your size and the type of diving you will be doing. Consult your PADI Instructor or Dive Center for assistance in choosing the best tank for your needs.

Preparation for Use — Aside from attaching the tank to the rest of your scuba system, the only preparation required for a tank is having it filled from a proper air source. Attachment will be discussed in the Confined-Water Training Preview.

Maintenance — Because scuba tanks and their tank valves form a single unit, the maintenance and care of both valves and tanks will be discussed together at the end of the section on tank valves.

Exercise 1-12

Scuba Tanks

1. A scuba tank safely stores _____ air for breathing. ☐ a. low-temperature ☐ b. high-pressure

2. Three common tank sizes are _____, _____, and _____ cubic feet.
   ☐ a. 300, 200, 100 ☐ b. 25, 15, 10 ☐ c. 80, 71.2, 50

3. Scuba tanks are made of either: ☐ a. copper or aluminium. ☐ b. aluminium or steel.

4. The numbers highlighted on the illustrated tank indicate the:
   ☐ a. date of hydrostatic test — month/year. ☐ b. working pressure. ☐ c. serial number.

How did you do?   *1. b   2. c   3. b   4. a.*

Objectives

After reading this section on tank valves, you will be able to:

1. State the purpose of a tank valve.

2. Identify the two types of tank valves.

3. State the function of a J-valve.

4. State the function of the burst disk in a tank valve.

Figure 1-50
There are two basic types of tank valves: 1) the K-valve, which has a simple on/off valve, and 2) the J-valve, which has a mechanism to warn of low air pressure.

Tank Valves

Purpose — The tank valve turns the airflow from the tank on and off.

Styles — There are two basic types of tank valves: 1) the K-valve, which is a simple on/off valve, and 2) the J-valve, which has a built-in mechanism intended to signal you when tank pressure is low.

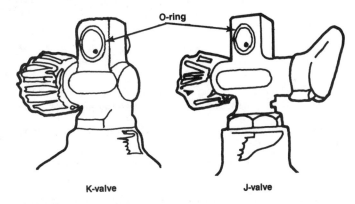

K-valve   J-valve

The J-valve contains a spring-operated shutoff valve that is held open by tank pressure until the pressure drops to approximately 300-500 psi. When the tank pressure drops below that point, the spring is no longer held open by the pressure, and it starts closing the valve, causing breathing resistance to increase. This signals you that tank pressure is low. You then pull down a lever on the valve to manually restore normal air flow.

The lever should be in the up position at the start of the dive and pulled down when breathing becomes difficult. Do not rely on a J-valve as the only warning that you are low on air, because the lever could accidentally be left in the down position at the start of the dive or knocked down during the dive. The only reliable way to monitor your tank pressure is to use a submersible pressure gauge, which will be discussed later in this module.

All tank valve openings are surrounded by a rubber O-ring whose purpose is to make a seal between the scuba tank and the scuba regulator when attached to the tank.

Features — A safety feature required on all valves is a burst disk. Burst disks relieve over pressurization in the tank, a situation that could occur from overfilling the tank or exposing it to excess heat. If the pressure gets too high, the burst disk opens, releasing the air to prevent a dangerous situation from occurring.

Materials, Selection and Preparation — Virtually all modern scuba tank valves are made of chrome-plated brass. Generally, the tank you select will come with a valve already in place. No special preparation is required.

Exercise 1-13

Tank Valves

1. A tank valve allows you to turn the airflow from the tank on and off. ☐ True ☐ False

2. The illustration depicts a: ☐ a. K-valve. ☐ b. J-valve.

3. The K-valve is equipped with a built-in reserve mechanism. ☐ True ☐ False

4. The function of the burst disk is to:
☐ a. allow you to attach your regulator to the tank.
☐ b. relieve pressure in the tank due to overfill or exposure to excess heat.

How did you do? *1.* True *2.* a *3.* False. The K-valve is an on-off valve only. The J-valve is equipped with a built-in reserve mechanism. *4.* b.

Objectives

After reading this section on the handling and maintenance of tanks and valves, you will be able to:

1. List two safety precautions for handling scuba tanks during transportation or at a dive site.

2. Describe the proper method of turning a tank valve on and off.

3. Explain the best way to pre-

Handling and Maintenance of Tanks and Valves

Handling — Scuba tanks are heavy, unstable when left standing and tend to roll when lying down. Always block tanks to keep them from rolling. A falling or rolling tank can damage not only its valve, but objects or people it runs into. Always keep tanks secure and never leave them standing unattended. If tanks must be left standing up, they should be secured to keep them from being knocked over.

When transporting tanks, lay them down horizontally and block or tie them.

vent water from entering a scuba tank.

4. State the purpose of a scuba tank visual inspection and pressure test.

Figure 1-51
When transporting tanks, lay them down horizontally and block or tie them.

Maintenance — Besides being rinsed on the outside with fresh water, dried and stored out of the sun like the rest of your equipment, tanks and valves have some special maintenance and storage considerations.

The tank valve should operate easily and smoothly. If there is any difficulty in operation, don't try to lubricate the valve. Have it serviced by a professional dive store. *Always close valves gently and avoid over-tightening.* Closing a valve too tightly can damage its high-pressure seal.

Tanks are filled with totally dry air because if moisture gets inside a tank, rust or corrosion will form rapidly on its inner surface. It is also important to prevent water from entering your tank while diving. The best way to be sure water stays out of your tank is to never allow it to be completely emptied of air pressure.

If, however, the tank pressure should somehow be exhausted completely, close the valve immediately to keep moisture out. Water can even enter an empty tank by backing up through a regulator, so having the regulator attached is not a safeguard. Also, avoid bleeding the air from your tank quickly, because this can cause internal condensation.

Tanks should only be filled with compressed air for breathing — never oxygen. The tank should be cooled in water during filling and be filled slowly. If it has a J-valve, the lever should be in the down position for filling. Tanks should only be filled to the rated pressure, since overfilling

Figure 1-52
Tanks are filled with totally dry air to prevent rust or corrosion from forming on their inner surfaces. Have tanks filled properly at a reputable air source, such as a professional dive store.

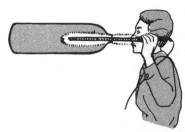

Figure 1-53
Proper maintenance of a scuba tank includes an annual visual inspection by a professional to check for possible internal corrosion or rust.

can lead to metal fatigue and shorten the life of the tank.

If your tank has a rubber or plastic boot, check underneath it periodically to make sure corrosion is not forming. Because tanks are susceptible to rust and corrosion, the inside must be *visually inspected by a professional at least once a year.* To do this, the tank is slowly drained of air and the valve is removed. The interior is then inspected using a special inspection light. (This service must only be performed by a trained professional at a qualified service center — do not empty the tank yourself.) Once the tank passes the visual inspection, a sticker is affixed to the tank with the date of the test. Professional dive facilities will not fill a tank without a current visual inspection sticker.

Tanks are also subject to metal fatigue, so *periodically a tank must be pressure tested* in what is called a *hydrostatic test.* During the test, the tank is evaluated for signs of fatigue and stress. When a tank passes the hydrostatic test, signifying that it can safely hold air at its rated pressure, the test date is stamped into the metal. Professional dive facilities will not fill a tank lacking a current hydrostatic test date. Your instructor will tell you what local or national standards relate to your cylinder hydrostatic testing. Standards vary from country to country.

Proper storage is another important part of tank maintenance. Scuba tanks should be stored in a cool place because the pressure of compressed air rises when exposed to heat. Full scuba tanks left in a hot trunk, for example, can have the pressure rise high enough to rupture their burst disks.

Tanks should always be stored with between 100-300 psi of air in them to keep moisture from entering. If a tank is stored without use longer than six months, have the tank refilled, since the air inside can turn stale.

With proper handling and maintenance, a scuba tank and valve can safely be used for many years.

Exercise 1-14

Handling and Maintenance of Tanks and Valves

1. Always keep tanks secure and never leave them standing unattended.
   ☐ True ☐ False

2. If a tank valve is closed forcefully or overtightened:
   ☐ a. It can damage the valve's high-pressure seal. ☐ b. You can avoid leaks during transportation.

3. The best way to prevent water from entering your scuba tank is to:
   ☐ a. Dry the tank thoroughly immediately upon exiting the water.
   ☐ b. Never allow it to be completely emptied of air pressure.

4. The purpose of a scuba tank visual inspection is to _____ ☐ a. Make sure corrosion is not forming.
   ☐ b. Check the quality of the air inside the tank.

How did you do? *1. True. 2. a 3. b 4. a.*

Objectives

After reading this section on backpacks, you will be able to:

1. State the purpose of a backpack.

2. Name two desirable features of a backpack.

Backpacks

Purpose and Styles — A backpack is designed to securely and comfortably hold a tank on a diver's back. This is usually done with a frame to hold the tank, shoulder straps and a waist strap. A number of different configurations are available, but most backpacks today are built into jacket and back-mounted style BCDs.

Features — Two desirable features on a backpack are 1) quick-release straps and 2) a quick-change tank retaining band.

The quick-release straps are usually found on one of the shoulder straps (unless there are no shoulder straps, such as when the backpack is part of a jacket-style BCD) and the waist strap. The quick-change retaining band allows you to move the backpack from one tank to another quickly and easily.

Materials, Selection and Preparation — Because the majority of backpacks are part of the BCD, the material used will be appropriate to the design of the BCD, and you

Figure 1-54
Backpacks hold the scuba tank securely and comfortably on a diver's back. Most modern backpacks are built into the BCD.

will select your backpack when you choose your BCD. When you adjust your BCD to prepare it for use, you are simultaneously preparing your backpack.

Most backpacks that are not part of a BCD are made of high-impact plastic and use nylon webbing for the shoulder and waist straps. To adjust one of these, lengthen or shorten the shoulder and waist straps to approximately the right length. With the backpack attached to a scuba tank, have someone help you try it on and make any final adjustments for a snug but comfortable fit.

Maintenance — Avoid lying your tank down on top of the backpack, especially if it's part of your BCD. Rinsing and checking to see that all fittings are secure is the only maintenance required.

Exercise 1-15

Backpacks

1. A backpack:
   - ☐ a. allows you to carry extra equipment on your dive.
   - ☐ b. holds the scuba tank securely and comfortable in place on your back.

2. Quick-release straps are not a desireable feature of a backpack. ☐ True ☐ False

How did you do? *1. b   2. False. Quick-release straps are a desireable feature of a backpack.*

Objectives

After reading this section on regulators, you will be able to:

1. State the purpose of a regulator.

2. Identify the following parts of a regulator: first and second stages, dust cover and purge button.

3. State the most important feature for consideration when selecting a regulator.

4. Outline three important points to remember when rinsing a regulator after use.

Regulators 📖

Purpose — A regulator is designed to reduce the high-pressure air of the scuba tank to a level that is usable. It delivers air to the diver only when the diver inhales.

Styles and Features — The modern scuba regulator is a very simple and reliable device with only a few moving parts. They have two *stages:* a first stage that attaches to the

Figure 1-55
Modern scuba regulator first and second stages.

📖 See *The Encyclopedia of Recreational Diving*

scuba tank and a second stage that has a mouthpiece. High-pressure air from the scuba tank is reduced sequentially in each stage. The first stage reduces the high tank pressure to an intermediate pressure of 100 to 150 psi above the surrounding water pressure. The second stage reduces the intermediate pressure to that needed for comfortable breathing. Easy breathing is the most important feature of a regulator.

Regardless of make, all modern regulators are relatively similar in basic structure. Familiarization with regulator terminology and how it functions will help you understand further explanations regarding regulators.

Look at the simplified drawings of a regulator's second stage for a view of the regulator's basic function and parts. The second stage is similar to a cup covered with a diaphragm (the diaphragm is simply a sheet of rubber). Additional parts of the second stage are a lever-operated inlet

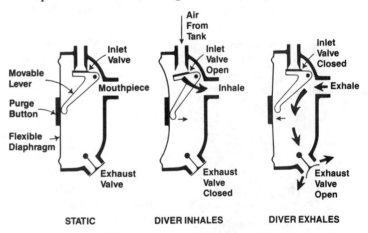

Figure 1-56
The function of the regulator second stage.

valve, a mouthpiece and an exhaust valve. As you inhale, the diaphragm is sucked inward, which opens the inlet valve by pushing down on the lever. This delivers your air (see Figure 1-56 *Diver Inhales).* When you stop inhaling, air pressure inside the second stage forces the diaphragm outward, releasing the lever and allowing the valve to close (see Figure 1-56 *Diver Exhales).* Note that you can manually control the flow of air at any time by pressing the purge button.

When you exhale, the exhaust valve opens and the air vents out through the exhaust tee (see Figure 1-56 *Diver Exhales).* The exhaust valve is a one-way valve that remains closed when you're not exhaling, keeping water out of the regulator.

The regulator you will use during confined-water training has an attached submersible pressure gauge that allows

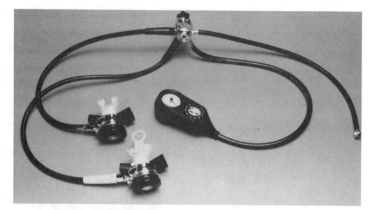

Figure 1-57
Typical regulator with alternate air source, submersible pressure gauge, and low-pressure inflator hose.

260A

Figure 1-58
Virtually all modern regulator first stages are made from chrome-plated brass, and second stages are made from chrome-plated brass, high-impact plastics or a combination of both.

you to determine how much air you have in your tank (this gauge will be discussed in detail shortly). The regulator will also have an extra second stage, called an *alternate air source* (alternate air sources may also be part of your BCD inflation/deflation hose). The alternate air source is used to simplify sharing air with another diver, should the need arise. You can often identify the alternate air source by its longer hose and brighter color. Alternate air sources are discussed in greater detail in Module Two. Finally, your regulator will have a hose with a coupling device at the free end. This hose connects to the low-pressure inflator of your BCD.

Materials — Although there are several manufacturers of popular regulators, virtually all regulators are made from the same basic materials. The first stage is generally made from chrome-plated brass, and the second stage may be made from brass, high-impact plastics or a combination of both. Parts like mouthpieces and exhaust tees are generally made from neoprene or silicone.

Selection — As mentioned earlier, the single most important feature in choosing a regulator is *ease of breathing,* both inhaling and exhaling. Choose an easy-breathing regulator by comparing flow rates and breathing resistance. When selecting your regulator, be sure to purchase the alternate air source at the same time. Again, your PADI Instructor and Dive Center can assist you in your selection.

Preparation — Aside from the assembly of your scuba unit (to be discussed in the Confined-Water Training Preview), a new regulator requires no special preparation other than the attachment of accessories. Attaching accessories should be done by a trained professional and will usually be taken care of when you purchase your regulator.

Maintenance — Your regulator needs to be rinsed after each use with the rest of your equipment, but it's usually best to soak it first, then rinse it with running water. When soaking and rinsing your regulator, keep these three points in mind: 1) Be sure the dust cover is firmly in place to keep water out of the first stage; 2) Do not use high-pressure water to rinse your regulator — only gently flowing water; and 3) Do not depress the purge button during rinsing, because this would open the second stage inlet valve and allow water to flow up the hose into the first stage.

Figure 1-59
When rinsing your regulator: be sure the
dust cap is firmly in place, that you use
only gently flowing water, and that you
don't depress the purge button.

During rinsing and soaking, water should be flushed through any holes in the first stage (except the high-pressure inlet covered by the dust cap, of course) and inside the second stage mouthpiece. It is a good precaution to attach the regulator to the scuba tank after rinsing and to purge the regulator briefly to blow out any water that may have entered the first stage accidentally.

Keep your regulator free of sand, mud and debris. To prevent damage to the hoses, when storing or packing your regulator, allow the hoses to form large, gentle curves rather than tight loops. Avoid pulling on them when the regulator is attached to the tank. It is better to store your regulator lying flat than to hang it by one of the stages or a hose.

An important part of regulator maintenance includes professional servicing at least once a year. With proper soaking, rinsing and storing, and with annual servicing, your regulator should provide many years of dependable service.

Exercise 1-16

Regulators

1. A regulator reduces the high-pressure air of the scuba tank to a level that is usable. ☐ True ☐ False

2. Identify the indicated part on the regulator illustration. ☐ a. Second stage ☐ b. First stage

3. The most important feature for consideration when selecting a regulator is:
   ☐ a. number of hoses. ☐ b. ease of breathing.

4. When rinsing a regulator, it's important to remember to:
   ☐ a. Put the dust cover firmly in place. ☐ b. Depress the purge button.

How did you do? *1. True 2. a 3. b 4. a.*

Objectives

After reading this section on submersible pressure gauges, you will be able to:

1. **State the purpose of the submersible pressure gauge.**

*Figure 1-60
Submersible Pressure Gauge.*

Submersible Pressure Gauge (SPG)

Purpose — The submersible pressure gauge (SPG) allows you to continuously monitor the amount of air in your tank during a dive, in much the same way that your car's gas gauge tells you how much gas you have. The SPG tells you how much air you have at the beginning of your dive and during your dive, permitting you to plan your dive so you can return safely to your exit point without running out of air. The SPG is mandatory equipment for all scuba diving.

Like the gas gauge in your car, the SPG is a passive device: you must get in the habit of watching it for it to have value. Develop the habit of checking your submersible pressure gauge frequently while diving.

Styles, Features, Materials, Selection — Although SPGs all have the same purpose, there are a few basic styles and features. These range from gauges that simply tell you your air pressure, to electronic gauges that incorporate other instruments. (These other instruments will be discussed in Module Two.) Have your PADI Dive Center or Instructor help you select the best SPG for your needs. Because the SPG is mandatory equipment, you should simultaneously purchase it with your regulator.

Preparation — The only preparation required is to have the SPG attached to the regulator, which should be done by your professional dive store when you purchase the SPG and regulator.

Maintenance — The SPG is a precision instrument and deserves careful handling. Do not drop or bang it, and be careful to avoid lying a tank or other heavy object on top of it.

Because the SPG remains attached to your regulator,

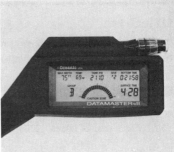

Figure 1-61
Submersible pressure gauges are often part of consoles that incorporate other instruments.

Figure 1-62
The SPG may be part of an electronic gauge that incorporates other instruments.

simply rinsing and soaking it along with the regulator takes care of its maintenance. When you take your regulator in for annual servicing, be sure to ask your serviceman to inspect the SPG as part of the servicing.

Equipment Identification

You should mark all your personal equipment for easy identification using special diving equipment markers. These may be marking paint, crayons or colored tape, among others.

Marking your equipment will prevent frustration and confusion when similar equipment, adjusted to different sizes, is being used by several divers, like on a boat or during confined-water training sessions. Equipment identification also helps distinguish one diver from another under water.

Exercise 1-17

Submersible Pressure Gauge (SPG)

1. The submersible pressure gauge:
   ☐ a. allows you to continuously monitor the amount of air in your tank during a dive.
   ☐ b. indicates the pressure of the water.

How did you do?   *1.* a.

The Buddy System

You should always dive with a buddy who stays nearby at all times. A buddy provides general assistance in putting on and checking your equipment before the dive; in helping

Objectives

After reading this section on the buddy system, you will be able to:

1. List three reasons for diving with a buddy at all times.

remind you of your depth, time and air supply limits; and in giving you emergency assistance in the unlikely event you need it. Your buddy will get the same assistance from you, and both of you will feel more secure diving together than alone.

Diving is a social activity — diving with someone adds to the fun. Together, you and your buddy will share experiences and witness the immense variety of scenes the underwater world displays. You may be surprised how many new friends you meet through diving and the buddy system.

Figure 1-63
The Buddy System

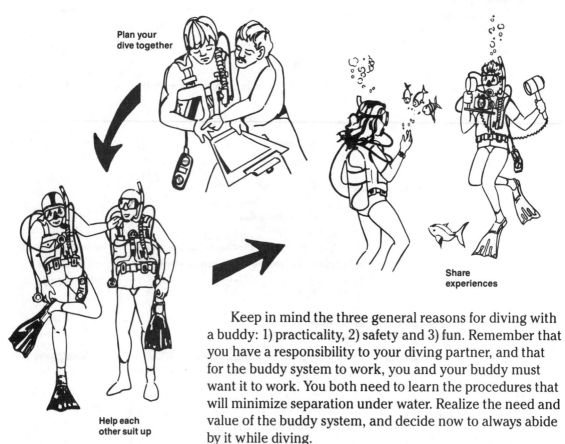

Plan your
dive together

Share
experiences

Help each
other suit up

Keep in mind the three general reasons for diving with a buddy: 1) practicality, 2) safety and 3) fun. Remember that you have a responsibility to your diving partner, and that for the buddy system to work, you and your buddy must want it to work. You both need to learn the procedures that will minimize separation under water. Realize the need and value of the buddy system, and decide now to always abide by it while diving.

Exercise 1-18

The Buddy System

1. There are practical reasons for diving with a buddy, one of these is the assistance he can provide in putting on and checking your equipment before the dive. ☒ True ☐ False

How did you do? *1. True.*

Confined-Water Training Preview — Module One

If you've never used scuba equipment before, you're about to have the most fun and excitement you've ever had in the water. You're about to breathe under water for the first time.

Those first breaths are exhilarating. Chances are, you will remember this first session in the water for the rest of your life.

Besides breathing with scuba for the first time, you'll be learning some underwater skills that you'll find both easy and fun. During the session, your instructor will always be close at hand, ready to assist you if necessary. If you have a question or would like assistance, don't be afraid to ask.

Figure 1-64
If you've never used scuba equipment before, you're about to have the most fun and excitement you've ever had in the water.

Figure 1-65
During the confined-water training session, your instructor will be close at hand. If you have a question or need assistance, don't be afraid to ask.

Read the following preview information carefully. This information will provide you with the general knowledge you will need to successfully participate in confined-water training. Knowing the information will make participating in the session more enjoyable, help you meet the performance requirements, and insure that the time you spend in the water is put to its best possible use.

The performance requirements listed here are those skills that must be successfully completed during the confined-water training of Module One. Read these requirements carefully so you will have an idea of what will be expected of you at this session.

Performance Requirements
Confined-Water Training — Module One

By the end of the confined-water training for Module One, you will be able to:

1. Correctly attach and remove a regulator from a scuba tank.

2. Correctly prepare, don and adjust mask, fins, snorkel, BCD, scuba and weights.

3. Orally inflate a BCD to about half full and then fully deflate it while at the surface in shallow water and in water too deep to stand up in.

4. Demonstrate proper compressed-air breathing habits, remembering especially to breathe naturally and not hold your breath at any time.

5. Recover a regulator hose from behind your shoulder while under water.

6. Clear a regulator while under water by exhalation and purge-button methods.

7. Clear a partially flooded mask while under water.

8. Swim under water with scuba equipment while maintaining control of both direction and depth.

9. Demonstrate a descent and ascent using the appropriate 5-step method.

10. Demonstrate proper disassembly and maintenance procedures of scuba equipment while on the pool deck.

Scuba Equipment Assembly

Before you can experience breathing under water for the first time, you must assemble your scuba equipment: tank, backpack and regulator. Assemble your scuba equipment carefully; remember that it is your *life-support equipment* while under water.

Putting the Backpack on the Tank — Whether or not your backpack is part of an integrated BCD, attaching it to the tank is essentially the same. Use the following steps:

1. Slide the backpack onto the tank from the top.

2. Before securing the backpack to the tank, orient the valve opening so that it faces toward the backpack.

The top of most backpacks should be about even with the base of the tank valve.

3. Secure the backpack onto the tank with its band and locking mechanism. Locking mechanisms vary, so have your instructor show you how your particular backpack's locking mechanism works.

4. Once you have positioned and locked the backpack, check to see that it is securely attached to the tank. To do this, lift the tank off the ground two or three inches by holding on to the top of the backpack. Give the tank a little shake. If the backpack does not move up and down on the tank, it's secure. If there is movement, readjust the band around the tank for a tighter fit.

Figure 1-66
Be sure to orient the backpack so the tank valve opening faces it. The top of most backpacks should be about even with the base of the tank valve.

Attaching the Regulator to the Tank — After the backpack is securely fastened to the tank, attach the regulator.

Figure 1-67
Remove the tape or cap from the tank valve (discard tape properly).

Figure 1-68
Verify that the O-ring is properly seated and undamaged.

Figure 1-69
Open the tank valve for a moment to blow out any accumulated water or dirt.

Proceed as follows:

1. The tank valve opening may be covered by a piece of tape or a plastic cap. If so, remove the tape or cap (discard tape properly — please do not litter).

2. Examine the tank valve opening. It should be surrounded by a rubber O-ring. Be sure the O-ring is seated properly. It should be clean and free from cuts or nicks. If a new O-ring is needed, see your instructor.

3. Open the tank valve slowly — just for a moment — to blow any accumulated water or dirt from the valve opening. The valve turns on counterclockwise and off clockwise, just like a water tap.

4. Remove the dust cap from the regulator first stage by unscrewing the knob on the first stage.

Figure 1-70
Place the tank between your legs with the backpack facing away from you.

Figure 1-71
Position the first stage on the valve so that the valve opening matches the regulator opening.

Figure 1-72
The regulator first stage should be mounted so the second stage hose leads to the right.

5. Set the tank between your legs with the backpack facing away from you. Position the first stage of the regulator on the tank valve so that 1) the valve opening matches the opening on the regulator first stage *and* 2) the second stage hose leads to the right. Remember, the second stage hose always goes over the right shoulder.

6. Tighten the first stage screw onto the valve until it is just finger tight. If the valve is a J-valve, the reserve lever should be in the up position.

7. If you are using an integrated BCD (back-mounted and jacket-style), attach the hose from the regulator to the low-pressure inflator Your instructor will show you how to connect this hose to the inflator. If you're using a front-mounted style BCD, you will connect this hose after you are wearing the BCD and scuba unit.

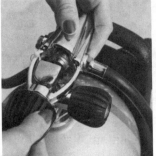

Figure 1-74
Attach the hose from the regulator to the low-pressure inflator. This is usually easier if you do it before you turn the air on. If you're using a front-mounted BCD, you'll attach the hose after you have the unit on.

Figure 1-73
Tighten the first stage screw until it's just finger-tight.

Turning on the Air and Checking the Unit — You should now be ready to turn on the air. Hold the submersible pressure gauge in your left hand, facing away from you for safety. Next, turn the air on slowly and listen for leaks. If

Figure 1-75
For safety, hold the SPG away from you when you turn the air on.

you hear a small leak, the O-ring may be dirty or defective. Ask your instructor to show you how to inspect and replace it. Open the valve all the way, then turn it back about a half turn.

Check the tank pressure using the submersible pressure gauge. By checking the pressure rating of the tank and comparing the reading on the SPG, you can determine about how full the tank is.

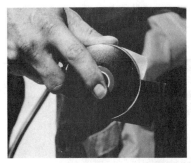

Figure 1-76
Check the tank pressure using the submersible pressure gauge.

Figure 1-77
Test the regulator by momentarily pushing the purge button. The air should flow freely and stop when you release the purge button.

Test the regulator by pressing the purge button momentarily. The air should flow freely and stop when you release the button. A slight hissing from the second stage may stop if the purge button is pressed or the mouthpiece opening is blocked momentarily. If it does not, notify your instructor.

Check the exhaust valve by exhaling into the regulator. Exhalation should be easy. If exhalation is difficult, the exhaust valve may be stuck — notify your instructor. If both the purge and exhaust valves function properly, take a few breaths from the regulator as a final check. The regulator should breathe easily and smoothly.

After assembling and checking your scuba system, do not leave it standing unattended while you don other equipment. Carefully lay it down, backpack up. It is also a good idea to lay the regulator on top of the backpack to keep it off the ground, away from sand and dirt.

Your instructor will be at hand while you put your scuba equipment together. If you have any problems or questions, don't hesitate to ask for assistance.

Preparation of Additional Equipment

Your mask, snorkel and fins should be prepared prior to the confined-water training session. As you read earlier, this equipment should be properly adjusted and marked. This will save time and reduce confusion during the session. Other equipment, such as the BCD and weight belt, will be adjusted prior to putting them on. If you need assistance or have questions while adjusting your equipment, see your instructor.

Adjusting the BCD — Regardless of the type of BCD you

Figure 1-78
Check the exhaust valve by exhaling into the regulator. It should be easy to exhale.

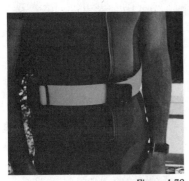

Figure 1-79
Adjust your weight belt so the weights are distributed evenly and the length is no more than 6-8 inches longer than needed to fit your waist.

Figure 1-80
Donning equipment is easier if you and your buddy help each other. Generally, it's best to don your equipment in this order: wet suit, BCD/scuba unit, weight belt, mask and snorkel, and fins.

use during confined-water training, it must be adjusted to feel snug and comfortable. Adjust the BCD following the procedures outlined earlier in the section on BCDs.

After you have your BCD properly adjusted, examine the various controls and familiarize yourself with their operation. If you have a question or need assistance, ask your instructor.

Adjusting the Weight Belt — You may use a weight belt in this confined-water training session. If a weight belt is to be used, your instructor will tell you approximately how much weight to use. Distribute the weights evenly on the belt and adjust the belt length to be no more than six to eight inches longer than needed to fit your waist. (You will learn more about weight belts in Module Two.)

Donning Equipment

Being familiar with how to put your equipment on will help the confined-water training session flow in an unhurried, enjoyable manner. Your instructor will give you additional specifics that relate to using your equipment, so always wait to put on your equipment until you are instructed to do so. In general, though, you'll don your equipment in this order: wet suit, BCD/scuba unit, weight belt, mask and snorkel, and fins.

Wet Suit — Wet-suit jackets or vests may be used during your confined-water training to keep you warmer in colder water and to help you become familiar with their use and buoyancy effects. Wet suits will be discussed in detail during Module Two, but for this session, you only need to know a few points.

Except when wet-suit pants are worn, the wet-suit boots are the first items to put on. Work the boots on slowly,

Figure 1-81
Work the boots on slowly, wiggling and twisting your foot in as you pull the boot up to the top of your ankle.

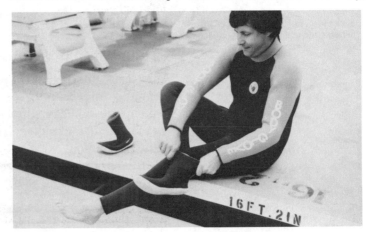

Figure 1-82
Put the wet-suit jacket on one arm at a time. Work the sleeve all the way up to your armpit before starting on your other arm.

a little at a time, wiggling and twisting your foot in as you work the top of the boot up onto your ankle.

If a wet-suit jacket is used, put it on one arm at a time. Work the sleeve all the way up to your arm pit before starting on your other arm. Pull or stretch the seams as little as possible. It may seem difficult to get the jacket on at first, but with practice it gets easier.

Next, fasten the crotch flap (if present) to hold the sides of the jacket together at the bottom, then zip the jacket up. With a proper fit, the suit should feel snug and somewhat restrictive. The restriction will ease when you get in the water, and after using the wet-suit jacket a bit, you'll get used to how it feels.

If you don't use a wet-suit jacket or vest during the session, it's recommended that you wear some sort of covering, such as a T-shirt, sweatshirt or body suit, to keep the tank and BCD straps from chaffing your shoulders.

Buoyancy Control Device — If a front-mounted BCD is used (the type not integrated with the backpack), it should be put on before the scuba unit. If a jacket- or back-mounted style BCD is used, it will be put on simultaneously with the scuba unit.

Scuba Unit — Before putting on the scuba unit, first prepare the backpack harness straps. If shoulder straps are present, all quick releases should be connected and the straps should be adjusted to your approximate size. The waist belt should be unfastened until you put the unit on.

The safest and easiest way to put your scuba unit on is to have your buddy hold the unit while you slip into it like a coat. Doing this for the first time in this session, your

Figure 1-83
The safest and easiest way to don your scuba tank or unit is to have your buddy hold it.

instructor will probably have you do this standing in shallow water. Before your buddy releases the weight of the unit onto your back, be sure to straighten any twisted straps and remove hoses or accessories trapped beneath the straps. Your buddy should then lower the unit onto your back and assist you in locating the waist belt on each side.

At this point, bend forward and balance the tank on your back to take the strain off the harness. It is easier to adjust and secure the unit in this position than when standing upright. Check to be sure that the waist belt release opens to the *left*.

After the tank is secure, stand upright and tilt your head back to check the height adjustment of the tank. If your head can touch the valve, the tank is probably too high in the backpack and should be repositioned. Take the tank off and readjust the height of the backpack.

Figure 1-84
After donning the scuba unit, tilt your head back to be sure your head can't easily touch the tank valve.

If you're using a front-mounted style BCD, connect the low-pressure inflator hose after you have the unit on and adjusted.

Weight Belt — Depending on the BCD and scuba unit you are using, your instructor may have you put on the weight belt either before or after donning the scuba unit. Regardless of whether you put the weight belt on before or after the scuba unit, you must be able to remove it quickly and easily. This means that the weight belt must be free and clear of all other equipment. Your instructor will advise you on the best way to ensure that the weight belt is clear for easy removal.

To put the weight belt on before entering the water, hold the buckle end in your left hand and the free end in your right hand. Step over it and then bend forward, posi-

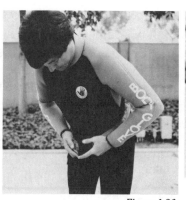

Figure 1-85
To don the weight belt, start by holding the buckle end in your left hand and the free end in your right hand, then step over it.

Figure 1-86
Bend forward, positioning the belt to rest across the small of your back. This makes it easy to buckle.

Figure 1-87
In this manner your weight belt can be released by the right-hand. Check to be sure no hoses, straps or accessories are trapped under the belt.

tioning the belt across the small of your back. By donning the belt in this manner, you take the strain off the front portion of the belt so you can easily position the belt and secure the buckle.

Be sure you wear the weight belt so that it can be released by the right-hand. This is a standard release position. Generally, if you have the buckle on the left-hand side, the release opens to the right. Note that the weight-belt release and the scuba-unit waist belt should open in opposite directions to help prevent confusion.

After you have the weight belt on, be sure it is snug but not tight. Check that no straps, accessories or regulator hoses are trapped under it. Loosen and secure the weight belt several times until you can do it confidently without looking. Under water, with a mask and BCD on, it's difficult to see your waist, so you'll want to be sure you can operate the weight belt by touch.

Finally, make sure the weights are evenly distributed on the belt and are not interfering with the operation of the quick-release buckle. It also helps to have the weights slightly forward on your hips to make you more stable when swimming.

Figure 1-88
Use antifog compounds to prevent condensation from forming inside your mask. Rub the compound over the inside surface of the mask, then rinse it quickly with water.

Mask — Condensation will fog the inside of your mask unless the glass is coated with a substance to prevent the fogging. Commercial antifog compounds are recommended, though saliva will work if none is available. Put some compound on the inside portion of the glass, rub it in and around, then rinse the mask quickly with water.

Now you're ready to put your mask on. Position it on your face with one hand, while using your other hand to

Figure 1-89
Put the mask on by positioning it on your face with one hand, while using your other hand to pull the strap over to the back of your head.

pull the strap over to the back of your head (see Figure 1-89). You should have adjusted your mask and snorkel before the session, but check the fit after putting the mask on.

Develop the habit of keeping your mask on your face until you exit the water. Propping the mask on your forehead should be avoided because it can result in losing your mask when diving in open water. Also, in many areas, a mask propped on the forehead is recognized as a signal of distress.

Fins — Fins are usually the last piece of equipment you don. Always put your fins on at the water's edge; walking in fins is clumsy and can be hazardous. If you must walk with fins (whether in or out of the water), shuffle your feet and walk backwards, always looking over your shoulder to see where you're going.

Figure 1-90
Walking in fins is clumsy and can be hazardous. If you must walk in fins, shuffle your feet and walk backwards, always looking over your shoulder to see where you're going.

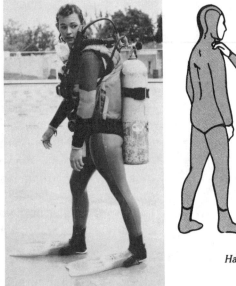

Figure 1-91
Have your buddy steady you as you put on your fins.

Wet your feet (or boots) and fins to make them easier to don. Have your buddy steady you as you put on one fin at a time as shown in Figure 1-91. Be sure to work your foot well into the foot pocket before pulling the heel portion of the fin in place.

Equipment Inspection

You and your buddy should develop the habit of inspecting each other's equipment for correct positioning, adjustment and function before entering the water. Also, you and your buddy should be familiar with the location and operation of each other's BCD controls and releases.

Figure 1-92
You and your buddy should develop the habit of inspecting each other's equipment before entering the water.

BCD Inflation and Deflation

With your equipment correctly donned and inspected by your buddy, you'll be ready to start learning some skills in the water. You will want to know how to inflate your BCD at the surface so that you can remain upright at the surface to rest, talk, listen or make equipment adjustments without having to tread water. An inflated BCD will also provide you with support while swimming at the surface. Whenever you're at the surface, you should have your BCD partially inflated.

There are two ways to inflate your BCD: orally and through the low-pressure inflator mechanism connected to your regulator. To orally inflate the BCD:

1. Take a breath.
2. Place the mouthpiece on the end of the BCD hose into your mouth.
3. Open the inflation valve (usually by pressing a button).
4. Blow about two thirds of the air in your lungs into the BCD hose.
5. Release the inflation valve button.

Figure 1-93
Inflating the BCD at the surface.

Figure 1-94
When inflating your BCD with the low-pressure inflator, use short bursts to permit easy control.

Your mouth and the inflator do not need to be above the surface during inflation. In fact, it requires energy to lift yourself out of the water, and that energy should be conserved. Simply lift your chin to take a breath, then put your face back into the water, blowing into the mouthpiece below the surface. Do this several times and you will be sufficiently buoyant to keep your head above water without kicking. Be sure to release the inflation valve button between breaths, so the air does not flow back out of the BCD.

To inflate the BCD using the low-pressure inflator mechanism, find the control that allows air to flow from the tank into the BCD (be careful not to accidentally press the control that allows air to vent from the BCD). Put air in your

BCD in short bursts to permit easy control of inflation.

Whether inflating your BCD orally or with the low-pressure inflator, you will find that full inflation is usually unnecessary and may even be uncomfortable. Filling your BCD about half full is generally adequate for resting or swimming at the surface.

Figure 1-95
To deflate the BCD, get into a vertical position and press the exhaust valve while making it the highest point on the BCD.

To deflate the BCD, get into a vertical position and simply depress the exhaust valve while making it the highest point on the BCD. For most BCDs, this is as simple as holding up the exhaust valve on the end of the BCD hose or, on some BCDs, you may use a specially designed "dump" valve for convenient deflation.

Introduction to Scuba

After learning to inflate and deflate the BCD, you'll be ready to use scuba and take that first memorable breath under water.

Before you go under for the first time, pay attention to your instructor. Communications are limited under water, so your instructor may give you hand signals to watch for.

As you breathe from scuba for the first time, remember to breathe slowly, deeply and continuously. Keep in mind the primary rule in scuba — never hold your breath. While under water, keep your eyes on your instructor at all times, watching for his or her signals.

Figure 1-96
When breathing under water for the first time, remember to breathe slowly, deeply and continuously.

Regulator Clearing

Once you're comfortable with breathing under water, your instructor will teach you how to remove the regulator from your mouth and replace it. When you remove the regulator from your mouth, it fills with water. This isn't a problem, though, because you can easily clear the water from it. There are two standard methods for clearing a regulator: 1) by exhaling into it (the exhalation method) and 2) using the purge button (the purge method).

The exhalation method is as easy as it sounds. Simply blow into the regulator with the second stage in an upright position so the exhaust valve is the lowest point. Air blown into the second stage from your lungs will force the water out through the exhaust valve. Remember that you must exhale before inhaling, and that the regulator must be in an upright position.

To use the purge method, place the second stage in your mouth in an upright position and block the mouthpiece opening with your tongue to prevent water from being blown into your mouth and throat. Next, push the purge button on the regulator to release air from the tank into the second stage. This air will force the water out through the exhaust valves, clearing the regulator so you can breathe normally.

Most divers use the exhalation method, reserving the purge method for when they need to clear the regulator but have little air in their lungs. Only a small amount of air is needed to clear a regulator, so you'll usually have enough air in your lungs to use the exhalation method.

As you practice this skill, keep the regulator mouthpiece turned downward when you remove it from your mouth. If you turn it upward, air may flow freely from it and be wasted (this is called *free flowing*); simply turn the mouthpiece downward and it will stop.

Figure 1-97
To clear the regulator using the purge method, come to an upright position, block the mouthpiece with your tongue and press the purge button momentarily.

Figure 1-98
Any time the regulator is not in your mouth under water, begin blowing a small continuous stream of bubbles by making an A-a-a-h-h-h sound.

You also need to begin developing an important habit while you practice regulator clearing. *Any time the regulator is not in your mouth under water, begin blowing a small, continuous stream of bubbles by making an A-a-a-a-a-h-h-h sound.* You must never hold your breath with compressed air in your lungs. As you've already learned, ascending with compressed air trapped in your lungs can cause serious lung damage due to overexpansion. By making the *A-a-a-a-h-h-h* sound whenever the regulator is not in your mouth, the airway to your lungs will be kept open, and the expanding air will easily escape.

Regulator Recovery

Once you know how to clear the regulator, you'll want to learn how to locate it quickly and effortlessly in the unlikely event that it should accidentally come out of your mouth

*Figure 1-99
Recovering the regulator
using the arm-sweep method.*

under water or when switching from your snorkel to the regulator on the surface. There are two methods you may use to recover your regulator: 1) the *arm-sweep* and 2) the *reach*.

To recover your regulator using the arm-sweep method, first come to an upright position and lower your right shoulder. Next, extend your arm out to your side and behind you until you can touch your tank. Sweep your arm forward, while extended, until the regulator hose hits your arm. Grasp the hose while sliding your hand downward toward the second stage. Once the second stage is found, put the regulator back in your mouth and clear it.

To recover the regulator using the reach method, first

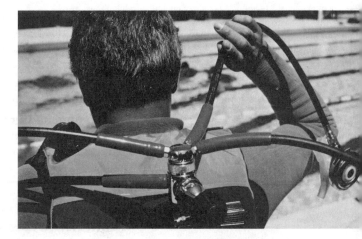

Figure 1-100
Recovering the regulator using
the reach method.

reach back behind you and find where the regulator hose is attached to the first stage. Once you find the proper hose, follow it with your hand until you locate the second stage. Put the regulator back in your mouth and clear it. When using the reach method of recovery, you may find it helpful to lift the bottom of your tank with your left hand, pushing it up and to the right. This makes it easier for your right hand to reach the first stage and find the hose.

You will practice both methods of recovery during this confined-water training session. *Remember to make the A-a-a-a-h-h-h sound underwater whenever the regulator is not in your mouth.*

Mask Clearing

By the time you've finished practicing regulator clearing and recovery, you may have noticed that a little water tends to trickle into your mask from time to time. Fortunately, clearing your mask is easy. During this confined-water training session, you will practice clearing the water from a *partially* flooded mask.

Figure 1-101
To clear a mask without a purge valve, hold the top of the mask firmly in place and look up slightly while exhaling through your nose.

To clear water from a mask without a purge valve, simply hold the top of the mask firmly against your forehead, then look up slightly while exhaling through the nose. The air from your nose will force the water out the bottom of your mask. *Note: Begin exhaling before tipping your head back to prevent water from running into your nose.*

If your mask has a purge valve, begin by holding the mask snugly against your entire face and looking down, making the purge valve the lowest point in the mask. Next, begin exhaling through your nose. The air will force the water out through the purge valve.

Figure 1-102
To clear a mask with a purge valve, hold the mask firmly in place and look down while exhaling through your nose.

Mask clearing is easiest when you exhale steadily and

continuously. Before you try to clear your mask under water, practice exhaling an entire breath slowly and steadily through your nose.

Mask clearing is most efficient when little or no air escapes in the process. Since the volume of a mask is small compared to your lungs, you may be able to clear your mask several times on just one breath.

Use of Fins

When you have successfully practiced clearing a partially flooded mask, your instructor will have you practice swimming with scuba on. The standard kick for diving is the *flutter kick,* but it's different than the short, quick kick used when swimming without fins. When using fins, slow your kick and lengthen the stroke. The idea is to have the fins pointed behind you, moving slowly and powerfully up and down from the hip to make use of the powerful thigh muscles. Your legs should be extended and your knees should

Figure 1-103
The flutter kick used for diving is longer and slower than the short, quick kick used without fins.

bend only slightly. The power portion of the stroke is downward. If you are kicking properly, you will feel the pull of the tendons on the top of your foot where it meets the ankle.

The fins only provide propulsion when they are submerged, so keep them below the water when swimming at the surface. Kick down farther, and up less, while arching your back upward to force your legs downward. You may find it practical to swim on your back or side, making possible a wider kick while keeping the fins submerged.

Speed is not the objective when swimming with scuba, so don't try to swim rapidly. Arm movements actually reduce momentum under water when you're using fins, so keep your arms still and trailing at your sides.

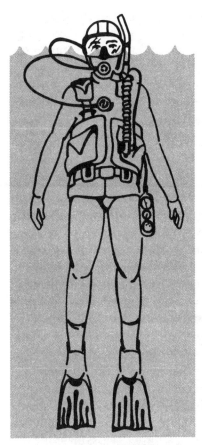

Figure 1-104
You are neutrally buoyant at the surface when you can float at eye level without kicking.

Neutral Buoyancy at the Surface

As you learned in the section on buoyancy, learning to maintain neutral buoyancy is an important diving skill. During this confined-water training session, your instructor will show you how to use your BCD to establish neutral buoyancy at the surface in water too deep to stand up in. Practicing this skill will allow you to become more familiar with your BCD and show you how to rest at the surface comfortably if you are slightly overweighted.

You will begin the exercise by moving to deeper water and completely deflating your BCD — you will probably need to kick to stay at the surface. Next, slowly add small amounts of air to your BCD, either orally or using the low-pressure inflator.

Your objective is to add just enough air to your BCD so you float at eye level without kicking. You will then be neutrally buoyant at the surface. If you have to add a lot of air to attain neutral buoyancy, you're carrying too much lead weight.

Equalization and Underwater Swimming

Your instructor will give you a chance to practice swimming with fins and equalizing your ears before you start practicing the actual scuba descent and ascent procedures you'll be using for the rest of the course. To do this, the instructor will have you swim back and forth from shallow to deeper water. Relax as much as possible, swimming slowly to conserve air and energy. Equalize your ears as soon as you submerge and frequently as you move to deeper water.

While swimming under water, your direction is controlled by moving the trunk of your body. If you arch your

Figure 1-105
Equalize your ears as soon as you submerge and frequently as you move into deeper water.

back upward, you will go up; if you bend it downward, you will go down; if you angle it right or left, you will turn accordingly. Arm movements are only helpful for making sharp turns.

Descending Under Water

Your instructor will have you practice making correct descents into the deep end of the pool or confined water. There are five steps to a correct descent that you should practice and learn, because you will use them repeatedly throughout the course and while diving.

1. You and your buddy should signal to each other that your are ready to descend.

2. Orient yourself to some surface object for reference.

3. Remove the snorkel from your mouth and replace it with your regulator mouthpiece. This should be done without lifting your head from the water. Remember to clear the regulator before taking a breath. (*Note: You will actually learn snorkel-to-regulator exchanges in Module Two, so for this session only, use the regulator the entire time.*)

4. Check the time at the beginning of your descent. There are time limitations at certain depths, and time begins as soon as you submerge — you'll learn more about time limits later. If you don't have an underwater watch during this training session, look at your wrist just prior to descent to simulate noting the time. Doing so will help you develop the habit of always checking the time before descending.

5. Slowly deflate your BCD and exhale to initiate a feet-first descent. Equalize your ears immediately upon submerging and do so frequently during descent.
Always maintain complete control of your descent so that

Figure 1-106
You will practice all five steps of a correct descent during confined-water training.

you can stop or ascend at any time. To control your descent, be conscious of your lung volume and the amount of air in your BCD. Descend slowly, keeping your fins beneath you so you can kick upward if you need to.

Ascending

There are also five steps in making a proper ascent that you will learn and practice. These are:

1. You and your buddy should signal each other that you agree to ascend.

2. Note the time of your ascent. If you do not have a watch, simulate checking the time by looking at your wrist.

3. Extend one hand over your head for protection and put your other hand on the BCD exhaust valve control.

Figure 1-107
Correct ascents also have five steps, which you will practice during confined-water training.

4. Look up and around, slowly rotating during your entire ascent.

5. Swim up slowly, at a rate no faster than one foot per second, while breathing normally.

As soon as you and your buddy reach the surface, you will want to inflate your BCD so you can float comfortably and effortlessly.

Exit from the Water

There are several methods of exiting the water and you'll learn the most common ones during this course. For this session, begin by positioning yourself in shallow water and stand up. Next, remove your equipment and place it on the pool's edge. Your instructor will demonstrate the equipment removal procedure he would like you to use prior to exiting the water.

Equipment Disassembly and Care

When you are finished using your scuba equipment, it is necessary to disassemble it for rinsing and storage. First, you need to remove the regulator from the tank. To do this, turn off the air by turning the tank valve clockwise, then push the purge button on the regulator until you hear that the pressure is completely released. This relieves the pressure in the regulator — if you fail to do this, the pressure will make it almost impossible to remove the regulator.

After relieving the pressure, remove the regulator, being careful to not allow water to drip into the high-pressure inlet on the first stage. Thoroughly dry the regulator dust cap and position it over the high-pressure inlet, then gently tighten the first stage screw to hold the dust cover firmly in place.

Once the regulator is removed and the dust cap secured, wrap loose tank straps around the backpack and buckle them. This keeps the straps from dragging and tangling. Remember to set the tank down (not on the backpack or BCD) so it can't fall over. Once the session is completed, don't forget to rinse all of your equipment with fresh water.

Figure 1-108
When you finish the confined-water training session, disassemble your equipment, rinse it and store it properly. A few minutes of care will insure your equipment lasts and remains reliable.

Summary

You are now ready for the confined-water training session for Module One. The new skills you will be practicing are:

1. Scuba equipment assembly
2. Equipment preparation
3. Donning equipment
4. BCD inflation and deflation
5. Introduction to scuba
6. Regulator clearing
7. Regulator recovery
8. Mask clearing
9. Use of fins
10. Neutral buoyancy at the surface
11. Equalization and underwater swimming
12. Descending under water
13. Ascending
14. Exiting from the water

Two

☐ **Adapting to the Underwater World**

☐ **Respiration**

☐ **Diving Equipment**

☐ **Diving Communications**

☐ **Buddy System Procedures**

☐ **Confined-Water Training Preview**

Figure 2-1

Adapting to the Underwater World

In the confined-water training session of Module One, you made your first venture into the underwater world and experienced new sensations, such as being almost weightless and breathing under water. You probably noticed some differences in how things look or sound when you're under water, too.

As an air-breathing creature, you have evolved for life on land. Above the water, you see, hear and move about in a familiar and comfortable manner that seems normal because you're adapted to an air environment.

Under water, though, you're in a new world, where seeing, hearing, staying warm and moving are different. This is because water is 800 times more dense than air, affecting

69

light, sound and heat in ways that we aren't used to.

To give you a greater understanding of the aquatic environment, this section focuses on the changes you experience in vision, hearing, heat loss and motion while under water. Understanding these changes and becoming familiar with them permits you to adapt to them as you learn to dive.

Underwater Vision 📖

Sight-seeing is a big part of what diving is all about. You will go diving for a myriad of reasons, yet your primary purpose will probably be to *see* new environments, aquatic life and

Objectives

After reading this section on underwater vision, you will be able to:

1. State how an object's apparent size is affected under water.

2. Explain how water affects light intensity and colors.

Figure 2-2
Under water, you're in a new world, where seeing, hearing, staying warm and moving are different than in air.

natural phenomena. Since seeing is so important, you need to know how the liquid environment affects vision.

To see clearly under water, you need a mask because the human eye cannot focus without an air space in front of

Figure 2-3
The human eye can't focus without an air space in front of it.

Figure 2-4
With a mask, you can see clearly because it provides the air space your eyes need to focus properly.

Figure 2-6
The magnification effect of water is demonstrated by a pencil in a glass of water. The submerged half looks larger and closer than the exposed half.

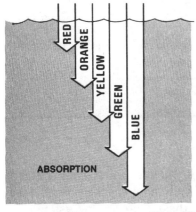

Figure 2-7
Water absorbs color as depth increases.

it. Your mask provides this air space. Without the mask, you can see large objects, but they will be blurred and indistinct because your eyes cannot bring the rays of light into sharp focus. Only by wearing a mask can you see sharply.

Light travels at a different speed in water than in air. When light enters the air in your mask from the water, the change in speed causes its angle of travel to shift slightly.

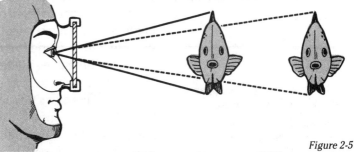

Figure 2-5
Under water, objects appear 25% larger and closer.

This causes a magnification effect that makes objects under water appear 25% larger and closer.

Water has other effects on light. As you descend, there is less light. This is due to several facts: some light reflects off the water's surface, some is scattered by particles in the water, and some is absorbed by the water itself. However, water does not absorb light uniformly.

White light, such as sunlight, is actually composed of various colors mixed together. The colors are absorbed one by one as depth increases (Figure 2-7): first red, followed by orange and yellow. Since each color is part of the total light entering the water, less light remains as depth increases and each color is absorbed. For these reasons, deeper water is darker and less colorful. Red, orange or yellow objects often appear brownish, gray or black. To see true colors, divers sometimes carry underwater lights with them.

Exercise 2-1

Underwater Vision

1. Underwater, the _____ effect makes objects appear 25% _____ and closer.
   - ☑ a. magnification, larger   ☐ b. particle, smaller

2. Colors are absorbed by water. The color that is absorbed first is _____
   - ☐ a. blue.   ☐ b. orange.   ☑ c. red.

How did you do?   *1.* a   *2.* c.

Objectives

After reading this section on underwater hearing, you will be able to:

1. Explain how hearing is affected under water.

Underwater Hearing 📖

The underwater world is not a silent world. You'll hear many new and interesting sounds, like snapping shrimp, grunting fish, and boat engines passing in the distance. Sound travels farther in water than in air, so you'll be able to hear things over much longer distances than you are used to above the surface.

Sound also travels about four times faster in water than in air. Because of this, you may have trouble determining the direction a sound is coming from. Under water, sound seems to come from all directions at once.

Speech is virtually impossible under water because your vocal cords do not work in a liquid environment. Communication by sound is usually limited to attracting the attention of another diver by rapping on your tank with a solid object, such as your knife. The diver will hear the rapping, but may not be able to tell where the sound is coming from

Exercise 2-2

Underwater Hearing

1. Sound travels ___4___ times faster in water than in air, and under water you may have trouble determining the _direction_ a sound is coming from. ☐ a. 2, depth ☑ b. 4, direction

How did you do? *1. b.*

Objectives

After reading this section on heat loss in water, you will be able to:

1. Compare the rate of body heat loss in water to body heat loss in air.

2. Describe what action a diver should take if he begins to shiver continuously under water.

Heat Loss in Water 📖

Diving stops being enjoyable if you get chilled under water — in fact, even a small loss of body heat has the potential to be a serious health threat. For these reasons, understanding about heat loss in the water is important.

In air, body heat is lost as it rises from the skin into the air, as it is carried away by air currents, or as perspiration cools the skin through evaporation. Water conducts heat away from your body about 20 times faster than air does, meaning that for a given temperature, water has a far greater cooling effect. Even seemingly warm 86°F water can become chilly after a while.

The loss of body heat in water can quickly lead to a serious condition unless you use insulation to reduce the heat loss. Insulation through the use of exposure suits is recommended for diving in water 75°F or colder. (Expo-

📖 See *The Encyclopedia of Recreational Diving*

sure suits are discussed in more detail later in this module.) Just as you dress according to the temperature and conditions when you go outdoors, you must dress appropriately for diving. For comfort and to prevent excessive heat loss, you will probably want to wear some form of insulation at all times.

Even with this insulation, you can get chilled after being under water for some time. Continuous shivering is a warning signal telling you that heat loss has reached a critical level. When you begin to shiver continuously, *get out of the water, dry off and seek warmth.*

Figure 2-8
Water conducts heat away from your body about 20 times faster than air. Even seemingly warm 86°F water can become chilly after a while.

Exercise 2-3

Heat Loss in Water

1. Water conducts heat away from your body approximately _____ times faster than air does.

    ☑ a. 20 ☐ b. 55

2. If you begin shivering continuously under water, you should swim faster to warm up.   ☐ True ☑ False

How did you do? *1. a 2. False. If you begin to shiver continuously, get out of the water, dry off and seek warmth.*

Objectives

After reading this section on motion in water, you will be able to:
1. Describe how a diver should move under water to compensate for the increased resistance of water.

Motion in Water

One of the best aspects of diving is that it can be so relaxing. There's little reason for hurrying. By learning how to move about without breathlessness, cramping or fatigue, you learn to relax during a dive.

Due to the greater density of water, resistance to movement in water is much greater than in air. If you've ever tried to run in waist-deep water, you've experienced this. In overcoming this increased resistance while diving, the best way to conserve energy is to move slowly and steadily. Avoid rapid and jerky movements that waste energy. Take your time.

The amount of surface area you expose to the water affects the amount of energy you use to swim. A streamlined object presenting a small frontal area needs less energy to move at a given speed than does an object with a large frontal area. Streamline yourself as you move through the water. When you and your equipment are streamlined, you save energy because you are pushing against less water (see Figure 2-9). As much as possible, swim through the water in a horizontal position.

Trying to swim fast or work hard in the water will cause you to tire quickly. Learn to pace yourself, take it easy and relax while diving. These are important aspects of your diver training.

Figure 2-9
Streamlining saves energy by reducing the amount of water you have to push against.

Exercise 2-4

Motion in Water

1. When swimming through the water, you should move:
   ☑ a. slowly and steadily to conserve energy.   ☐ b. quickly and rapidly to see more.

How did you do?   *1.* a.

Respiration

Unlike a fish, which is capable of obtaining the oxygen necessary for sustaining life directly from the water, you must take an air supply with you when you venture beneath the surface. Although you are breathing air, you must learn the best *way* to breathe when diving.

By understanding something about how you breathe, you can learn the proper method of breathing for diving. This is an important step in adapting to the underwater environment.

Breathing Efficiency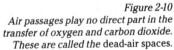

Each breath of air you take contains oxygen — the gas needed to sustain life. When the air reaches your lungs, your blood absorbs oxygen to carry to the cells of your body and releases waste carbon dioxide gas carried away from the cells. When you exhale, the waste carbon dioxide is carried out. The two gases transfer only within your lungs. The air passages to and from your lungs — your mouth, throat and windpipe — contain air that plays no direct part in the transfer of oxygen and carbon dioxide.

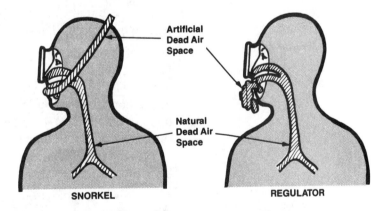

Figure 2-10
Air passages play no direct part in the transfer of oxygen and carbon dioxide. These are called the dead-air spaces.

These are called *dead-air spaces*. Snorkels and regulators *increase* the amount of dead-air space that naturally exists in your body by increasing the volume of the air passages.

When you inhale, the first air drawn into your lungs is air left in the dead-air spaces from your previous breath. This air is high in carbon dioxide. If you take shallow breaths, each breath has a relatively high amount of carbon dioxide because you inhale proportionately little fresh air. You are essentially rebreathing the air from your dead-air spaces. Shallow breathing is not very efficient because so little of the air you breathe in and out actually gets to take part in the exchange of oxygen and carbon dioxide.

If you breathe deeply on the other hand, you draw in much more fresh air. In this case, there is a much greater proportion of fresh air reaching the lungs on each breath.

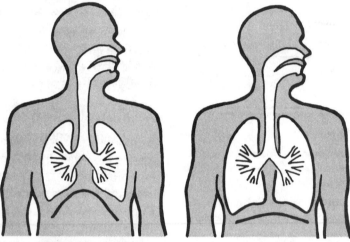

Figure 2-11
Shallow breathing is not very efficient because little of the air you breathe in and out actually takes part in the exchange of oxygen and carbon dioxide. Deep breathing brings a greater proportion of fresh air into the lungs with each breath.

SHALLOW BREATHING   **DEEP BREATHING**

This means deep breathing is more efficient breathing.

It is important to breathe efficiently while diving, whether breathing through scuba or through a snorkel. Because this equipment increases the dead-air space, the amount of air you must move to get fresh air into your lungs and stale air out is also increased. The proper breathing pattern for diving is consistently slow and deep breathing. When using scuba, you should inhale more slowly and deeply than normal, and exhale more slowly and deeply than normal. You should breathe the same way when using a snorkel, but you may need to exhale sharply and rapidly from time to time to blow water out of it.

By breathing efficiently and limiting your activity while diving, you will be comfortable. If you overexert yourself, you may create a feeling of air starvation.

Exercise 2-5

Breathing Efficiency

1. For maximum breathing efficiency under water, always breathe slowly and deeply.   ☑ True   ☐ False

How did you do?   *1. True.*

Objectives

After reading this section on overexertion, you will be able to:

1. Name eight symptoms of diving overexertion.

2. Describe how to prevent diving overexertion.

3. Describe what a diver should do if he becomes overexerted while diving — either at the surface or under water.

Overexertion

If you attempt to maintain an elevated activity level while diving — like swimming against a current, swimming long distances or carrying excessive weight — you may experience overexertion. Symptoms of overexertion are fatigue, labored breathing, a feeling of suffocation, weakness, anxiety, headache, muscle cramping or a tendency to panic.

It is always best to prevent overexertion. Know your physical limits and pace yourself to avoid breathlessness. Move slowly and avoid prolonged exertion. If you experience symptoms of overexertion under water, stop all activity, breathe deeply and rest. Hold on to an object for support if possible.

If you experience overexertion at the surface, establish buoyancy and stop moving. Rest and catch your breath. Once you have recovered, proceed at a slower pace.

Figure 2-12
If you experience the symptoms of over-exertion, stop, breathe deeply and rest.

Exercise 2-6

Overexertion

1. Of the eight symptoms of diving overexertion, check those listed here:
   ☐ a. itching   ☑ b. anxiety   ☑ c. muscle cramping   ☐ d. feeling of elation

2. To prevent diving overexertion, you should:
   ☐ a. use your hands for propulsion as often as possible.   ☑ b. know your physical limits and pace yourself.

3. If you become overexerted under water, you should:
   ☑ a. stop, breathe and rest.   ☐ b. ascend immediately to the surface and signal for assistance.

How did you do?   *1.* b, c   *2.* b   *3.* a.

Airway Control and Breathing Goals

It is not unusual for a small amount of water to occasionally be present in your regulator or snorkel, particularly after clearing it. This normally poses no problems because proper airway control helps you avoid accidentally drawing a few drops of the water into your throat.

Proper airway control means to: 1) Always inhale slowly if water has entered your regulator, snorkel or mouth, so it won't be pulled into your throat; 2) Always inhale cautiously and slowly after clearing your snorkel or regulator; and 3) Use your tongue as a splash guard by placing it on the roof of your mouth when water begins to enter. These methods will help prevent you from taking in water and choking. Once you take a breath, you can expel the water from your mouth, regulator or snorkel the next time you exhale.

If you ever lose control of your airway and accidentally inhale some water, hold your snorkel or regulator in place with one hand and cough through the mouthpiece. Stay calm. Swallowing the inhaled water may also allow you to quickly resume breathing and regain control of your airway. Airway control while diving is easy to learn and important to develop. It typically becomes a natural habit with a little experience.

To summarize, these are your goals for breathing under water: Always breath slowly and deeply, strive to develop airway control and always breathe continuously when using scuba.

Exercise 2-7

Airway Control

1. Of the three techniques used for airway control, check those listed here:

☑ a. Always inhale slowly.   ☐ b. Clench your teeth before inhaling.   ☑ c. Use your tongue as a splash-guard by placing it on the roof of your mouth.

How did you do?   *1. a, c.*

Diving Equipment

In Module One, you learned about masks, snorkels, fins, BCDs and scuba equipment (tank, valve, regulator, backpack and submersible pressure gauge). In this module, you'll become familiar with exposure suits and their accessories, weight systems, alternate air sources, diving knives, equipment bags and diving instruments.

Exposure Suits

Purpose — Exposure suits are valuable in virtually all diving activities, and serve to reduce heat loss and to protect you from minor scrapes, stings and abrasions.

Objectives

After reading this section on exposure suits, you will be able to:

1. State two reasons for wearing an exposure suit while diving.

2. Describe how a dry suit and a wet suit work to keep a diver warm.

3. Explain why a wet suit must be designed to fit snugly.

4. Identify the two properties an exposure suit may lose due to increased water pressure at depth.

5. Identify three factors that must be considered when selecting an exposure suit.

6. List four procedures used in caring for an exposure suit.

Figure 2-13
Exposure suits reduce heat loss and protect you from minor scrapes, stings and abrasions.

Exposure Protection Doesn't Mean Reef Protection

When divers explore the fragile environment around corals, sponges and other aquatic life without the protection of exposure suits, they tend to be cautious. After all, they must watch what they touch to prevent abrasion or a minor sting.

With exposure suits, however, divers may not be quite so careful, and that means potential harm to the environment. Though most divers wouldn't intentionally kick or rub against the reef and its inhabitants, exposure suits make it more difficult to tell when accidental contact is being made. Often, divers don't realize that even a light touch can harm or kill some organisms. Breaking off a ten-inch piece of coral, for example, can destroy a decade of growth.

By being aware of the fragile environment and using some simple techniques, you can minimize

accidental damage to the reef:

• *Swim next to the reef.* This avoids damage from the downstroke of your fins.

• *Watch your buoyancy.* By staying neutral, you avoid the tendency to drag along the reef where your legs and feet can wreak destruction on a small scale.

• *Turn sideways when you look under ledges.* Divers sometimes forget that their tank adds some height. If you turn sideways, you will reduce the likelihood of bashing your tank against the reef.

In general, avoid touching the living reef. Keep in mind that just because you are safe from the reef doesn't mean the reef is safe from you.

Styles

There are three basic styles of exposure suits, each with its own characteristics of how much exposure protection it provides. These are the body suit, the wet suit and the dry suit.

Body Suits — Among the most recent form of exposure protection are body suits, which are usually made from colorful Lycra® or nylon. Body suits provide full-length abrasion protection, but only minimal insulation, and are therefore worn only in tropical waters. Out of the water, body suits also provide a comfortable means to protect yourself from sunburn.

Figure 2-14
Body Suits

Wet Suits — Wet suits are by far the most common form of exposure suit. The wide variety of wet-suit patterns and thicknesses make wet suits suitable insulation in water as cold as 50°F to as warm as 86°F.

Wet suits reduce heat loss in two ways: 1) by putting a layer of insulation against your skin, and 2) by reducing the

Figure 2-15
Wet Suits

amount of cold water that circulates over your skin. Wet suits get their name because you get wet while wearing them — water enters through the wrist, ankle and neck areas into the space between your skin and the insulating material of the suit. Once in the suit, the water remains trapped. Because this water is colder than your skin, it absorbs body heat until a state of equilibrium is reached.

As long as the layer of warmed water remains in place, it takes relatively little body heat to keep it warm. If water

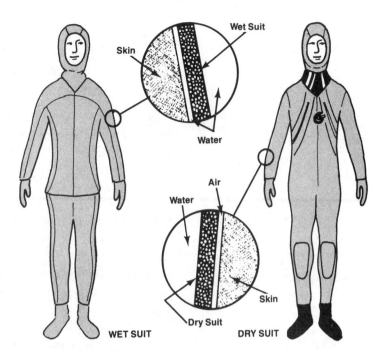

Figure 2-16
A wet suit traps water next to your skin and keeps it from circulating with cold external water. A dry suit keeps water out altogether.

circulates in and out of the suit, however, an excess amount of heat will be lost in warming the newly admitted cold water. This is why a snug fit is a critical factor in a wet suit.

Dry Suits — Dry suits provide insulation by keeping you dry. They are the warmest exposure protection used by recreational divers and are especially useful for diving in water colder than 50°F.

Because air conducts heat relatively poorly, the dry suit

Figure 2-17
Dry Suit

keeps you warm by keeping you dry. With some dry suits, special garments are worn underneath for extra warmth.

Since dry suits are filled with air, they need to be equalized as you change depth, just like other air spaces. For this reason, dry suits come equipped with a method of adding and venting air. Some have BCD-type inflation/deflation hoses, while others have specialized inflation/deflation valves. Regardless of the type of inflation device, most dry suits fill with air directly from the tank via a low-pressure inflator similar to those found on BCDs.

Dry-suit diving requires special instruction. If you will be using dry suits during this course, your instructor will provide you with an orientation to their use. If you don't learn to use a dry suit during this course, seek specialized instruction before attempting to use one for the first time.

Features — Of the three styles of exposure suits, the wet suit has the widest array of available features. This is because of the very diverse environments in which wet suits can be used. Common wet-suit options include length, thickness, color, pads for the knees and elbows, pockets, and zipper position. Some of these features are also available on dry suits.

Materials — As mentioned earlier, body suits, which are the simplest exposure suits, are made of thin nylon or Lycra. Wet suits and dry suits, on the other hand, have to be made from materials that insulate.

Wet suits are made from closed-cell neoprene foam. *Closed-cell* refers to the fact that the individual gas bubbles inside neoprene foam are not interconnected. For this rea-

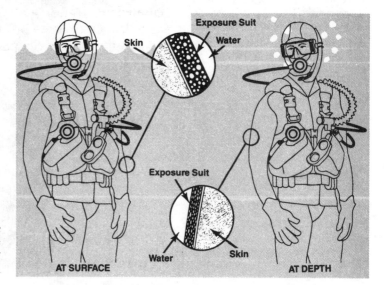

Figure 2-18
As you descend, water compresses the bubbles in a neoprene suit, making it less buoyant.

son, water can't flow through a wet suit like a sponge.

Since wet-suit material is comprised of thousands of tiny closed-cells, or bubbles, it's quite buoyant. In fact, a wet suit is so buoyant at the surface that it will float a person comfortably. Without weight to offset the suit's buoyancy, it's quite difficult to get below the surface.

Neoprene foam provides excellent insulation. However, as you descend, water pressure compresses the bubbles in the neoprene, making the suit thinner. Consequently, a wet suit has less buoyancy and provides less insulation the deeper you descend. To compensate for the loss of buoyancy, you will add air to your BCD, and to be sure you have adequate warmth, you must choose a wet suit thick enough to insulate you at the depth you'll be diving.

Many dry suits are made of neoprene, too, but use a watertight zipper as well as neck and wrist seals to keep the inside of the suit dry. The neoprene provides most of the insulation, with extra insulation added by the layer of air.

Other dry suits are made from coated fabrics and have no built-in insulation. These suits are designed to be worn with special thermal undergarments — in fact, without the undergarments, you would chill wearing such a dry suit, even in moderately warm water. Yet, by using undergarments of varying thickness and type, you can remain comfortable in temperatures ranging from 75°F to close to the freezing point of water.

Because they are filled with air, all dry suits are much more buoyant than wet suits. With a dry suit, however, the loss of insulation and buoyancy due to compression at depth can be minimized. Loss of insulation may be compensated for through the use of undergarments and the addition of air between the suit and the skin. Compensation of buoyancy loss is accomplished by adding air to the dry suit as well as the BCD.

Figure 2-19
Some dry suits require the use of special thermal undergarments.

Selection — The exposure suit you select will depend almost entirely on the environment you intend to be diving in. The most important considerations — regardless of whether you choose a body suit, wet suit or dry suit — are warmth, fit and comfort.

An exposure suit should be one of the first pieces of equipment you obtain because it makes the difference between a cold, miserable dive and a fun, comfortable dive. Your PADI Instructor or Dive Center can help you choose the best exposure suit and features for your needs.

Preparation — Body suits and wet suits generally require

Figure 2-20
Rinse your exposure suit
after use, then turn it inside out
to dry on a nonmetal hanger.

no special preparation before use. Some dry suits do require preparation, however. Consult the owner's manual included with the suit.

Maintenance — There are four basic steps to general exposure suit maintenance: 1) rinse, 2) dry inside out, 3) store without folds on a wide hanger, and 4) lubricate zippers and fasteners.

As you learned in Module One, all diving equipment should be rinsed after use, including your exposure suit. After rinsing, turn the suit inside out to dry. Always store your suit out of direct sunlight on a wide non-metal hanger.

Avoid folding your suit tightly or leaving it folded for extended periods. Doing so will cause the closed-cells in neoprene to collapse at the creases, reducing their ability to insulate. Coated-fabric dry suits may stick together if folded or stored too long in a tight place.

Lubricate fasteners and zippers periodically with silicone spray or some other nonpetroleum lubricant. Minor suit repairs can be made easily with special cement available from dive stores.

Exercise 2-8

Exposure Suits

1. The two reasons for wearing an exposure suit are:
   - ☐ a. to reduce heat loss.
   - ☐ b. to protect the diver from minor scrapes, stings and abrasions.
   - ☐ c. to allow the diver to contact coral without harm to either the diver or the coral.

2. A wet suit keeps a diver warm by preventing water from coming in contact with the diver's skin.
   - ☐ True ☐ False

3. A snug fit is crucial in a wet suit because:
   - ☐ a. a tight wet suit will help keep the body streamlined.
   - ☐ b. it prevents excess water circulation around the body and helps keep the body warm.

4. A wet suit may lose which of the following two properties at increasing depths?
   - ☐ a. Flexibility ☐ b. Buoyancy ☐ c. Insulation

5. When selecting an exposure suit, you should check for warmth, fit and comfort.
   - ☐ True ☐ False

6. Of the four procedures used in caring for a wet suit, check those that appear here:
   - ☐ a. Rinse. ☐ b. Dry inside and out. ☐ c. Clean zippers with alcohol.
   - ☐ d. Store unfolded, on a hanger.

How did you do? *1. a, b 2. False. A wet suit keeps a diver warm by adding a layer of insulation against the skin and by reducing the amount of water that circulates over the skin. 3. b 4. b, c 5. True. 6. a, b, d.*

Objectives

After reading this section on exposure suit accessories, you will be able to:

1. State the need for a hood and identify three basic types.

2. Explain why it is important not to wear a tight-fitting hood.

3. List two reasons for wearing diving gloves.

4. List three reasons for wearing wet-suit boots while diving.

Exposure Suit Accessories

Your need for exposure protection includes your head, hands and feet as well as the rest of your body. You get this protection through exposure suit accessories — namely hoods, gloves and boots.

Hoods — Up to 75% of your total body heat can be lost through your head if it's left unprotected. This is why hoods provide important thermal protection in water below 70°F. Hoods also provide abrasion protection for the head and neck areas.

All hoods, even those used with coated-fabric dry suits, are typically made from neoprene foam. They come in a variety of thicknesses and three basic types: 1) bibbed hoods, 2) non-bibbed hoods and 3) hooded vests.

Bibbed hoods are attached to a broad flange, or "bib," that is tucked in under the neck of the wet-suit jacket. The flange helps create a snug fit between your neck and the jacket, and helps minimize water circulation by reducing the amount of water entering around the neck. Non-bibbed hoods don't have the flange and are commonly worn with dry suits. For diving in extremely cold water in a wet suit, you may elect to use a hooded vest. A hooded vest incorporates a hood attached to a sleeveless neoprene vest, providing a good neck seal and extra insulation for your chest area.

Figure 2-21
Bibbed Hood

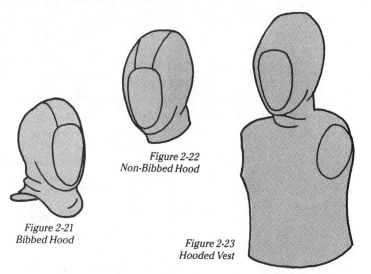

Figure 2-22
Non-Bibbed Hood

Figure 2-23
Hooded Vest

Select a hood that fits snugly, but not too tightly. A hood that's too tight can cause changes in your heart rate due to compression of the arteries in your neck. Consider comfort and fit when you select your hood.

See *The Encyclopedia of Recreational Diving*

Gloves — Your hands are not very well insulated, making them highly susceptible to heat loss. In colder water, your hands may become numb and lose dexterity if they are unprotected. This can cause difficulty in operating your equipment and in other safety-related tasks. Your hands are also vulnerable to objects that can sting or cut.

For these reasons, some form of hand protection is recommended for nearly every kind of diving. Depending

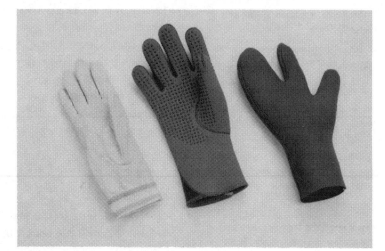

Figure 2-24
Diving gloves.

on the water temperature, you may use lightweight noninsulating gloves (for protection only), wet-suit gloves (for insulation and protection) or thick wet-suit mitts (for extra insulation in very cold water). Your PADI Dive Center or Instructor will assist you in proper glove selection.

Boots — Wet-suit boots are generally worn while diving for three reasons: 1) warmth in water below 70°F, 2) protection against cuts, scrapes and bruises while walking to, from and around your entry/exit points and 3) to prevent abrasion by adjustable-strap fins.

Boots are constructed from neoprene foam and usually have semirigid soles. The soles are typically molded from hard rubber and have textured surfaces for better traction and protection. The soles of many boots cover the heel and toe, and are made in pairs contoured separately for the right and left feet. Some boots have side-entry zippers, which helps when putting them on but may allow greater water circulation around the feet.

Diving boots fit by size, much like shoes, and should be comfortable without being excessively large or small. Your instructor or dive store will assist you in choosing properly fitting boots.

Figure 2-25
Wet-suit boots with side-entry zippers.

Exercise 2-9

Exposure Suit Accessories

1. A hood provides abrasion protection for the head and neck areas. ☐ True ☐ False

2. The following illustration shows a: ☐ a. bibbed hood. ☐ b. non-bibbed hood. ☐ c. hooded vest.

3. When selecting a hood, you should choose one that fits very tight. ☐ True ☐ False

4. Diving gloves should be worn:
    ☐ a. because they keep your hands warm and protected from stings and cuts.
    ☐ b. on all dives.

5. Wet-suit boots should be worn because:
    ☐ a. they make it easier to swim without fins.
    ☐ b. they protect your feet from abrasion and provide warmth.

How did you do?   *1. True   2. a   3. False. Aside from being uncomfortable, a too-tight hood can cause changes in your heart rate due to the compression of arteries in your neck. Choose a hood that fits snug, but not too tight. 4. a, b   5. b.*

Objectives

After reading this section on overheating, you will be able to:

1. Name six ways to prevent overheating before a dive when wearing an exposure suit.

Overheating

Before moving on to the next piece of equipment, there is a final, important note regarding exposure suits and their accessories. Since exposure suits reduce the loss of body heat, they can also cause a diver to build up too much body heat when they are worn out of the water on warm days. There are six steps to follow to prevent overheating.

1. Prepare all your equipment before putting on the exposure suit. Put the suit on at the last possible moment.

2. Once you have the suit on, limit your activity as much as possible.

3. Stay out of the sun as much as possible.

4. Keep your hood off as long as possible.

5. Leave your jacket unzipped until you are ready to enter the water.

6. Cool off by entering the water one or more times during the suiting up process.

Exercise 2-10

Overheating

1. Of the six ways to prevent overheating before a dive, check those listed here.

    ☐ a. Put your suit on in the water.   ☐ c. Cool off by entering the water during the suiting-up process.
    ☐ b. Stay out of the sun.   ☐ d. Put your boots on last.

How did you do?   *1. b, c.*

Objectives

After reading this section on weight systems, you will be able to:

1. Identify the two variations in weight system design.

2. Name the most important feature of any weight system.

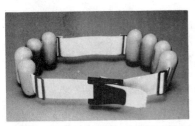

Figure 2-26
The most common weight system is the weight belt.

Figure 2-27
The most important feature of a weight belt or weight system is a quick-release device that can be operated with one hand.

Weight Systems

Purpose — If you're like most people, you naturally float in water, and if you wear a wet suit or dry suit, you're even more positively buoyant. To offset your natural and exposure suit buoyancy, you must use a weight system. When used properly, a weight system only counteracts the tendency to float; it doesn't *cause* you to sink, it *allows* you to sink.

Styles, Features and Materials — The primary component of a weight system is lead, which is so heavy and dense that a small quantity easily offsets positive buoyancy. Although all weight systems share the use of lead, they vary in design — depending primarily on whether weights are integrated into the scuba system (usually the backpack) or worn separately on a weight belt. Wearing the weights correctly, as well as the right amount of weight, has a tremendous bearing on your underwater safety and comfort.

Weight belts are the most commonly used weight system. They are typically made from a 2-inch-wide piece of nylon webbing or solid neoprene rubber. The belt is threaded through individual weights especially designed for use on diving weight belts. Some weight belts have compartments or pockets that hold lead shot or solid weights. Regardless of the design of the belt, *the most important feature is a quick-release device that can be operated with one hand.* Most weight belt quick releases are plastic or metal buckles.

Integrated weight systems vary widely from manufacturer to manufacturer and range from shot-filled compartments to pockets for solid lead weights. Like the weight belt, *its most important feature is a quick-release mechanism that can be operated with one hand.*

Remember, all weight belts or weight systems must be worn clear of all other equipment and have a quick-release device to allow immediate and quick removal with one hand.

Selection — Choosing the optimum weight system will depend on the type of equipment you use and the environment in which you dive. Check with your PADI Instructor or Dive Center for advice in selecting the best weight system for your needs.

Preparation — During confined-water training for this module, your instructor will show you how to determine

Setting Up the Weight Belt

When setting up a nylon-webbing weight belt, begin by determining the proper length you will need. The free end of a properly adjusted belt protrudes about 6 to 8 inches from the fastened buckle when worn. A new weight belt may have to be trimmed to the correct length.

Start by measuring the belt around your waist while wearing your exposure suit. Next add 2 to 4 inches to compensate for webbing length used up running through the weights and their retaining clips (small clips that keep the weights from sliding out of place on the belt), and 6 to 8 more inches to fold under the buckle. This extra length will allow you to lengthen the belt later, if necessary.

After determining the correct length, you are ready to cut the belt. If you're unsure about your measurement, you may wish to mark your intended cut, then thread on your weights and buckle to check the fit before you actually start cutting.

After cutting the belt to the right length, you'll need to singe the cut edge to keep it from unraveling. A butane lighter works well for this. Before singeing, you may want to round the corners first, to make it easier to pass the end of the belt through the buckle.

With the edge singed, you're ready to figure out where to put the weights. The off-limits areas are the center of your back (where the tank will sit) and within 4 inches of the buckle on either side (which could interfere with buckle operation). Any place else is fine.

Try to divide your weight evenly, so that each side is a mirror image of the other. An unevenly weighted belt can be uncomfortable. Once you have determined the best place for your weights, use retaining clips so they won't slide around when you're handling the belt. See the accompanying illustration for proper use of weight retaining clips.

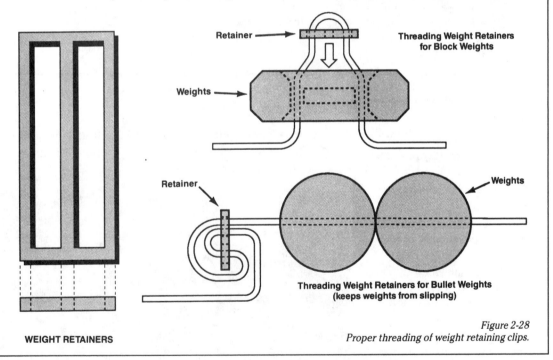

Retainer

Threading Weight Retainers
for Block Weights

Weights

Retainer

Weights

Threading Weight Retainers for Bullet Weights
(keeps weights from slipping)

Figure 2-28
Proper threading of weight retaining clips.

WEIGHT RETAINERS

the correct amount of weight for your weight system (this is explained in the Confined-Water Training Preview).

If you're using a weight belt, thread the weights on and adjust the length so that 6-8 inches of belt protrudes beyond the buckle when it's in place. Be sure not to place any of the weights too close to the buckle or they may keep it from closing securely.

Maintenance — Most weight systems require very little maintenance, aside from a brief rinse after use. Integrated weight systems may have additional requirements, however, so consult the instructions provided by the manufacturer.

Weight systems do require some care in handling. Carelessly dropping a weight belt can break or bend the belt's buckle and easily damage anything it's dropped on. Weights accidentally dropped on a foot can cause injury. Handle weight systems with care to avoid damage to equipment and accidental injury.

Exercise 2-11

Weight Systems

1. Weight systems can be integrated into the scuba system or worn as a weight belt. ☐ True ☐ False

2. The most important feature of any weight system is:

   ☐ a. room for adjustment to increase or decrease weight.

   ☐ b. a quick-release device that can be operated with one hand.

How did you do?   *1. True*   **2.** *b*

Objectives

After reading this section on alternate air sources, you will be able to:

1. Define *alternate air source*.

2. Identify two types of alternate air sources that require the help and cooperation of another diver.

3. Identify the alternate air source that does not require the help and cooperation of another diver.

4. State why it is important to specially mark an extra second stage used as an alternate air source.

5. Describe where an alternate air source should be attached to a diver.

Alternate Air Sources

Purpose — Divers who find themselves either very low on air or totally out of air can use one of several alternative procedures to safely reach the surface. (All these alterna-

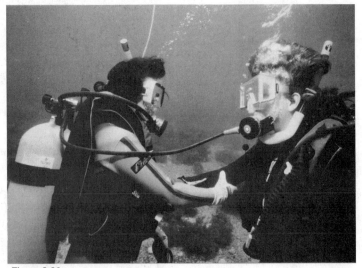

Figure 2-29
An alternate air source is any second stage you may use, other than your own primary second stage, to make an ascent while continuing to breathe normally.

tives will be discussed in a later module.) Among the most desirable choices in very-low-on- or out-of-air situations is the use of an *alternate air source*. An alternate air source is any second stage you may use, other than your own primary second stage, to make an ascent while continuing to breathe normally.

Styles and Features — The use of some alternate air sources requires the help and cooperation of another diver, while others may be used independently by the out-of-air (or low-on-air) diver and do not require the assistance of another diver.

Alternate air sources that require the help of another diver can be grouped into two categories: 1) alternate air source second stages and 2) alternate inflator regulators.

An *alternate air source second stage* (also called an "octopus") is simply an additional second stage attached to the first stage of a regulator. (See Figure 2-30.) For ease of use by an out-of-air diver, an alternate air source second stage typically has a hose longer than the primary second

Figure 2-30
The most common alternate air source is the alternate air source second stage. Also called an "octopus".

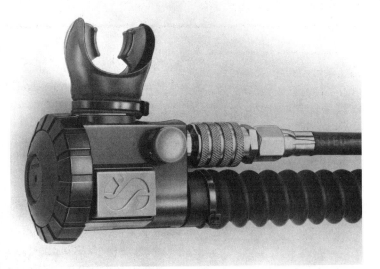

Figure 2-31
The alternate inflator regulator combines the functions of a low-pressure BCD inflator and a second stage.

Figure 2-32
Another version of the alternate inflator regulator utilizes a conventional second stage secured in line with the low-pressure inflation hose.

stage on the regulator.

An *alternate inflator regulator* combines the functions of a low-pressure BCD inflator and a second stage. (See Figures 2-31 and 2-32.) An alternate inflator regulator is found at the end of the BCD hose. In this case, the out-of-air diver usually uses the buddy's primary second stage, and the buddy switches to the alternate inflator regulator.

A *pony bottle* is an alternate air source that does not require the assistance of another diver. A pony bottle is a small scuba tank normally strapped alongside your main tank, with its own independent regulator.

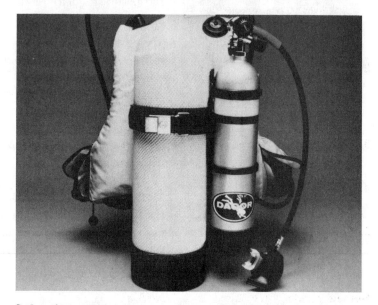

Figure 2-33
The pony bottle is an alternate air source consisting of a small tank with a regulator.

Selection — Alternate air source second stages and alternate inflator regulators are the most popular alternate air source choices because they are less expensive and less bulky than pony bottles. Some divers, though, prefer the added security that a pony bottle offers in some diving situations. Your PADI Dive Center or Instructor will be glad to help you decide on the most appropriate alternate air source.

Preparation — Regardless of the type of alternate air source you select, it's important to prepare it for use by properly marking and securing it.

An alternate air source should be conspicuously marked, such as with a bright color, so it can be quickly and easily identified by a diver needing air. Also, it should be secured in plain view to your chest in the triangular area between your mouth and the lower corners of your rib cage (see Figure 2-34). The method used to secure the alternate air source should hold it firm, but allow quick release so it will be immediately accessible if it is needed. Never allow your alternate air source to dangle freely because it will tend to snag, be difficult to locate and may fill with mud and debris.

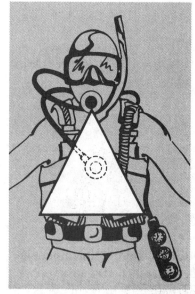

Figure 2-34
An alternate air source should be secured in plain view in the triangular area between your mouth and the lower corners of your rib cage.

Maintenance — Alternate air sources should be maintained like any other regulator and/or scuba tank.

Exercise 2-12

Alternate Air Sources

1. An alternate air source is:
   ☐ a. a diving compressor.
   ☐ b. any second stage you may use, other than your primary second stage, to make an ascent while continuing to breathe normally.

2. _____ and _____ are the two types of alternate air sources that require the help and cooperation of another diver.
   ☐ a. Alternate air source second stages, alternate inflator regulators
   ☐ b. Pony bottles, attached alternative scuba systems

3. _____ is the type of alternate air source that does not require the help and cooperation of another diver.   ☐ a. A pony bottle ☐ b. An alternate inflator regulator

4. It is important to specially mark an extra second stage used as an alternate air source so that it can be quickly and easily identified by a diver needing air.   ☐ True   ☐ False

5. An alternate air source should be:
   ☐ a. secured to your chest in the triangular area between your mouth and the lower corners of your rib cage.
   ☐ b. tucked under your weight belt.

How did you do?   *1.* b   *2.* a   *3.* a   *4.* True   *5.* a.

Objectives

After reading this section on low-pressure inflators, you will be able to:

1. State the purpose of a low-pressure inflator.

Low-Pressure Inflator

Purpose — By now, you're probably already familiar with low-pressure inflators after reading about BCDs. As discussed there, low-pressure inflators allow quick, easy one-hand inflation of the BCD with air directly from the tank.

Figure 2-35
The low-pressure inflator allows quick, easy BCD inflation with the regulator still in your mouth.

The low-pressure inflator is mandatory equipment for this course.

Styles, Features, Materials and Selection — The low-pressure inflator is normally an integrated part of the BCD, so you'll not normally have to make a separate selection. If you get a BCD that doesn't have a low-pressure inflator, you can have one added to it easily. Your PADI Instructor or Dive Center can help you choose your BCD and low-pressure inflator.

Preparation — After you select a low-pressure inflator, you'll need to have its hose installed to your regulator. This should be done by your professional dive store. The only other preparation is to connect the low-pressure inflator during equipment assembly, like you did in the confined-water training session of Module One.

Maintenance — Following the normal maintenance procedures for your BCD will encompass the maintenance of the low-pressure inflator.

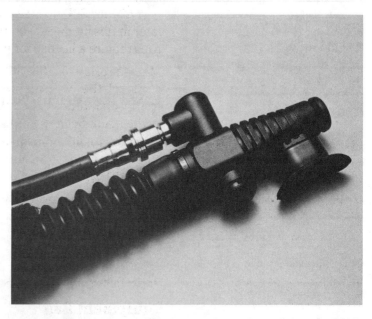

Figure 2-36
Pre-dive preparation of the low-pressure inflator includes connecting the hose from the regulator, like you did in the confined-water training session of Module One.

Exercise 2-13

Low-Pressure Inflators

1. Low-pressure inflators allow you to inflate your BCD orally. ☐ True ☐ False

How did you do? *1. False. Low-pressure inflators allow quick, easy one-hand inflation of the BCD with air directly from the tank.*

Objectives

After reading this section on diving knives, you will be able to:

1. State the purpose of a diving knife and explain how it is not to be used.

2. Identify three features that should be considered when selecting a diving knife.

Diving Knife

Purpose — Diving knives are practical tools, providing you with a means to measure, pry, dig, cut and pound under water (always being mindful not to harm aquatic life). A diving knife is not intended to be, nor should it be, used as a weapon.

Styles, Features and Materials — Diving knives come in a wide variety of styles and sizes. They differ from other knives primarily in the metal used to make them and the design of the blade and handle. At minimum, a diving knife should: 1) be made from stainless steel, 2) have both a sharp cutting edge and serrated sawing edge, and 3) come with a sheath or holder.

Selection — Choose a diving knife that has the three minimum features. You may also want to consider the design of the sheath, which may give you a choice in wearing the knife on the inside of your calf, on the thigh, arm or weight belt, or carrying it attached to an instrument console that is part of your SPG (instrument consoles will be discussed later in this module). You should be aware that some countries require a license for possession of a knife.

Maintenance — Although diving knives are made of stainless steel, they will still rust. Be sure to rinse your knife in fresh water after use and sharpen it occasionally according to the manufacturer's instructions.

Exercise 2-14

Diving Knives

1. A diving knife should be used: ☐ a. to pry, dig and pound under water. ☐ b. as a weapon.

2. A diving knife should have a sharp cutting edge and a serrated sawing edge; should come with a sheath or holder; and should be made of rustproof stainless steel. ☐ True ☐ False

How did you do? *1. a* *2. True.*

Objectives

After reading this section on equipment bags, you will be able to:

1. State the purpose of an equipment bag.

2. Explain how to pack an equipment bag before a dive.

Equipment Bag

Purpose — An equipment bag is an essential means of transporting and temporarily storing all your diving equipment. It helps you keep your equipment together when working in crowded areas such as aboard a boat.

Styles, Features, Materials and Selection — Your equipment bag should be large and strong enough to hold and protect all your equipment except your tank and weight belt. (The tank and weight belt could damage other equip-

Figure 2-37
Your equipment bag should be large
enough to hold all your equipment except
your tank and weight belt.

ment in the bag and should be carried separately.) The bag should be made of heavy-duty fabric that is impervious to seawater and resists rotting. The bag should have a strong zipper that won't corrode. Many equipment bags have features such as shoulder straps, pockets and padding.

Preparation — The equipment bag is prepared for use by proper packing. Always pack your equipment in the reverse order in which it will be needed. When you are done packing, the first items you will need will be on top and the last items needed will be on the bottom. Additionally, after the

Figure 2-38
By packing your equipment bag
in reverse order, the first items you
need will be on top.

dive you should make a habit of putting your equipment directly into the bag so it doesn't become lost or mixed with another diver's equipment. Proper use of your equipment bag will minimize confusion and possible equipment loss.

Maintenance — Your equipment bag should be emptied and rinsed inside and out after each use. Allow it to dry before storing it.

Exercise 2-15

Equipment Bags

1. An equipment bag should not be used when working in crowded areas, such as on a boat. ☐ True ☐ False

2. You should pack your equipment:
   ☐ a. in the same order in which it will be needed.   ☐ b. in the reverse order of which it will be needed.

How did you do?   *1. False. An equipment bag* should *be used when working in crowded areas.* **2.** *b.*

Objectives

After reading this section on diving instruments, you will be able to:

1. State the five types of reference information that can be obtained from diving instruments.

2. Compare and contrast the two types of underwater timepieces used for diving.

3. Explain why a depth gauge is needed when diving.

4. List three reasons for using an underwater compass.

*Figure 2-39
Four important diving instruments are the underwater timepiece, the depth gauge, the compass and the submersible pressure gauge.*

Diving Instruments 📖

Part of successfully adapting to the underwater world requires keeping track of time, depth, direction, temperature and air supply. Diving instruments meet this need, giving you reference information at a glance.

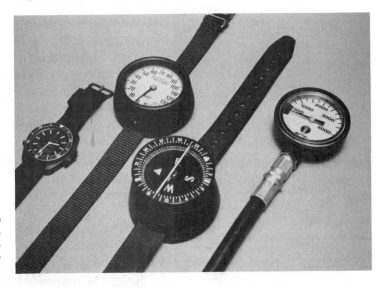

Underwater Timepieces — Depending on how deep you descend, every dive has a time limit that must not be exceeded. (You will learn more about these limits in Module Four.) For this reason, you need an underwater timepiece while diving. At a minimum, an underwater timepiece must be depth-rated (meaning it's made specifically for diving) and able to measure elapsed time.

There are two types of underwater timepieces: 1) watches and 2) timers. Underwater watches may be used for diving and nondiving purposes, while underwater timers can only be used for diving.

Underwater watches are available in analog models

(time displayed by pointers) or digital models (time displayed numerically). Some watches combine both types. Analog watches measure elapsed time against a rotating scale (called the *bezel*) you set at the beginning of the dive; digital watches measure elapsed time with a stopwatch function. Both types must be checked at the start and end of the dive.

Dive timers are essentially pressure-activated stopwatches that automatically start when you begin your descent and stop when you return to the surface. All dive timers measure elapsed time, with some models designed to measure the time between dives, too. Dive timers are available in analog and digital models.

Underwater timepieces should be handled with care and rinsed after each dive. Timepieces generally need to be cleaned and lubricated annually by a qualified service technician, unless specified otherwise by the manufacturer.

Depth Gauge — As mentioned in the discussion on timepieces, there are limits based on the time and depth of your dive. The timepiece tells you how long you've been diving; the depth gauge tells you how deep you are. A depth gauge is therefore necessary equipment to make certain specific depth limits are not exceeded.

Depth gauges come in a wide variety of types, styles and price ranges. Like underwater timepieces, there are both analog and digital models. Generally speaking, the inexpensive gauges are adequate for shallow diving, while the more expensive gauges are required for accuracy at deeper depths.

Treat your depth gauge like any other precision instrument. Protect it from rough handling and rinse it after each dive, following the manufacturer's instructions. Some depth gauges can be damaged by exposure to the reduced pressures at altitude, so they should be kept in pressure-tight containers when flying or when driving through mountains.

Compass — A compass helps you know where you are and where you're going. It provides you with navigational information so you know your direction of travel relative to where you start or end your dive. It helps you to follow a designated course and may even be useful in low-visibility conditions, such as fog, when swimming back to shore at the surface.

A diving compass is liquid-filled and unaffected by pressure. The preferred type of compass has a reference mark called the lubber line and index markers that can be aligned over the compass needle to maintain a directional heading. (Use of the compass will be presented in Module Five.)

As with other diving instruments, rinse the compass after each dive and make certain to keep it out of direct sunlight.

Thermometer — Although not an essential diving instrument, a thermometer is useful for providing water temperature information. Temperature information is helpful in keeping records of water conditions and planning future dives by helping judge what exposure protection is required. There are several types of underwater thermometers on the market to choose from.

Submersible Pressure Gauge (SPG) — The SPG was discussed in Module One, but is listed here because it's a mandatory diving instrument for all dives. See Module One for details on the SPG.

Instrument Console — Diving instruments can be worn individually on your wrist, or they can be combined into a console attached to your SPG. This puts all your information in one convenient place for quick reference. A console also makes diving easier because wrist-mounted gauges often interfere with gloves or wet-suit zippers, are difficult

Figure 2-40
Instrument consoles put all your information in one convenient place for quick reference.

to strap on, and can snag on tank harnesses when you're putting on the scuba unit. Consoles eliminate some steps from the suiting-up process and protect fragile instruments during use and storage.

Instrument consoles shouldn't be allowed to dangle freely because they may become entangled, are prone to damage and may be difficult to locate. Your PADI Instructor will show you how to secure your console.

Integrated instruments — A popular approach to instrumentation is to integrate several instrument functions into one gauge, allowing consoles to be more compact and

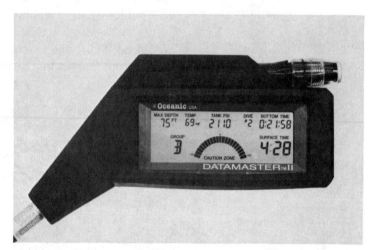

Figure 2-41
Dive computers combine the function of several gauges and go one step farther by telling you when you need to ascend. You'll learn more about dive computers in Module Five.

convenient. Some models integrate depth and time information, while others report tank pressure, maximum depth, current depth, bottom time, surface time and the dive number all on a single gauge.

Dive computers — Dive computers are another development in diving instrumentation. Many of the computers on the market provide depth and time information, and go one step further by calculating your depth/time limits and telling you when to ascend. Dive computers will be discussed further in Module Five.

Summary

Diving instruments give you the reference information you need to plan your dives and dive safely. Without them, you can become disoriented and exceed the safe limits of time and depth. Most instruments are considered standard equipment for general diving conditions, and in some conditions, they are considered mandatory.

Exercise 2-16

Diving Instruments

1. Of the five types of reference information that can be obtained from diving instruments, check those listed here: ☐ a. Direction of current ☐ b. Air supply ☐ c. Time ☐ d. Depth

2. _____ watches measure elapsed time against a rotating scale, while _____ watches measure elapsed time with a stopwatch function. ☐ a. Analog, digital ☐ b. Digital, analog

3. A depth gauge is needed:
   ☐ a. to make certain preplanned dive depth limits are not exceeded. ☐ b. only on dives below 30 feet.

4. One of the three reasons for using an underwater compass is to:
   ☐ a. help you follow a designated course under water. ☐ b. help you monitor your air supply.

How did you do?   *1.* b, c, d *2.* a *3.* a *4.* a.

Diving Communications

Although sound travels well in water, voice communication is virtually impossible under water except with elaborate electronic communications systems. Due to the expense and other drawbacks of these systems, they are not commonly used by recreational divers. As a result, nonverbal methods of communication must be used.

Figure 2-42
Recreational divers use visual communications such as hand signals or writing on a slate.

Figure 2-43
PADI Standard Hand Signals

PADI STANDARD HAND SIGNALS

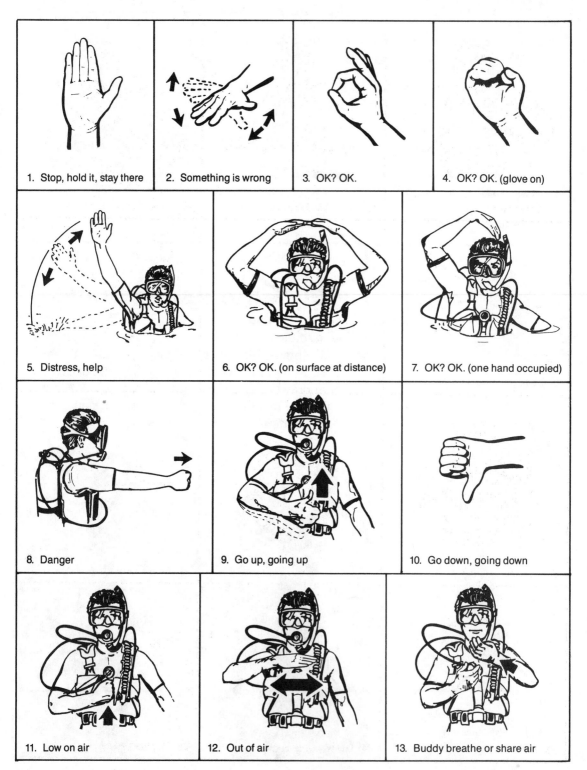

1. Stop, hold it, stay there
2. Something is wrong
3. OK? OK.
4. OK? OK. (glove on)
5. Distress, help
6. OK? OK. (on surface at distance)
7. OK? OK. (one hand occupied)
8. Danger
9. Go up, going up
10. Go down, going down
11. Low on air
12. Out of air
13. Buddy breathe or share air

COMMONLY USED HAND SIGNALS

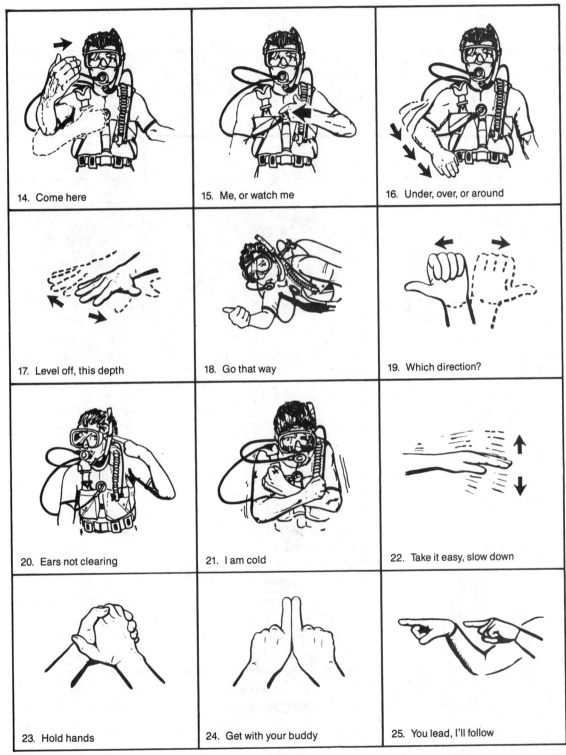

14. Come here

15. Me, or watch me

16. Under, over, or around

17. Level off, this depth

18. Go that way

19. Which direction?

20. Ears not clearing

21. I am cold

22. Take it easy, slow down

23. Hold hands

24. Get with your buddy

25. You lead, I'll follow

Objectives

After reading this section on communications, you will be able to:

1. **Describe two ways of gaining the attention of another diver under water.**

2. **Describe two ways of communicating with another diver under water.**

3. **Identify the meaning of the 25 standard hand signals.**

4. **Describe what a diver should do if he hears an underwater recall signal.**

Gaining Attention

Before you can communicate with another diver, you must have his attention. Gently touch him or rap on your tank with your knife or other hard object.

Figure 2-44
Rapping on your tank is an easy way to gain the attention of another diver.

Communication Under Water

After gaining your buddy's attention, you can communicate by writing on a slate or by using hand signals. Various types of slates are available from retail dive stores. The standard underwater hand signals are illustrated on the preceding pages. You should learn the meaning of each of these hand signals. Additionally, you should review hand signals and other forms of communication with your buddy before the dive to avoid misunderstandings and confusion under water.

Communication at the Surface

On the surface, you can use hand or audible signals. Several hand signals for surface communication are also illustrated on the following pages. Avoid waving your arm at the surface as a greeting — waving is recognized as a distress signal. A whistle is recommended as a standard piece of surface communication equipment because it works well to gain attention, produces a loud noise without expending much energy (as opposed to yelling) and emits a sound that carries well.

Underwater Recall

Some dive charter boats use an electronic underwater recall device to gain the attention of submerged divers. When activated, a recall device emits a siren-like sound through an underwater speaker. If you hear this sound, you should cautiously surface and look to the boat for instructions. Do not swim toward the boat until the captain signals that it is okay to do so.

Exercise 2-17

Diving Communications

1. You can gain the attention of another diver under water by:
   ☐ a. waving your arms until he notices you. ☐ b. gently touching him or rapping on your tank.

2. You can communicate under water by:
   ☐ a. writing on a slate or using hand signals. ☐ b. taking your regulator out of your mouth and yelling.

3. Of the 25 standard hand signals, identify the meaning of those illustrated here.

   a. _____ b. _____ c. _____

4. If you hear an underwater recall signal while boat diving, you should:
   ☐ a. swim under water to the boat. ☐ b. cautiously surface and look to the boat for instructions.

How did you do? *1.* b *2.* a *3.* a. OK, b. Let's go up, c. out of air *4.* b.

Objectives

After reading this section on buddy system procedures, you will be able to:

1. State the responsibility every diver has to his buddy.

2. List the eight considerations that must be discussed between dive buddies when planning a dive.

3. Explain the procedure that should be followed if contact with a buddy is lost under water.

Buddy System Procedures

In Module One, you learned about the importance and value of the buddy system. By understanding the responsibilities, considerations and procedures of the buddy system, you can make it work to your best advantage.

Your responsibility as a buddy is to help avoid problems and assist your partner as needed. You are an extra set of eyes and hands for your buddy, as he is for you. By coordinating your efforts before, during and after a dive, together you can optimize your diving safety and enjoyment.

You and your buddy should agree on an objective for each dive and work together toward that objective. With the specific objective in mind, you should both:

1. Establish entry and exit points and techniques.
2. Choose a course to follow.
3. Agree upon a maximum time and depth limit.

Figure 2-45
*You and your buddy should plan
your dive together and agree on a
common objective.*

4. Establish and review communication procedures.
5. Establish an agreed-upon air pressure for returning to the surface.
6. Discuss the technique you will use to stay together.
7. Agree on what to do if separated.
8. Discuss what to do if an emergency arises.

Remember: *Plan your dive together and dive your plan together.*

Figure 2-46
*Part of planning the dive with
your buddy should include entry and exit
points, and techniques.*

During the dive, you and your buddy are responsible for keeping track of each other and providing each other with assistance whenever possible. In general, you and your buddy should be no more than a few feet apart during the dive. Staying together is easier if you and your buddy agree to maintain a relative position and follow a general direction until you both acknowledge a change in course. If separated, you should search for each other for not more than one minute, then surface to reunite if you haven't located each other.

For safety, practicality and fun, use teamwork while diving. Choose your buddies carefully and work with them to develop techniques that enhance safety and enjoyment. Remember, one of the fundamental rules of diving is "never dive alone." The buddy system only works when divers stay together.

Exercise 2-18

Buddy System Procedures

1. As a buddy, you are responsible for helping your buddy avoid problems and assisting him as needed.

   ☐ True ☐ False

2. Of the 8 considerations that must be discussed between dive buddies when planning a dive, check those listed here:

   ☐ a. Discuss what to do if an emergency arises.
   ☐ b. Agree upon maximum time and depth limits.
   ☐ c. Establish and review communication procedures.

3. If you and your buddy lose contact under water, you should:

   ☐ a. search for each other for not more than 1 minute, then surface to reunite if you haven't located each other.
   ☐ b. return to the boat or shore and wait for your buddy to return.

How did you do?   *1.* True   *2.* a, b, c   *3.* a.

Confined-Water Training Preview — Module Two

During the confined-water training session for Module Two, you'll be using scuba for the second time. You will find that you're more comfortable with breathing under water, and that what seemed strange and new to you has become more familiar.

In this session, you'll be learning new underwater skills that will contribute to successfully becoming a qualified diver. Just as you did for the confined-water training session in Module One, read the following preview carefully so you'll have the general knowledge you'll need to participate in this session.

The following list of performance requirements are the skills that you must successfully complete during confined-water training for Module Two.

Performance Requirements
Confined-Water Training — Module Two

By the end of the confined-water training for Module Two, you will be able to:

1. Perform the predive safety check.

2. Demonstrate appropriate deep-water entries.

3. Clear a snorkel of water by using the blast method and resume breathing through it without lifting the face from the water.

4. Exchange snorkel for regulator and regulator for snorkel repeatedly while at the surface, without lifting the face from the water.

5. Swim a distance of at least 50 yards at the surface, while wearing scuba and breathing through the snorkel.

6. Completely remove, replace and clear the

mask of water while under water.

7. Breathe under water for not less than one minute while stationary and not wearing a mask.

8. Adjust the amount of weight worn to achieve neutral buoyancy at the surface with the BCD deflated.

9. Demonstrate the cramp removal technique.

10. In water too deep to stand up in, perform a tired-diver tow for 25 yards.

11. In water too deep to stand up in, exit by first removing the weight belt, scuba unit and fins (if necessary), then climbing out using the most appropriate means.

The PADI Predive Safety Check

Few things in diving are more embarrassing than jumping into the water, for example, without your weight belt or without your air turned on. To reduce the likelihood of having equipment problems in the water, always have your equipment inspected for adjustment and function by your buddy before you enter the water. You should do the same for your buddy.

To inspect your buddy's equipment:

1. Check the BCD. It must be snugly adjusted with all releases firmly secured. Also check to see that it operates properly, including the low-pressure inflator and the oral inflator.

2. Check the weight belt. It should have a right-hand release and be free and clear of other equipment and straps for easy and fast one-hand removal.

3. Check all releases. You should be familiar with the operation and location of all the releases on his equipment.

4. Check the air supply. Check that the air is turned on,

Figure 2-47
Conduct the Predive Safety Check before
*each dive: **B**egin (BCD) **W**ith (Weight belt)*
***R**eview (Releases) **A**nd (Air Supply & Air*
*Sharing Procedures)**F**riend (Final okay).*

what the tank pressure is, if the regulator is functioning, if the J-valve (if used) lever is in the up position, if the hoses are untangled and untrapped by straps, and where the alternate air source is and how it is used.

5. Give the final OK. After completing the above checks, give an overall inspection looking for things like dangling straps or missing equipment.

Conduct this inspection before every dive. The sequence and steps are easily remembered by using the phrase: "Begin With Review And Friend."

Buoyancy Control Device	**B**egin
Weight Belt	**W**ith
Releases	**R**eview
Air Supply & Air Sharing Procedures	**A**nd
Final OK	**F**riend

Entering the Water

Special entry techniques are needed in specific diving situations, but in general, the best entry is usually the easiest, with as little impact with the water as possible. If you can wade or lower yourself in, that's best. The idea is to enter without becoming disoriented or knocking any equipment loose. Some general rules for entries include:

1. Be sure the entry area is clear.

2. Have your BCD about half-inflated so you'll be buoyant.

3. Be sure your buddy is prepared to enter.

4. Hold your mask firmly in place if there is a possibility of it becoming dislodged.

5. After entering, clear the entry area and wait for your buddy. Watch while your buddy enters.

The *controlled seated entry* may be used to enter from a platform that is just a few inches above the water — like a dock or pool side. To perform this entry (see Figure 2-48), sit on the platform with your feet dangling in the water.

Figure 2-48
The controlled seated entry is suitable for entering the water from a low, stable platform such as a dock or poolside.

Turn slightly so you can place both hands on the platform on the same side of your body. Then, using your arms for support, gently lower yourself into the water while turning to face the platform. Once in and comfortable, let go of the platform and clear the entry area.

When you must enter the water from a height of several feet, you'll usually use a *giant stride entry.* To do a giant stride entry, first make sure all your equipment is secured, be sure your BCD is about half-inflated, place your regulator in your mouth and hold your mask tightly in place. Make sure your buddy is ready to go, check the area below, then simply step out with one foot.

Your legs should remain spread until contacting the water. By pulling your legs together as you hit the water,

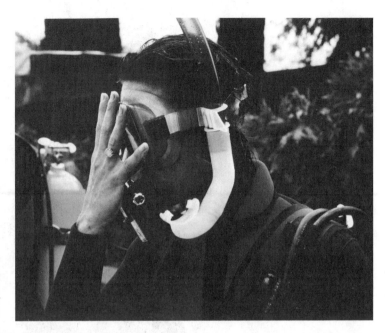

Figure 2-49
When making a giant-stride entry, be sure to hold your mask and regulator firmly in place.

you'll keep yourself from submerging as far as you would if you entered the water with both feet together. Once in the water, give the OK signal, swim clear of the entry area and wait for your buddy to enter.

Your instructor will give you a chance to practice the controlled seated entry, the giant stride or other appropriate methods for entering water too deep to stand up in.

Figure 2-50
Your legs should remain spread until you contact the water when making a giant stride. Pulling your legs together as you hit the water will keep you from sinking deep.

Snorkel Breathing and Blast Clearing

If you've ever tried to tread water for a long time, you know that keeping your head above water gets very tiring. Your snorkel lets you lie face down in the water, completely motionless, while breathing. This basic resting position is stable, comfortable and much easier than treading water.

Figure 2-51
Your snorkel lets you lie facedown in the water while you rest and breathe.

Develop the habit of assuming the resting position at the surface because it helps you to conserve energy. If you must sit upright in the water to talk or look around, inflate your BCD to provide support and conserve energy.

Breathe slowly, deeply and cautiously through your snorkel. Bite gently on the mouthpiece, letting your lips seal around it and hold it in place. Whenever you put the snorkel in your mouth, be sure to exhale before inhaling in case there's water in it.

To clear water from the snorkel, such as when you surface, simply exhale forcefully and sharply into the snorkel. This will "blast" the water up and out of the barrel. The blast method of clearing will remove nearly all the water from the snorkel. Any small amount of water left will be inconsequential if you inhale slowly and cautiously, and may possibly be removed by a second blast.

Remember: When using the blast method to clear a snorkel, the exhalation must be quick and forceful, as though you are shooting a giant pea-shooter. This method will also work to clear any water sloshing into the snorkel while swimming at the surface.

Snorkel clearing will become automatic with experience. If you're unable to clear the snorkel sufficiently with

Figure 2-52
To clear water from the snorkel, simply exhale sharply and forcefully into it to blow the water out.

the first blast, it's quite easy to take another breath and clear it. Although there is some water left in the snorkel, if you inhale slowly and use airway control, you can essentially "bubble" the air through the water until you have enough air for another blast. The ability to breathe past water demonstrates airway control and proper snorkel-clearing technique.

Snorkel/Regulator Exchanges

Quite often, the place you want to dive is some distance from the boat or shore. To save tank air, breathe through your snorkel, relax and watch the underwater environment as you swim out. Once you reach the dive site, exchange your snorkel for your regulator.

To do this effortlessly, locate your regulator and hold it in your right hand. Then, without lifting your head from the

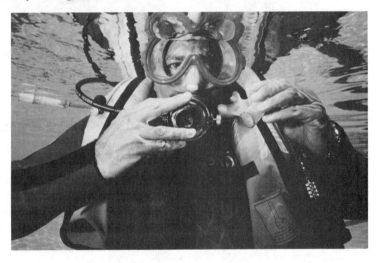

Figure 2-53
Make snorkel/regulator exchanges without lifting your head out of the water.

water, remove your snorkel from your mouth, put in your regulator, clear it and begin breathing.

When you surface after your dive, exchange your regulator for your snorkel. Again, you should do this without lifting your head from the water to conserve energy. Take and hold a deep breath from the regulator, remove it from your mouth and replace it with the snorkel. Blast the water from the snorkel and inhale cautiously as you resume breathing.

When you can perform these exchanges smoothly, you'll be learning to dive correctly — with minimal effort.

No-mask Breathing

Because it's possible for your mask to become dislodged or

Figure 2-54
With a little practice, you'll discover that
breathing without a mask is as easy as
breathing with a mask.

flooded under water, you need to learn how to keep breathing while your nose is exposed to the water. With thought, concentration and practice, you'll easily learn to breathe through your mouth while keeping water out of your nose.

At first, you may find it easier to inhale through your mouth and exhale through your nose. After you are comfortable with that, practice inhaling and exhaling through your mouth only. If you feel water entering your nose, just exhale slightly to force the water out.

With a little practice, you'll discover that breathing without a mask is as easy as breathing with one. Once you have mastered this skill, you can be confident that you'll remain in complete control if your mask should become flooded or dislodged.

Mask Replacement Under Water

If your mask is dislodged under water, keep the mask skirt unobstructed when you replace the mask on your face. Hair or the edge of your hood trapped under the skirt can cause the mask to continuously flood as you try to clear it.

To replace your mask under water, first hold your mask firmly by the front and make sure the strap is out of the way by looping it forward over the back of the hand holding the mask (Figure 2-55).

Next position the mask carefully against your face for a good seal. If you hold the mask with one hand, you can use

Figure 2-55
Hold the mask firmly with the strap looped over the back of your hand.

Figure 2-56
Position the mask against your face and clear it like you did in your first confined-water training sesssion.

Figure 2-57
After clearing the mask, position the strap while holding the mask firmly in place. Some people prefer to position the strap before clearing the mask.

Figure 2-58
You want to wear just enough weight so you float at eye level with a deflated BCD and holding a normal breath.

your free hand to be sure the area under the mask skirt is clear.

Once the mask has been properly positioned, you may either immediately clear the mask like you did in the first confined-water training session (Figure 2-56), or you may replace the strap and clear it. Some people find that replacing the strap first makes mask clearing a little easier; others find that clearing the mask before replacing the strap helps them be sure they've properly seated the mask. Your instructor will advise you on which technique to use.

Proper Weighting

As you've learned in the Knowledge Development portions of this module and Module One, how much weight you need depends on your weight and size, the equipment you wear, and whether you're diving in fresh or salt water. Without an exposure suit, you may need only a few pounds of weight, if any at all. With an exposure suit, the amount of weight you need can vary, but a good approximation for typical cold-water wet suits is approximately 10% of your body weight (slightly more for dry suits). For example, if you weigh 140 pounds, you'll probably need about 14 pounds of weight.

This is an approximation only. With all your equipment on and with your BCD deflated, you want to wear just enough weight so you float at eye level while holding a nor-

mal breath. This is considered optimal weighting for several reasons:

1. You can begin a slow, feet first descent by merely exhaling.

2. When you return to the surface, you'll have slight positive buoyancy.

3. It will minimize the necessary buoyancy adjustments while diving.

Consider the disadvantages of diving with too much weight: To begin with, you have to wear the extra weight while you walk around on the boat or beach with your equipment on. When floating at the surface, you find yourself caught between your BCD, which is pulling you up, and your excessively heavy weight belt, which is pulling you down. Finally, to remain neutrally buoyant under water, you have to swim around with a lot of air in your BCD, creating unnecessary drag.

To determine proper weighting:

1. Wear all your equipment.

2. Enter water too deep to stand up in and deflate your BCD completely.

3. Hang vertical and motionless in the water while holding a normal breath.

4. Add or subtract weights until you float at eye level while holding a normal breath.

5. As a final test, exhale. You should sink slowly.

If you have trouble determining your weight, ask your instructor to help you.

Surface Snorkeling

As mentioned in the discussion on snorkel/regulator exchanges, you'll spend a lot of time using your snorkel to save tank air while you swim to a particular dive site. During this confined-water training session, you will work on fine-tuning your surface snorkeling skills while wearing all your scuba equipment.

When snorkeling at the surface with scuba equipment, watch your body position. Keep your arms at your side and the top of the snorkel out of the water. Always swim slowly and relaxed with your fins below the surface for maximum efficiency.

Cramp Removal

A cramp is a painful, involuntary muscle contraction,

Figure 2-59
You can stretch a cramped calf muscle by grasping the tip of your fin and pulling it toward you.

which, as a diver, you may experience in your leg or foot muscles. Cramps are caused by working the muscle too hard, by restricted circulation, or by cold. Fins can contribute to cramping if they are too large and stiff for your body size. With fitness, proper fin selection, practice, proper insulation and by pacing your activity, you can avoid cramps.

If you get a cramp while diving, stretch and massage the cramped muscle to increase circulation. If you have a leg cramp in your calf muscle, you can stretch it by grasping the tip of your fin and pulling it toward you. After relieving the cramp, rest the muscle before continuing at a slower pace.

During this confined-water training session you'll practice using your fins to stretch a cramped calf muscle.

Tired-Diver Tow

One day, you may be swimming on the surface with a diver who becomes tired, out of breath and unable to swim to the boat or shore. You can lend assistance by helping the diver establish positive buoyancy and using either the tank valve tow (Figure 2-60), or the modified tired-swimmer carry (Figure 2-61).

Your instructor will demonstrate these tows and allow you time to practice them.

Figure 2-60
Tank valve tow.

Figure 2-61
Modified tired-swimmer carry.

117

Deep-Water Exit

At times it may be necessary to remove your weight belt, scuba unit and fins to exit the water. You will practice this skill in this session so you'll be familiar with it before you attempt it in an actual diving environment.

To make a deep-water exit, keep the regulator in your mouth and partially inflate your BCD. If you are wearing a front-mounted BCD, disconnect the low-pressure inflator. Remove your weight belt and hand it to an assistant. Next, slide out of the scuba unit — it is usually easiest to slide it off one shoulder first. Once the unit is off, position it so the assistant can easily lift it from the water by grasping the tank valve.

Remove your fins last, but only if necessary. On a low platform, your fins may help you lift yourself out of the water. If you must remove your fins, to climb a ladder for example, make sure you have firm contact with the exit point so you won't drift away. In open water, try to exit when the waves will help lift you onto the platform, boat or rocks.

Your instructor will first demonstrate this skill before having you practice it in the deeper section of the pool or confined-water area.

Figure 2-62
When making a deep-water exit, hand up your weight belt first, then your scuba unit.

Summary

You are now ready for the confined-water training session for Module Two. The new skills you'll be practicing are:

1. Predive Safety Check
2. Controlled Seated and Giant Stride Entry
3. Snorkel Breathing and Clearing
4. Snorkel/Regulator Exchanges
5. No-mask Breathing
6. Mask Replacement Under Water
7. Proper Weighting
8. Surface Snorkeling
9. Cramp Removal
10. Tired-Diver Tow
11. Deep-Water Exit

Get from dive Master
specifically dyplees ← not wacn cool. always aress for the coolest part of the dive

① temperature
② currents
③ aquatic plants & animals
④ visibility → interms of feet
Lheavier the bottom composition the better the settling

Three

☐ **The Diving Environment**

☐ **Dive Planning**

☐ **Boat-Diving Procedures**

☐ **Problem Management**

☐ **Confined-Water Training Preview**

☐ **General Open-Water Skills**

☐ **Open-Water Training Preview — Dives 1-3**

Objectives

After reading this section on the diving environment, you will be able to:

1. List six general environmental conditions that can affect divers in any aquatic environment.

2. State the three ways to obtain an orientation to an unfamiliar aquatic environment.

The Diving Environment

In your first two confined-water training sessions, you experienced the underwater environment for the first time. Although your experience has been limited to a swimming pool or confined water, you've probably already begun to notice some of the underwater conditions that affect divers, like temperature and water clarity.

Just as the swimming pool or confined water has its underwater conditions, every dive site has environmental conditions that may affect you as a diver and that may vary from day to day — depending on weather, climate and other factors. These conditions are:

1. Temperature
2. Visibility

3. Water movement
4. Bottom composition
5. Aquatic life
6. Sunlight

This section of Module Three will give you a brief *overview* of these conditions, as well as some general information about both saltwater and freshwater diving environments.

Perhaps one of the greatest appeals of diving comes from the diversity of environments you can explore. You

Figure 3-1
This fantastic view of the Earth was seen by the Apollo 17 crewmen as they traveled toward the moon. Shown in the photograph are the Mediterranean Sea area, the Antarctic ice cap and almost the entire African coastline. Photo courtesy of NASA.

may have opportunities to explore rivers, lakes, quarries, ponds, tropical seas or temperate oceans. Each environment has its own unique characteristics and its own unique attraction. Weather, climate and season may affect the environmental conditions, so your diving experience at a specific site can vary, depending on the time of year.

During the classroom discussion on diving environments, your instructor will give you some details about the dive site where you'll be making your first open water dives. Listen closely to your instructor and read this section carefully so you may maximize your enjoyment when you make your first dive in open water.

Important Note: *When you're planning to dive in an area* *for the first time, always obtain instruction in the local area or dive under the supervision of an experienced local diver. One of the best ways of coming to know more about an unfamiliar aquatic environment is to participate in a PADI Discover Local Diving experience, which generally increases diving safety for divers unfamiliar with an area.*

Discover Local Diving is a guided tour with a PADI Instructor, Assistant Instructor or Divemaster. More information about this program will be presented in Module Five.

Exercise 3-1

The Diving Environment

1. The six environmental conditions that may affect you as a diver are temperature, visibility, water movement, bottom composition, aquatic life and sunlight. ☒ True ☐ False

2. One way to obtain an orientation to an unfamiliar aquatic environment is to go diving in the area with an experienced local diver. ☒ True ☐ False

How did you do?   *1. True   2. True.*

Water Temperature

Objectives

After reading this section on temperature, you will be able to:

1. Explain how temperature changes with depth.

2. Describe a *thermocline*.

3. Explain how to dive in an area known to have a thermocline.

From the discussion on exposure suits in Module Two, you're aware that water temperature plays the major role in how much insulation you'll need to wear to enjoy a dive. The amount of insulation you'll need will vary with where you dive, because water temperature can vary greatly from one climate to another and from one depth to another.

Natural water temperature ranges from 28°F in Arctic regions to 85°F in the tropics. Within a given region, however, water temperature usually varies less than 15°20°/ throughout the year.

Water temperature also changes with depth, generally getting colder as you descend. While descending, you may encounter an abrupt transition to distinctly colder water. This is called a *thermocline*. The temperature difference above and below the thermocline may be as great as 15° to 20° F. Sometimes you can see visual distortion at the thermocline that looks like the shimmering you see rising from a hot asphalt road. This effect is caused by the mixing of two temperature layers.

Thermoclines may be found at any depth in both fresh and salt water. They tend to be commonly encountered in

Figure 3-2
Water temperature changes with depth, generally getting colder as you go deeper. An abrupt transition to colder water is called a thermocline.

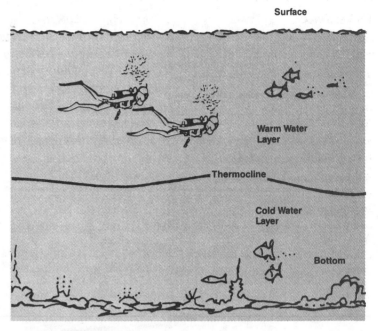

Figure 3-3
You should choose your exposure protection based on the temperature of the water at the depth you plan to dive.

freshwater lakes, ponds and quarries.

To keep from getting chilled, you should base your exposure protection on the temperature of the water at the depth you're going to dive. Since bottom temperatures and thermoclines may be hard to predict, ask your PADI Instructor or Dive Center for local information.

As you learned in Module Two, loss of body heat while diving can cause problems. For this reason, diving in extremely cold or icy water requires not only proper exposure protection, but special training and experience as well. You may find special courses locally that can provide you with supervised training in cold water diving.

Exercise 3-2

Water Temperature

1. Generally, the deeper you dive the _____*B*_____ the water will be. ☐ a. warmer ☐ b. colder

2. A *thermocline* is: ☐ a. a mixing of fresh and salt water.
   ☒ b. an abrupt transition to distinctly colder water while descending.

3. To avoid getting cold while diving, exposure protection should be:
   ☐ a. based on the temperature of the water at the surface.
   ☒ b. based on the temperature of the water at the depth you plan to dive.

How did you do?   *1. b*   *2. b*   *3. b.*

Objectives

1. Define *underwater visibility*.

2. Name the four principle factors affecting underwater visibility.

3. State three effects that restricted visibility has on divers.

4. Explain how to avoid the problems associated with diving in clear water.

Visibility

In the discussion on masks, you learned that diving is a visual activity, so it makes sense that water clarity — or visibility — has a tremendous influence on your dive plan.

As a diver, you need to know how to keep from reducing the visibility, how to measure underwater visibility (so you can record it in your dive log and so you can have a common reference when discussing visibility with other divers), and when not to dive if visibility is extremely poor.

Underwater visibility is defined as how far you can see, horizontally, under water. Visibility can range from 0 to more than 200 feet. Some principle factors affecting visibili-

Figure 3-4
Visibility has a tremendous influence on your dive plan.

ty are: 1) water movement, 2) weather, 3) suspended particles and 4) bottom composition. Waves, surf and currents churn sediment up into the water, reducing visibility. Muddy rain runoff commonly clouds visibility. In certain conditions, microscopic animals (plankton) and plants (algae) suspended in the water proliferate until they cloud the water — oceanic plankton blooms called *red tides* can be so extreme as to kill animals and turn the water reddish. If disturbed by the kick of a diver, the wash from a boat or other water movement, fine bottom sediment can swirl into the water, quickly ruining visibility.

The effects of some visibility conditions are obvious; while others are more subtle. In limited visibility, it's difficult to stay with your buddy and to keep track of where you are and where you're going. You may feel disoriented when you can see neither the surface nor the bottom for reference.

To effectively dive in limited visibility, stay very close to your buddy where you can watch each other. Use your compass to keep track of your position and heading (using your compass will be discussed in Module Five), and it is recommended that you use a reference line from the surface for ascending and descending to prevent disorientation. If visibility is extremely poor, postpone your dive until it improves. Diving in extremely limited visibility requires special training and experience. Much of this training and experience may be obtained by taking the PADI Underwater Navigator course and the PADI Search and Recovery Diver course. See your PADI Instructor or Dive Center for details on these courses.

Surprisingly, diving in extremely clear water can cause problems, too. Because of water's magnifying effect, the bottom will appear closer than it really is. You must use care to keep from accidentally exceeding depth limits by using an accurate depth gauge and referring to it frequently. Disorientation (vertigo) during descents and ascents without reference can be a problem in clear water as well as in limited visibility, so it is recommended that you use a line for descending and ascending.

Exercise 3-3

Visibility

1. *Underwater visibility* is defined as:
    ☐ a. how far you can see vertically.   ☒ b. how far you can see horizontally.

2. One of the principle factors affecting underwater visibility is:
    ☒ a. bottom composition.   ☐ b. the temperature of the water.

3. To avoid problems associated with diving in clear water:
    ☐ a. watch your compass constantly.   ☒ b. use an accurate depth gauge and refer to it frequently.

How did you do?   *1.* b   *2.* a   *3.* b.

Currents 📖

You have learned that you want to remain relaxed by swimming slowly and easily while diving. You learned that because water is dense and has a lot of resistance, you want to remain streamlined as you move through it. It follows then, that when diving in a current, you need to learn some

Objectives

After reading this section on currents, you will be able to:

1. State the four primary causes of surface and underwater currents.

2. Explain what a diver should do if he gets caught in a current and carried downstream past a predetermined destination or exit point.

3. State the direction in which a diver should begin his dive when a mild current is present.

4. Explain what a diver should do if exhausted and caught in a current at the surface.

special techniques to avoid breathlessness and exhaustion, using your air too quickly, and long, difficult swims back to a boat or shore.

Currents are mass movements of water and occur in many bodies of water to some extent. There are four main causes of currents. Large-scale currents are caused by : 1) winds blowing over the surface and 2) unequal heating and cooling of the water; other currents may be caused by 3) tidal movement and 4) waves.

Trying to swim against even a mild current can quickly tire and exhaust you. Since you have to work harder to swim against a current, you use your air faster. It is important to recognize and estimate the strength of local currents.

When there's a mild current at a dive site, begin your dive by slowly swimming *into* the current. At the end of the dive, the current will assist your return by drifting you

Figure 3-5
When there's a mild current, begin the dive by slowly swimming against it. At the end of the dive, the current will help you return.

back. Avoid long surface swims against even a mild current. You will find it easier to swim against a mild current along the bottom, where it is generally weaker than at the surface.

If you are accidentally caught in a current and carried past your destination or exit point, swim across (perpendicular to) the current. Don't try to fight it by swimming directly into it because that will lead to exhaustion. By swimming across the current, you may be able to swim out of it and then head back to your destination or exit point.

When diving from a boat, if you become caught in a current at the surface, establish buoyancy, signal for assistance and then wait for help. Above all, remain calm. Diving in strong currents and swift moving water like rivers requires special training and experience. You can get this training and experience from special courses in the areas where these conditions are common.

Exercise 3-4   # Currents

1. Of the four primary causes of surface and underwater currents, check those listed here:

   ☒ a. Unequal heating and cooling of the water.   ☒ b. Tidal movement.

   ☒ c. Winds blowing over the surface of the water.

2. If you get caught in a current and are carried downstream past your exit point, you should begin swimming perpendicular to the current   ☒ True   ☐ False

3. If a mild current is present at a dive site you should begin your dive by slowly swimming _____ the current.   ☐ a. with   ☒ b. into

4. If you are exhausted and caught in a current at the surface, you should just signal for assistance.
   ☒ True   ☒ False.

How did you do?   *1. a, b, c*   *2. True*   *3. b*   *4. False. If you get caught in a current at the surface you should first establish buoyancy, signal for assistance, and wait for help.*

Objectives

After reading this section on bottom compositions, you will be able to:

1. Name six types of aquatic bottom compositions.

2. Describe two ways to avoid contact with the bottom.

Bottom Compositions

You will spend most of your time under water near the bottom, so its composition may affect you in several ways. Various compositions include silt, mud, sand, rock, coral and vegetation. Of these, the most interesting diving areas tend to be in rock, coral and vegetation.

In the section on visibility, you learned that some bottom compositions are easily stirred up. Additionally, some compositions may require you to take precautions while entering and exiting, or while moving about under water. You may sink into a muddy bottom if you're trying to wade into the water. If you drop something, it may vanish into a soft silt or sediment bottom. Entanglement in submerged trees, bushes, man-made objects or aquatic plants is possible if you're not cautious. You can get cuts or scrapes from rocks or coral.

It is important to know the bottom composition of the dive site, any problems associated with that composition, and how to cope with the problems. You must be especially cautious when diving over bottoms covered with living

Figure 3-6
It is important to know the bottom compo-sition of the dive and any problems associated with that composition.

organisms such as coral reefs. As you learned in Module Two, many aquatic organisms are so delicate that even a light touch can damage or kill them, so this caution is for their sake as well as yours. For your benefit and the reef's, be concerned about contact with a coral or rock bottom, or any bottom with sensitive aquatic organisms.

Regardless of the bottom composition, you may avoid most contact problems through buoyancy control. When you're near the bottom, establish neutral buoyancy and secure all dangling equipment. Swim up off the bottom to avoid stirring up the sediment with your fins and reducing visibility. Try to avoid direct contact with the bottom.

Exercise 3-5

Bottom Compositions

1. Name six types of aquatic bottom compositions.

   Sand   Rock   Silt

   Submerged trees   Coral   Mud

2. When near the bottom, establish _____ buoyancy and _____.

   ☐ a. negative, watch where your knees touch. ☒ b. neutral, secure all dangling equipment.

How did you do? *1. silt, mud, sand, rock, coral and vegetation. 2. b.*

Objectives

After reading this section on aquatic animal and plant life, you will be able to:

1. Define the two basic types of interaction that humans have with aquatic life.

2. State how nearly all injuries from aquatic life are caused.

3. Describe what a diver should do if he sights an aggressive animal under water.

4. List nine simple precautions that minimize the likelihood of being injured by an aquatic animal.

5. Explain why local fish and game laws should be followed by all divers.

6. Describe what a diver should do if he becomes entangled in an aquatic plant.

Figure 3-7
Quiet, smooth movement is less likely to disturb aquatic animals and will reward you with more opportunities to observe their natural behavior.

Figure 3-8
It is your responsibility to be sure that your active interactions with aquatic life, whether intentional or accidental, have minimal negative impact on the organisms you interact with.

Aquatic Animal and Plant Life 📖

Interaction with aquatic life — In becoming a diver, you're becoming one of the fortunate people who gets to see the marvelous world of underwater life first-hand. You'll be interacting with many new and fascinating animals; some will swim up to you curiously, others will freeze or flee in your presence. You may swim among aquatic plants that tower over you like an earthbound forest. Your interaction with aquatic animals and plants carries both a privilege and a responsibility.

Interaction between divers and aquatic life can be considered either 1) passive or 2) active. Passive interaction means that just by being under water, you're interacting

with aquatic life. Because aquatic animals are very sensitive to their environment, approaching them can change their behavior and the natural rhythm of their life. Quiet, smooth movement — which is less likely to disturb them — will reward you with more opportunities to observe aquatic animals behaving naturally, rather than fleeing or hiding.

Active interaction means that you deliberately or accidentally make physical contact with aquatic life. Active interaction like bumping into sensitive coral can be detrimental to aquatic life, whereas active interaction like feeding fish can be beneficial. It is your responsibility to be sure that your active interactions with aquatic life, whether

📖 See *The Encyclopedia of Recreational Diving*
See *Touch The Sea*

Figure 3-9
The most common injuries from aquatic animals are from nonaggressive creatures, such as sea urchins.

intentional or accidental, have minimal negative impact on the organisms you encounter while diving.

Aquatic Animals — Nearly all aquatic animals are timid and harmless. Most are fascinating and enjoyable, but there are a few that you'll want to be cautious with.

Nearly all injuries involving aquatic life (plants or animals) result from a diver being careless. In fact, you'll find after you've been diving a while that injuries caused by aquatic life are rare, and almost all of those are minor. It takes only a little bit of understanding and care to avoid potential problems.

The most common injuries from aquatic animals are from animals that aren't aggressive. These injuries include puncture wounds from sea urchins, stings from jellyfish and their relatives, and cuts and scrapes from barnacles and coral. With these, simply watch what you touch and wear an exposure suit as protection from accidental contact. If you're not familiar with an organism, leave it alone.

Very few aquatic animals are outwardly aggressive. While it's true that almost any animal is potentially dangerous when provoked, the incidence of human injuries caused by attacks from aquatic animals is extremely low. The reputation of some animals as bloodthirsty killers, such as sharks and killer whales, is the result of distorted reports, which often become myths.

Virtually all injuries from animals that may seem aggressive, such as eels and stingrays, result from making the animal feel frightened and threatened. These creatures only act defensively, such as if you carelessly stick your hand in an eel's hole without looking first. If you see an animal like a shark (or some other potentially aggressive animal), remain still and calm on the bottom, and watch what

Figure 3-10
Virtually all aquatic animals that have the potential to cause injury can be easily avoided by using caution.

Figure 3-11
Before collecting any game, learn local fish and game laws so you can be aware of seasons, size and catch limits, and other restrictions.

it does. Chances are, its just passing through. If it stays in the area, calmly move away from the area by swimming along the bottom and exit the water.

To avoid potential problems with aquatic animals, follow these nine guidelines:

1. Treat all animals with respect. Never tease or intentionally disturb them.

2. Be cautious when diving in extremely murky water, where you may have trouble watching where you put your hands. If potentially aggressive animals are known to inhabit the area, they may mistake you for something other than a diver in murky water.

3. Avoid wearing shiny, dangling jewelry that may attract the interest of some animals.

4. If you are spearfishing, remove speared fish from the water immediately.

5. Wear gloves and an exposure suit to avoid stings and cuts.

6. Establish neutral buoyancy to keep off the bottom.

7. Move slowly and carefully.

8. Watch where you're going and where you put your hands.

9. Avoid contact with unfamiliar animals.

While there are a few animals you want to avoid problems with, there are also many animals you may seek as food or specimens. These include lobster, crab, abalone, scallops, fish, clams, conch and other shellfish to name a few. Before collecting any game, learn local fish and game laws so you can be aware of seasons, size and catch limits and other restrictions. Fish and game laws are intended to assure a continuing supply of these animals for future enjoyment. If local laws permit game taking, collect only what *you* can eat or use. Be reasonable in what you take, so that there can be game for divers to enjoy in the future.

Aquatic Plants — Aquatic plants range from giant forests of kelp common to New Zealand, California and other cool-water areas, to smaller grasses and algae in freshwater rivers and lakes. Plants provide food and shelter to aquatic animals, so you'll find diving around plants interesting and filled with animal life.

The one concern regarding diving in or near aquatic plants is a possibility of entanglement. Fortunately, this is not a serious problem. Most divers find that with a little training and experience, they move easily in and about aquatic plants without ever getting entangled. Keeping

*Figure 3-12
Diving around plants is interesting
since they provide food and shelter
for aquatic animals.*

your equipment streamlined helps minimize the chances of snagging or tangling.

In the unlikely event you do get entangled in a plant, remain calm. Work slowly to free yourself with your buddy's help. Don't struggle or fight with the entanglement. You'll find that pausing to think, then taking action, will be far more effective than brute force.

Exercise 3-6

Aquatic Animal and Plant Life

1. If you're trying to feed an aquatic animal, your interaction with the animal can be classified as:
   ☐ a. passive ☒ b. active

2. Nearly all injuries involving aquatic life, result from the aggressive nature of these animals.
   ☐ True ☒ False

3. If a potentially aggressive animal is sighted, you should:
   ☒ a. remain still and calm on the bottom, watching what it does. ☐ b. surface immediately.

4. Of the nine precautions that minimize the likelihood of being injured by an aquatic animal, check those listed here: ☒ a. Never tease or intentionally disturb the animal. ☐ b. Never look under a rock outcropping.
   ☒ c. Move slowly and carefully. ☒ d. Avoid wearing shiny, dangling jewelry.

5. Fish and game laws are intended to keep a diver safe from harm. ☐ True ☒ False

6. If you should accidentally become entangled in an aquatic plant you should:
   ☐ a. inflate your BCD to pull yourself free.
   ☒ b. not struggle or fight with the entanglement, work slowly to free yourself.

How did you do? *1.* b *2. False. Nearly all injuries involving aquatic life result from carelessness on the part of the diver. 3.* a *4.* a, c, d *5. False. Fish and game laws are intended to assure a continuing supply of these animals for future enjoyment. 6.* b.

Objectives

After reading this section on sunlight, you will be able to:

1. State three ways to prevent sunburn while out of the water, and two ways to prevent it while snorkeling.

Sunlight

The intensity of sunlight varies from one region to another, so you should take precautions to prevent sunburn. Prevention while out of the water includes wearing protective clothing, staying in the shade and using sunscreen. A cloudy day is no protection against sunburn, and sunburn is also possible in the water, especially while snorkeling. Wear an exposure suit and waterproof sunscreen to protect yourself while snorkeling. Be careful not to let sunburn ruin a dive trip or vacation.

Exercise 3-7

Sunlight

1. To prevent sunburn while snorkeling:

 ☐ a. keep water on your back. ☒ b. wear an exposure suit or protective clothing.

How did you do? *1. b.*

Objectives

After reading this section on fresh water and salt water, you will be able to :

1. Name the general considerations for diving in the two main environments of the aquatic domain.

Fresh Water and Salt Water

The aquatic domain consists of two broad categories of environment: fresh water and salt water. Each has different conditions, different animal and plant life, and different considerations, so with each you'll use different techniques and procedures. Also, depending on the environment, you may engage in different special activities. A summary of different areas, activities and precautions will help you see each environment in perspective and help you understand the importance of regional orientations.

Freshwater Diving — General diving areas in freshwater environments include lakes, quarries, springs and rivers.

Figure 3-13
Popular freshwater diving environments include lakes, springs, quarries and rivers.

You can engage in activities like photography, bottle collecting and artifact hunting, and also in specialty activities including wreck diving, ice diving, cavern diving and swift-water diving. Each of these specialties requires specific training and equipment that you should have before trying to participate in them.

General problems to consider in the freshwater environment include: currents, bottom compositions, limited visibility, thermoclines, cold water, entanglement, deep water and boats. Diving may also take place at altitudes above sea level, which requires special techniques and training.

As you have learned, fresh water is less dense than salt

Figure 3-14
Many special activities, such wreck diving, are enjoyed in both fresh- and salt-water environments.

water, so you are less buoyant in it. If you are making a dive in fresh water after diving in salt water, be sure to adjust your buoyancy accordingly. When diving through thermoclines, keep in mind that colder water is denser than warmer water, creating slightly more buoyancy.

Saltwater Diving — The saltwater diving environment is divided into three general areas: 1) temperate, 2) tropical and 3) arctic. Nearly all recreational diving takes place in the temperate and tropical areas. Activities in salt water include all general diving activities, plus photography, spearfishing, shell collecting and diving from man-made structures like jetties, piers, oil rigs, wrecks and artificial reefs. General considerations in this environment include waves, surf, tides, currents, coral, boats, deep water, marine life and remote locations.

Figure 3-15
Nearly all recreational diving in salt water takes place in temperate and tropical areas.

Figure 3-16
Without proper training, any environment that doesn't permit you to make a direct vertical ascent to the surface is extremely hazardous. Avoid these environments until you are properly trained and properly equipped.

Just a brief look at the possibilities in both freshwater and saltwater environments makes it obvious that diving conditions and activities vary from region to region. For safety and enjoyment when diving in a new area or engaging in a new activity, be sure you get a proper orientation.

Exercise 3-8

Fresh Water and Salt Water

1. Diving in high-altitude lakes:
   ☐ a. requires special air in your tanks.   ☒ b. requires special techniques and training.

2. When diving in fresh water you will probably need _____ weight than in salt water.
   ☐ a. more   ☒ b. less

How did you do?   *1. b   2. b.*

Diving in Overhead Environments

Whether you're diving in fresh or salt water, there are areas that don't permit direct vertical access to the surface. Some examples of these are inside shipwrecks, under ice and in caves or caverns. These are called *overhead environments.*

Although diving in many overhead environments is quite safe with proper training, **without proper training these areas are very hazardous.** For this reason, *do not enter a cavern, cave, wreck or any other overhead environment unless* *you are both properly trained and properly equipped.* Doing so would place you in an unnecessary and extremely hazardous situation.

Many overhead environments may seem inviting and safe, but any time you can't swim directly to the surface, you're in a special situation, *no matter what the circumstances.* Enjoy the fun and adventure of diving outside the overhead environment until you are trained to venture inside safely.

Objectives

After reading this section on ocean diving, you will be able to:

1. Explain how *surge* is created and how to avoid it.

2. Explain how *longshore currents* are created and what possible effects they may have on a diver.

3. Explain why a wave would break offshore.

4. Explain how a *rip current* is formed and list two ways to identify its location.

5. Describe what a diver should do if he gets caught in a rip current.

6. Explain the effect of an *upwelling* on local offshore diving conditions and describe what creates an upwelling.

Ocean Diving 📖

There is more diving activity in the world's oceans than anywhere else. More than likely, you'll make an ocean dive

Figure 3-17
There is more diving activity in the world's oceans than anywhere else.

at some point. Possibly even your first dive — or most of your diving — will be in the ocean. The ocean is a dynamic environment that is constantly changing and in motion. It can be calm and still at times and very powerful at others. Through respect and understanding, diving in the ocean can be extremely rewarding, and difficult situations can be avoided. For these reasons, a basic understanding of waves, surge, longshore currents, rip currents, upwelling and tides plays an important part in preparing for ocean diving.

Except for offshore currents, which are permanent large-scale currents like the North American Gulf Stream, most water motion that concerns you as an ocean diver involves waves. The wind forms waves as it blows over the

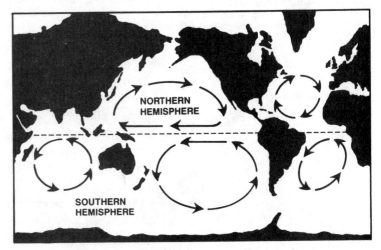

NORTHERN
HEMISPHERE

SOUTHERN
HEMISPHERE

Figure 3-18
Offshore currents are large-scale, permanent currents.

Figure 3-19
Most water motion that concerns you as a diver involves waves.

surface of the ocean. These waves can travel thousands of miles until they finally break in the shallow water of a beach. The size of a wave relates directly to the duration and strength of the wind causing it. A strong wind blowing continuously for several hours can make waves so large that diving conditions are unfavorable or hazardous.

A wave can travel along the surface of the water until it encounters shallow water. In shallow water, the lower por-

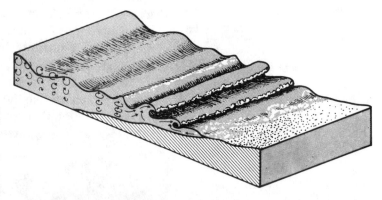

Figure 3-20
A wave travels along the surface until reaching shallow water, where the lower portion slows as it drags along the bottom. This causes the wave to peak up, become unstable and break as surf.

tion of the wave slows as it drags along the bottom, causing the top of the wave to peak up and become unstable. This makes the wave fall forward and break as surf. Surf is actually the spilling of a wave's energy onto a beach. The area where waves break is called the *surf zone*. Breaking waves can make entries and exits difficult unless you use special techniques. Diving through surf requires special training.

Waves break in water only slightly deeper than their height. An offshore reef, wreck or sand bar can create a shallow area that causes waves to break. These waves may then reform as they continue toward shore and break again

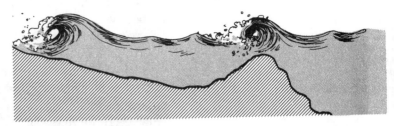

Figure 3-21
Because waves break in water only slightly deeper than their height, an offshore reef, wreck or sand bar can cause waves to break, reform, and then break again on shore.

on the beach. Some shallow areas offshore are popular dive sites, others are hazards to avoid. Knowing how to locate these shallow areas by watching the waves can help you develop your dive plan prior to entering the water.

When you dive in shallow water with waves passing overhead, you'll feel a back-and-forth movement of the water. This motion is called *surge*. Surge tends to move you back and forth through the water and can move you an appreciable distance as large waves pass overhead. Strong surge can be hazardous, but can be avoided by moving into deeper water. Avoid diving near shallow, rocky areas when a strong surge is present.

After a wave breaks on the beach, it flows back into the ocean under oncoming waves, causing what divers and swimmers call *undertow*. Undertow is nothing more than

Figure 3-22
Undertow is nothing more than the back-rush of a wave. It is not a current that pulls objects out to sea.

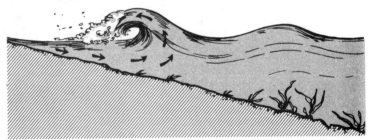

the backrush of a wave and usually dissipates at a depth no greater than three feet. It is *not* a current that can pull objects out to sea. On steep beaches with large waves, the backrush can be quite strong, making it hard to keep your balance during entries and exits. Avoid diving from beaches with extremely steep shorelines and high surf.

Waves typically approach the shore at a slight angle, pushing water down the shoreline. This water movement is called a *longshore current*. As you move through the surf zone, or if you're diving just offshore, a longshore current can move you parallel to the beach — away from your intended exit area. When diving in a longshore current, try to begin your dive up-current from your exit point, or dive

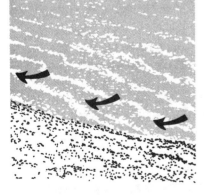

Figure 3-23
Waves approaching the shore at an angle push water down the shoreline, creating a longshore current.

into the current so you can drift back to the exit at the end of the dive.

Sometimes waves approach the shore from different directions. This causes the waves to either reinforce or nullify one another, causing wave sets. Wave sets are a series of large waves followed by a series of larger waves. When entering and exiting through wave sets, always time it so you pass through the surf zone while the smallest waves hit the beach.

Another current of concern in the ocean is a rip current. A rip current occurs when water piled up on shore by waves funnels back to sea through a narrow opening in a sand bar or reef. Rip currents are very strong and can be alarming if you get caught in one because they carry you

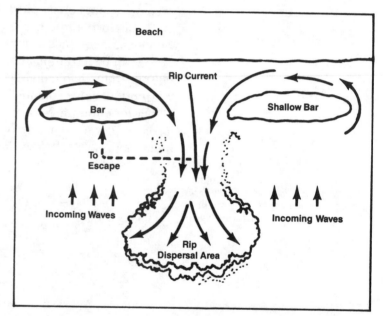

Figure 3-24
A rip current occurs when water piled up on shore by waves funnels back to sea through a narrow opening in a sand bar or reef.

away from shore very quickly. Rip currents can be recognized as a line of turbid, foamy water moving seaward. In addition, a rip current interrupts the normal wave pattern where it rushes seaward.

Avoid rips currents. In the event you get caught in a rip current, establish buoyancy, turn and swim parallel to shore until you clear the rip area, then resume your original course. Never try to swim directly against a rip current.

Upwelling is another important ocean current. An upwelling is a slow-moving current commonly caused by offshore winds pushing the warm surface water away from shore. As the surface water moves out to sea, deep water flows upward to take its place. The deeper water is usually

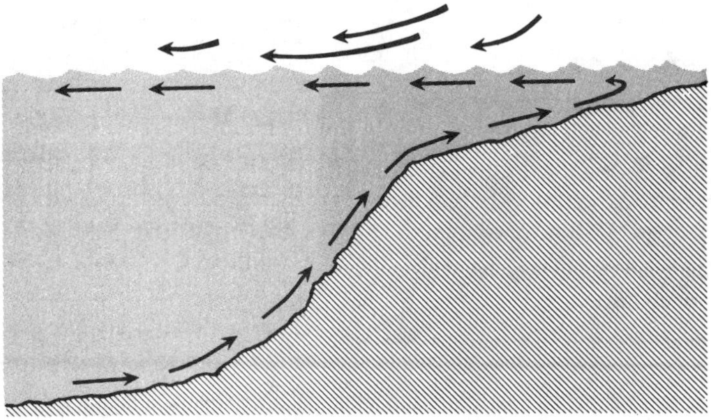

Figure 3-25
An upwelling is caused when an offshore wind blows the surface water out to sea, causing cooler, clearer deep water to flow up and take its place at the surface. An upwelling usually produces good diving conditions.

clear and cold, creating excellent, though cooler, diving conditions.

The movement of water in the surf zone may affect you in many ways: when entering, swimming at the surface, swimming under water or exiting. Avoid diving when the surf is large and rough. You need specialized surf training before attempting to dive in surf of any size. In surf training, you learn to judge conditions and use the correct techniques for entering and exiting through the waves. Stay out of the surf until you have had this training. Keep in mind that surf-diving techniques vary from area to area, and even from season to season in the same area.

Exercise 3-9

Ocean Diving

1. *Surge* is created by longshore currents. ☐ True ☐ False

2. If you get caught in a longshore current, you will be quickly swept away from shore. ☐ True ☐ False

3. A shallow offshore reef, wreck or sandbar can be detected by:
   ☐ a. surge ☐ b. waves breaking over it and then reforming as they continue toward shore.

4. Of the two ways to identify the location of a rip current, check those listed here:
   ☐ a. Fast moving water, parallel to shore ☐ b. A line of turbid, foamy water moving seaward
   ☐ c. Strong surf breaking offshore

5. If caught in a rip current, establish _____, turn and swim _____ to shore until you clear the rip area. ☐ a. where you are, up current ☐ b. buoyancy, perpendicular ☐ c. buoyancy, parallel

6. Upwelling:
   ☐ a. creates dangerous diving conditions. ☐ b. creates excellent, though cooler, diving conditions.

How did you do? *1. False. Surge is created by waves passing overhead in shallow water. 2. False. If you get caught in a longshore current, you will be moved parallel to the shoreline. 3. b 4. b 5. c 6. b.*

Objectives

After reading this section on tides, you will be able to:

1. Describe the three environmental conditions that can be changed by tidal movement.

2. Identify the tidal level best for diving.

Tides 📖

Sea coasts have a rhythmic rise and fall of water level called *tide*. Tides are caused by the gravitational pull of the moon and the sun on the waters of the earth and vary in time and height from place to place due to geographic configuration. The tides affect diving conditions by producing currents, changing depth and changing visibility.

Before diving, consult local tide tables and become familiar with the effects the tide has on local diving conditions. Generally speaking, the best diving conditions occur at high tide.

Exercise 3-10

Tides

1. Of the three environmental conditions that can be changed by tidal movement, check those listed here:
   ☐ a. Currents   ☐ b. Depth   ☐ c. Visibility

2. In general, the best diving occurs at what tidal level?   ☐ a. Low tide   ☐ b. Mean tide   ☐ c. High tide

How did you do?   *1.* a, b, c *2.* c.

Summary

Environmental conditions vary somewhat from one dive site to another, and often vary radically from one region to another. Exercise good judgment in evaluating diving conditions. Know the various conditions for the environment you'll be diving in. Use good judgment in evaluating the conditions of the environment. If they're poor or you're uncertain about your ability to handle the situation, don't make the dive. Seek an area orientation or training before trying to dive in an unfamiliar area and when the conditions are poor or require the use of unfamiliar skills.

Figure 3-26
Environmental conditions vary somewhat from one dive site to another, and often vary radically from one region to another.

Dive Planning

Objectives

After reading this section on dive planning, you will be able to:

1. State three reasons for planning a dive.

2. Outline the four stages of proper dive planning.

3. List the five steps to be followed during the advanced planning stage of dive planning.

4. List the four steps to be followed during the preparation stage of dive planning.

5. List the five steps to be followed during the last-minute preparation stage of dive planning.

6. List the seven steps to be followed during the pre-dive planning stage of dive planning.

Proper dive planning is your best assurance of an enjoyable dive. Through planning, you can avoid disappointments due to misunderstandings with your buddy, forgotten equipment or poor conditions at the dive site. Think of planning your dive as planning your fun. The following four stages of proper dive planning will assist you in organizing your dive: 1) advance planning, 2) preparation, 3) last-minute preparation and 4) pre-dive planning.

Advance Planning — The first steps in planning a dive start when you make the decision to go diving. These steps include: 1) selecting a buddy, 2) establishing a dive objective, 3) choosing a dive site, 4) determining the best time to dive and 5) discussing logistics with your buddy.

Pursuing a common objective, you and your buddy can work and stay together as a team. With the objective in

Figure 3-27
Before making a dive, consult local tide tables and become familiar with the effects the tide has on local diving conditions.

mind, such as taking underwater pictures or catching lobsters, you can choose an appropriate dive site. (Check your log book for relevant information if you've been to the site before. You'll learn more about log books in Module Four.) Plan an alternate dive site in case conditions are unfavorable at your primary site. Determine the best time to dive, taking into account variables like the tides and other activities in the area. Finally, discuss and agree on logistics, such as when to leave for the dive, how to get there, what to take and emergency contact information.

Preparation — Prepare for the dive by 1) inspecting all the equipment you'll be using, 2) making sure your tank is filled, 3) gathering all your equipment into one area and 4) using an equipment checklist to make certain something isn't forgotten (use the checklist in the Appendix). If you check your equipment well in advance, you should have ample time to fix or replace anything that is broken or missing. Finally, look for information on the dive site and current conditions.

Last-minute Preparation — Just before you leave to go diving, there are some last-minute items to take care of:

1. Get a current weather report.

2. File a dive plan with someone who isn't going with you, including information of when you expect to be back and what to do if you're delayed.

3. Gather last-minute items like a jacket, hat, sunglasses, wallet, lunch, ice chest, certification card and log book.

4. Pack your equipment bag so the first thing in is the last thing out, as described in Module Two.

5. Make a final check that you aren't forgetting anything.

Pre-dive Planning — Once you're at the dive site, take a few steps of planning *before* putting on your equipment:

1. Evaluate the conditions, preferably from an elevated vantage point.

Figure 3-28
Think of planning your dive as
planning your fun.

2. Decide whether or not conditions favor the dive and your objective. (If they don't, go to your alternate site, and if conditions are bad there, too, abort the dive. You should have a good, confident feeling about the dive.)

3. Decide on where to enter, the general course to follow, the techniques to use on the dive and where to exit.

4. Review hand signals and other communications.

5. Decide on what to do if you and your buddy become separated.

6. Agree on time, depth and air supply limits.

7. Discuss what to do if an emergency arises. The idea in pre-dive planning is to discuss and agree on as much as possible before the dive, while you can still communicate easily.

Dive the Plan — It doesn't make much sense to form a dive plan, then not use it. You and your buddy will find diving much safer, easier and more enjoyable when you stick with the decisions you made before the dive. Together you work toward your objective, knowing what each other will do because you discussed it before the dive. You can anticipate success if you stay with your dive plan.

A dive plan does not have to be complicated, but it should be followed. Get the most out of diving by planning your dive with your buddy, and then diving the plan.

Exercise 3-11

Dive Planning

1. One reason for planning a dive is to avoid disappointments due to poor conditions at the dive site.
   ☐ True ☐ False

2. The four stages of proper dive planning are: 1) advance planning, 2) _____, 3) last-minute preparation and 4) pre-dive planning. ☐ a. filing a dive plan ☐ b. preparation

3. Of the five steps to be followed during the advanced planning stage of dive planning, check those listed here:
   ☐ a. Choose a dive site. ☐ b. Discuss logistics with your buddy. ☐ c. Determine the best time to dive.
   ☐ d. File a dive plan with someone not going on the dive.

4. During the last-minute preparation stage of dive planning, review hand signals with your buddy.
   ☐ True ☐ False

5. Once at the dive site, evaluate the conditions, preferably from _____
   ☐ a. a boat. ☐ b. an elevated vantage point. ☐ c. the shoreline.

How did you do?   *1. True* *2. b* *3. a, b, c* *4. False. Reviewing hand signals should be done during the pre-dive planning stage so that the signals are fresh in your mind.* *5. b.*

Objectives

After reading this section on boat-diving procedures, you will be able to:

1. Outline three reasons for diving from a boat.

2. List five general considerations for equipment preparation before boat diving.

3. List four general considerations for personal preparation before boat diving.

4. Locate the following areas of a dive boat: bow (forward), stern (aft), starboard and port sides, leeward and windward sides, bridge, head and galley.

5. Outline four ways to minimize the effects of motion sickness while on a boat.

Boat-Diving Procedures

Diving from boats is tremendously popular, for many good reasons. Dive boats can often take you to dive sites with the best clarity, the most aquatic life, and the most interesting reefs. Boats can carry you to dive sites inaccessible from shore — in fact, in some regions the majority of the dive sites can only be reached by boat. Diving from a boat eliminates long, tiresome surface swims, dealing with surf, and hikes to and from the dive site. Chances are, you'll be doing some boat diving, so you'll want to know what to do to prepare for a boat dive and you'll want to understand

Figure 3-29
Diving from boats is popular because they can take you to the dive sites with the best clarity, the most aquatic life and the most interesting reefs.

basic boat terminology. It's also important to be familiar with general boat-diving procedures to help make your initial boat-diving experience pleasant.

Before heading out on a boat, spend some time getting ready:

1. Carefully inspect your equipment for potential problems, fill your tank and organize important spare parts.

2. Be sure your equipment has been well marked as described in Module One, because much equipment looks alike on a crowded boat.

3. Always use a dive bag for carrying your equipment to and from the boat.

4. Pack your equipment as described in Module Two — with what you need first on top.

5. Take ample warm and dry clothing. Be prepared because abrupt weather changes are not uncommon.

Prepare yourself as well as your equipment: 1) Be well rested, especially if the boat has an early departure scheduled, 2) avoid partying and drinking the night before, 3) don't eat foods you'll have trouble digesting, and 4) have your ticket, money, lunch and warm clothes all rounded up.

To find your way around a dive boat, it helps to know a few common boating terms. The *bow* is the front (pointed) end of the boat, and the rear is called the *stern.* If you are directed *forward,* that means to go toward the bow, and *aft* is in the direction of the stern. The *port* side of the boat is the left side, when you're standing facing the bow. The *starboard* side is on your right. (To help you remember, "port" and "left" have the same number of letters. Think of "left port.")

When the wind blows across the boat, the side the wind comes from is called the *windward* side and the side away from the wind is the *leeward* side. A boat's bathroom is called the *head,* and the kitchen is called the *galley.* The boat is controlled at the *helm,* which is found in the "control room" of the boat, called the *bridge* or *wheelhouse.* On charter boats, some areas may be off-limits to divers or off-limits when wearing equipment or wet exposure suits.

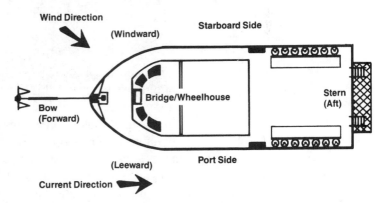

Figure 3-30
Typical charter boat layout.

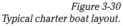

Always check with the crew or captain before entering the bridge, galley or sleeping area when you're wet.

When boat diving, always try to arrive at least a half hour before departure. This gives you time to check with the crew, sign in and secure your dive equipment. On some charter boats, you'll also pick out a bunk or a space in the cabin to stow your dry clothes and personal items.

If you tend to get motion sickness, take seasickness

medication before the boat gets underway and avoid greasy foods prior to boarding. It helps to stay in the fresh air on deck and to stand in the center of the boat while concentrating on a stationary object on the horizon. Try to stay busy while underway and be prepared to enter the water as soon as possible.

The ride to the dive site can take from a few minutes to several hours. Once the boat is anchored over the dive site, diving begins only after the OK has been given by the cap-

Figure 3-31
Listen closely to briefings and instructions given by the crew or captain of a dive boat.

tain or crew. Often a crew member will give a briefing about procedures at this time, so listen closely to his instructions. As you put your equipment on, be careful with heavy equipment. On a pitching boat, it's easy to lose your balance and hurt yourself. Avoid dropping tanks or weight belts because this can damage the boat deck. When putting on your scuba unit, always get a buddy to assist you. Step through your weight belt, rather than trying to swing it around your waist.

Be careful walking with equipment on. Equipment changes your center of gravity and can make keeping your balance awkward as you walk across a slippery, rolling deck. Don't try to walk across the deck with fins on. Put your fins on immediately before entering the water, using a rail or your buddy for balance.

When you and your buddy are ready to enter the water, check with the divemaster or a crew member. Leave the boat only at the places the crew indicates. The entry most commonly used from large dive boats is the giant stride, but from smaller vessels you may use a controlled seated entry or a back roll. Be certain the entry area is clear before entering.

Once in the water, have someone hand you accessories like cameras or spearguns. Note the current's direction so you can plan to swim into it on the bottom, and then make your descent, preferably along the anchor line or other line to the bottom. Once on the bottom, check your bearings and swim into the current. Plan your dive so you finish near the boat with enough air so you'll be back on board with 300 to 600 psi left in your tank. This will mean using careful navigation, which you'll learn more about in Module Five.

If you hear the boat's underwater recall system (discussed in Module Two) during the dive, remember that you should surface and look toward the boat for instructions. The crew may tell you to remain where you are or they may signal for you to return to the boat. Check with the crew before the dive about recall procedures.

At the end of the dive, surface in front of the boat, keeping one hand over your head for protection. When you break the surface, signal to the divemaster or crew that you're OK. Avoid swimming back to the boat immediately below the surface. If there are other boats underway in the area, they will not be able to see you.

In the unlikely event you surface and the boat is not in sight, stay calm and get buoyant. The boat may have slipped anchor or the captain may have needed to leave for an emergency. Relax and wait to be picked up. If the shore is near, slowly swim in that direction.

When you reach the boat's exit area, don't crowd it. Exit one at a time and stay clear of divers climbing the boarding ladder, because they can fall, drop a weight belt, or have a tank slip loose. Hand accessory equipment like cameras or spearguns up to crew members or other divers. Keep all your other equipment in place until you're aboard, except for your fins, which you will probably need to remove so you can climb the boarding ladder. Don't take off your fins until you have a firm hold of the boat, because the current can carry you away from it. Without your fins, you would have difficulty swimming back.

Once aboard, clear your equipment and accessories from the deck. A cluttered deck can cause people to trip, and equipment can be broken by being stepped on. Put your equipment in your equipment bag as you remove it, secure your tank and store accessories appropriately.

After the last dive, pack your equipment before the boat gets underway. On a charter boat, the crew or divemaster generally takes a visual roll call before moving the boat, which requires all divers to be present and to acknowledge only their own presence on board.

Watch experienced boat divers and learn from them. Follow proper boat-diving procedures and use safe diving techniques while diving from a private or charter boat. Doing so will make boat dives some of your best diving experiences.

Exercise 3-12

Boat Diving Procedures

1. The only reason you might want to dive off a boat is to eliminate long, tiresome surface swims.
   ☐ True ☐ False

2. Since equipment can't get sandy while boat diving, there is no need to use a gear bag. ☐ True ☐ False

3. The front end of the boat is called the _____ and the rear is called the _____.
   ☐ a. bow, stern ☐ b. stern, bow ☐ c. starboard, bow

4. If you are feeling seasick while on a boat, lay down near the bow of the boat. ☐ True ☐ False

How did you do? *1. False. There are other excellent reasons for boat diving. 2. False. You will need a dive bag to carry your equipment to and from a dive boat and to keep your equipment organized once on board. 3. a 4. False. It is best to busy yourself while underway and stand in the center of the boat.*

Problem Management

Diving is a safe recreation, and you'll find that if you and your buddy dive within your limitations, plan your dives and use safe diving techniques, you'll avoid a problem situation. Keeping yourself physically fit and maintaining your diving skills are also important in preventing problems. If a problem does arise, however, you'll want to be able to care for yourself and lend assistance to another diver.

This section will *introduce* you to some of the basic concepts in managing a diving problem. Keep in mind, though, that if you plan to dive where secondary assistance (paramedic, lifeguard, divemaster or instructor) is either remote or unavailable, you should have additional training in handling problems. This training includes learning first aid, cardiopulmonary resuscitation (CPR) and special procedures for handling diving-related problems.

CPR and first aid are excellent skills to have, not just for diving, but so you can help others no matter where you are.

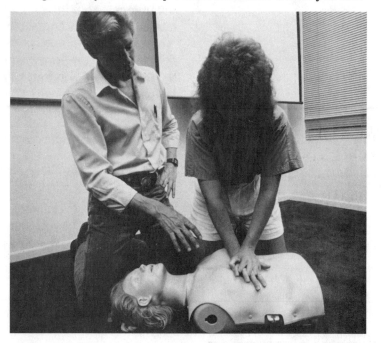

Figure 3-32
CPR and first aid are excellent skills to have, not just for diving, but so you can help others no matter where you are. The Medic First Aid course teaches you both CPR and first aid emergency care.

The Medic First Aid course offered by PADI gives you basic training in both CPR and first aid emergency care. Medic First Aid is available through PADI Instructors and Dive Centers.

To learn how to handle the specific and potentially complex problems that involve diving, plan now to enroll in a PADI Rescue Diver course. The Rescue Diver course makes you a more responsible diver by fine-tuning your ability to prevent problems and by developing skills to handle them if they should occur. Successful completion of the Rescue Diver course will increase your confidence in your personal diving ability.

For now, you should emphasize problem prevention and be prepared with emergency contact information, such as phone numbers for local paramedics and police, and radio frequencies for Coast Guard and other emergency services. Some areas have special telephone numbers specifically for handling diver emergencies. These services include the Divers Alert Network (DAN, serving the United States and Caribbean) and the Diving Emergency Service (DES, serving Australia, New Zealand and the South Pacific). In areas that don't have special diver emergency services, you'll want to have the number and contact information for the nearest recompression chamber as well as the appropriate emergency medical services. Be sure to carry change so you can use a pay phone in the event of an emergency. Your instructor will give you additional details about emergency contact information for the area where you will be diving.

In this section you'll learn how to prevent and respond to problems such as how to recognize when a diver needs assistance, how to assist another diver, how to respond to problems under water and how to deal with an unconscious diver.

Objectives

After reading this section on surface problem management, you will be able to:

1. Outline three ways to prevent or control most diving problems that occur on the surface.

2. Explain what should be done in the unlikely event that a diving-related problem occurs on the surface.

Surface Problem Management

Although diving is an underwater activity, the majority of diver distress situations take place at the surface. Surface problems can be prevented or controlled by 1) diving within your limitations, 2) relaxing while you dive and 3) establishing and maintaining positive buoyancy when you are at the surface.

Possible surface problems include overexertion, cramping leg muscles and choking on inhaled water. You learned about handling overexertion and leg cramps in Module Two. If you choke on water, hold your regulator or snorkel in place and cough through it — don't remove it from your mouth, and be sure to keep your mask in place. Swallowing sometimes helps relieve choking, too. Be sure you have

Figure 3-33
A diver who has a problem but is in control will generally ask for assistance.

sufficient buoyancy, because coughing lowers your lung volume, decreasing your tendency to float.

If a problem occurs at the surface, you should immediately establish buoyancy by either inflating your BCD or dropping your weight belt. Stop, think, then act. Avoid having to swim, tread water or exert yourself to stay above water, because you'll tire quickly. Don't hesitate to signal for help with a whistle or by waving. Getting assistance when you have a problem in the water is no different than getting assistance when you have a problem on land: it's the smart, safe thing to do. Get help when you need it and make it easier on yourself.

Exercise 3-13

Surface Problem Management

1. Of the ways to prevent diving problems while swimming at the surface, check those listed here:

   ☐ a. Always hurry to exit the water. ☐ b. Relax while you dive. ☐ c. Dive within your limits.

2. If a diving related problem occurs at the surface, you should immediately call for assistance.

   ☐ True ☐ False

How did you do? *1.* b, c. *2. False. If a problem occurs at the surface, you should immediately establish buoyancy. If the problem persists, then signal for help.*

Objectives

After reading this section on problem recognition, you will be able to:

1. Compare and contrast the appearance and actions of a diver who is under control with the appearance and actions of a diver who has, or is about to have, a problem.

Problem Recognition

Before you can help another diver, you have to know the diver needs help. You must immediately recognize the need for assistance, then follow your recognition with prompt action.

Divers who have a problem, but who are in control of their actions, look like divers without problems. Generally, you'll find they need assistance when they signal for it. A diver in control normally appears relaxed and breathes normally. Typically, he'll have all his equipment in place, be attentive and moving with slow, deliberate movements.

A diver who has allowed sudden, unreasoned fear to replace controlled, appropriate action with uncontrolled, inappropriate action has lost control and has panicked. The panicked diver, fearing drowning, typically struggles to hold his head high above the water, expending tremendous energy. He usually abandons his regulator and shoves his

Figure 3-34
The panicked diver typically struggles to hold his head high above the water, expending tremendous energy. He usually abandons his regulator and his mask. The panicked diver needs immediate help.

mask up on his forehead, requiring him to get even higher to breathe. A diver experiencing or about to experience a problem, who is out of control, will generally be anxious and breathing rapidly and shallowly. He pays no attention to his buddy or others and makes quick, jerky movements. His eyes are wide and unseeing. Divers exhibiting these signs need immediate help, because they will continue to struggle until completely exhausted and unable to remain afloat.

Exercise 3-14

Problem Recognition

1. Check all appropriate responses. A panicked diver, afraid of drowning, will typically:

☐ a. Drop his weight belt immediately ☐ b. Abandon his regulator and shove his mask up on his forehead

☐ c. Breathe rapidly and shallowly ☐ d. Look for his buddy ☐ e. Close his eyes.

How did you do? *1. b, c.*

Objectives

After reading this section on assisting another diver, you will be able to:

1. State the four basic steps to assisting another diver.

Assisting Another Diver

There are four basic steps to assisting another diver: 1) establish ample buoyancy, 2) calm the diver, 3) help the diver reestablish breathing control and 4) if necessary, assist the diver back to the boat or shore.

The first step in assisting another diver is to provide him with ample buoyancy. Ideally, this means throwing or extending some flotation to him, but if you can't do that, inflate the diver's BCD and/or discard his weight belt. Once you've established the diver's buoyancy, the next step is to

Figure 3-35
After helping him establish ample buoyancy, encourage a diver who is having problems to rest and, if necessary, assist him using the tank valve tow or the modified tired swimmer carry you learned in the last confined-water training session.

get him to calm down. Talk to the diver, offering encouragement and persuading him to relax and take it easy.

Help the diver reestablish breathing control by having him take deep, slow breaths. This will aid the diver in relaxing and regaining self-control. Give him time to recover and, if necessary, assist the diver using the tank valve tow or the modified tired-swimmer carry you learned in the last confined-water training session.

Figure 3-36
Tank valve tow.

Figure 3-37
Modified tired swimmer carry.

Exercise 3-15

Assisting Another Diver

1. The first step in assisting another diver is to:
   - ☐ a. take his mask from him so that he can breathe through his nose.
   - ☐ b. give him your regulator for air. ☐ c. provide him with ample buoyancy.

2. The second step in assisting another diver is to:
   - ☐ a. take his mask from him so that he can breathe through his nose. ☐ b. drop his weight belt.
   - ☐ c. talk to him, offering encouragement and persuading him to relax. ☐ d. yell for assistance.

How did you do? *1.* c *2.* c.

Objectives

After reading this section on underwater problem management, you will be able to:

1. Outline three ways to prevent or control most diving problems that may occur under water.

2. List four problems that may occur under water.

3. Arrange the five low-on-air/out-of-air emergency procedures in order of priority.

4. Explain how to breathe from a free-flowing regulator.

5. Explain what a diver should do if he becomes entangled under water.

Figure 3-38
To keep from running excessively low on or out of air, make a habit of checking your SPG frequently.

Underwater Problem Management

Few problems occur under water, and those that do can be prevented by 1) relaxing while you dive, 2) carefully monitoring your air supply and 3) diving within your limitations. Of the few problems that do occur under water, the most likely are 1) overexertion, 2) running out of or low on air, 3) regulator free flow and 4) entanglement.

Overexertion — In Module Two, you learned that overexertion can be prevented by moving and breathing slowly and deliberately, and by pacing yourself. You also learned to stop all activity, rest, relax and breathe slowly if you do get overexerted, so you can restore your normal breathing pattern.

Under water, overexertion can give you a feeling of air starvation because breathing resistance through the regulator increases as you go deeper. Although overexertion is the primary problem under water, you can prevent it by avoiding strenuous activity and by pacing yourself.

Running Low On or Out of Air — Running out of air is probably the easiest problem to avoid, and air stoppage due to a malfunction is extremely remote (more about this in a moment). To keep from running excessively low on or out of air, make a habit of checking your SPG frequently. Remember, your SPG will only help you if you watch it.

In the unlikely event your air either runs out or stops unexpectedly, it's still not a serious situation if you take a moment to consider your options and then act intelligently. Here are five options you can consider in a low-air situation, in their order of priority:

1. *Make a normal ascent.* If your tank isn't completely empty, you can often make a normal ascent. As you ascend, the water pressure surrounding you decreases, allowing you to get more air from your tank.

2. *Ascend using an alternate air source.* Use of an alternate air source, either an additional second stage from your buddy or your own pony bottle, is probably the easiest way to solve an out-of-air problem, and is your best all-around choice. Remember, to have this option, you must know how to locate the alternate, how to secure it and how to use it. Don't neglect these steps in your Pre-dive Safety Drill.

3. *Execute a controlled emergency swimming ascent.* If you either have no alternate air source available, or your buddy is too far away to provide it, and the water is 30 to 40 feet deep or less, you may decide to make an emergency

Figure 3-39
A controlled emergency swimming ascent simply involves swimming to the surface with all your equipment in place, while exhaling continuously by making an A-a-a-h-h-h sound.

Normal
alternate
controlled
Buddy
Buoyant

ascent. This simply involves swimming to the surface, exhaling continuously making an *A-a-a-h-h-h* sound into your regulator to release expanding air and to prevent lung-expansion injury. The emergency swimming ascent is not a difficult exercise, and you'll have a chance to practice it in the confined-water training session of this module.

4. *Buddy breathe with a single regulator.* If you're deeper than 40 feet and there's no alternate air source available, you may need to share air by passing one regulator back and forth between you and your buddy. This is called *buddy breathing.* Although this is more difficult to execute than using an alternate air source, it can be managed if you and your buddy remain calm and are familiar with the procedure. Once you begin buddy breathing, you and your buddy should continue all the way to the surface without attempting to switch to another out-of-air option. Your instructor may have you practice buddy breathing in Module Four. Keep in mind that sharing air with an alternate air source is far more preferable.

5. *Make a buoyant emergency ascent.* The final out-of-air option is the buoyant emergency ascent, which requires dropping your weights and/or inflating your BCD and exhaling continuously, making the *A-a-a-h-h-h* sound as you rise to the surface. This option should only be used when your buddy cannot be located, you have no alternate air source available, and it is doubtful that you can reach the surface by an emergency swimming ascent.

Remember to discuss out-of-air emergency options with your buddy *before* the dive, and stay close together so you can assist each other as necessary, especially as you go deeper. Consider an alternate air source a standard part of your and your buddy's equipment for all diving. Look after one another, watching your air supplies, breathing patterns, and time and depth limits. By remaining alert and monitoring each other, air supply problems can be avoided.

Regulator Free Flow — Today's regulators are extremely reliable; it's highly unlikely that a regulator malfunction would cut off your air. Modern regulators are designed to be fail-safe, which means a malfunction results in a free flow of air rather than a termination of air.

You can breathe from a free-flowing regulator if you follow a couple of procedures. First, don't seal your mouth on the regulator because the continuous flow of high-pressure air may cause lung-expansion injury. Instead, hold the regulator in your hand and press the mouthpiece to the outside of your lips. You can breathe the air you need while the excess escapes around the edge of the mouthpiece. You should begin your ascent immediately if your regulator free flows because your air supply will be used very quickly. When you reach the surface, turn off the air and don't use the regulator until it has been serviced by a qualified technician. If you maintain your regulator properly, keep it out of the sand or debris and have it serviced annually, you'll probably never have a free-flow problem.

Entanglement — As mentioned earlier in the discussion on aquatic plants, entanglement is rare. Besides plants, though, fishing line, tree branches and any loose line in the water has the potential to create entanglement problems. Prevent entanglement by moving slowly, being observant and keeping your equipment secure so it won't snag or tangle.

As long as you have air and are unhurt, entanglement really isn't considered an emergency. If you become entangled, simply stop, think, and then work slowly and calmly to free yourself. Get your buddy to help you and avoid twisting and turning because this simply worsens the tangles. If your scuba unit is tangled, you may have to remove the unit, keeping your regulator in your mouth, free it, and then put it back on. You will practice taking your unit off and putting it back on under water in Module Five. Entanglement is not a serious problem if you deal with it calmly.

Exercise 3-16 **Underwater Problem Management**

1. One way to prevent a problem from occurring under water is to dive within your limitations.
   ☐ True ☐ False

2. Of the few problems that do occur under water, check those that are most likely:
   ☐ a. Entanglement ☐ b. Eel attack ☐ c. Running out of air ☐ d. Regulator malfunction

3. If you run out of air at a depth of 35 feet and can't see your buddy, you should:
   ☐ a. make a buoyant emergency ascent. ☐ b. make a controlled emergency swimming ascent.

4. To breathe from a free-flowing regulator:
   ☐ a. place the regulator at your chest, breathing from the bubbles as they hit your face.
   ☐ b. press the mouthpiece to the outside of your lips and breathe the air you need, allowing the excess to escape.

5. If you get entangled under water, begin by cutting yourself free with your knife. ☐ True ☐ False

How did you do? *1.* True *2.* a, c *3.* b *4.* b *5.* False. If you get entangled under water, first stop, think and then work slowly and calmly to free yourself.

Objectives

After reading this section on the unconscious diver, you will be able to:

1. Outline the four general procedures for dealing with an unconscious diver in the water.

Near Drowning and The Unconscious Diver

Near drowning occurs when an unconscious, non-breathing, revivable diver has been submerged in water. It may be caused by such things as swallowing water, extreme fatigue, entanglement and lung overpressurization — all of which lead to panic, inefficient breathing, blockage of the throat, exhaustion, stoppage of the heart and unconsciousness.

With an unconscious diver, the primary concern is to make sure he is breathing and to render mouth-to-mouth ventilation if he isn't. If a diver is unconscious under water, he must be brought to the surface. Artificial respiration may be needed. If you suspect the diver's heart has stopped, CPR will be required. The victim will have to be removed from the water to perform CPR, because it can't be done effectively in water.

Here are the four general procedures to follow if a diver loses consciousness in the water:

1. Quickly bring the diver to the surface and check for breathing.

2. Establish ample positive buoyancy.

3. Get assistance as needed in providing resuscitation.

4. Help remove the diver from the water.

Assistance must continue once out of the water. The following steps should be followed once you have removed the unconscious diver from the water. These procedures also apply for a diver who, *after* diving, becomes unconscious or experiences symptoms of lung overpressurization injury. These symptoms may include difficulty breathing, confusion, lowered alertness, a change in the level of consciousness, unclear thinking, visual problems and chest pain.

1. Keep airway open and check for breathing. If necessary, start and continue mouth-to-mouth ventilation and/or CPR (if properly CPR qualified).

2. Observe the diver constantly.

3. If the diver doesn't require CPR or mouth-to-mouth ventilation, lay him level on his left side, supporting his head. This position should not be allowed to interfere with transportation or other aid, and should *not* be used if CPR is required.

Figure 3-40
With an unconscious diver, the primary concern is to make sure he is breathing and to render mouth-to-mouth ventilation if he isn't.

4. Administer oxygen if possible.

5. Keep the diver still and maintain a normal body temperature by protecting the diver from heat or cold.

6. Seek emergency medical assistance.

7. If unable to accompany the diver to medical treatment, write down as much background information as possible and attach it to him in a conspicuous place.

Exercise 3-17

The Unconscious Diver

1. If you find an unconscious diver under water, what should be done first? ☐ a. Determine his condition ☐ b. Quickly bring the diver to the surface and check for breathing ☐ c. Remove his tank.

How did you do? *1.* b.

Summary

Diving is safe and fun when you follow the rules. Nevertheless, people sometimes do break the rules and get into difficulty, and may require assistance. To be effective in helping a diver in distress, you need training beyond the scope of this course. Complete a Medic First Aid course to gain the skills that could one day allow you to help someone whereever you are, and take the PADI Rescue Diver course to gain the skills that will make you practiced in helping divers.

Confined-Water Training Preview — Module Three

You are about to begin your third session using scuba equipment. By now, you're probably finding that you're becoming comfortable and familiar with diving, and that many of the skills you have been practicing are becoming automatic. This means you're well on your way to becoming a diver.

In this session, you'll have a chance to expand upon some skills you learned in Module Two, practice some skills you already know, and learn some new ones — like alternate air source use and breathing from a free-flowing regulator. You will find these new skills are fun, easy and contribute to your confidence as a diver.

The performance requirements listed below are the skills that you must successfully complete during the confined-water training for Module Three. As you did in the first two modules, read the requirements now so you'll have an idea of what your instructor will be teaching you during the session.

Performance Requirements
Confined-Water Training — Module Three

By the end of the confined-water training for Module Three, you will be able to:

1. Swim under water without a mask for a distance of not less than 50 feet.

2. Independently establish neutral buoyancy under water by pivoting on the fin tips (both oral and low-pressure inflation).

3. Locate, secure and breathe for one minute from an alternate air source supplied by a buddy, both in a stationary and swimming position while under water.

4. Breathe effectively from a free-flowing regulator for not less than 30 seconds.

5. Simulate a controlled emergency swimming ascent by swimming horizontally under water for at least 30 feet while continuously exhaling by emitting a continuous sound.

No-mask Swimming

In the last confined-water training session, you learned to breathe under water without a mask on. If your mask were to come off completely while diving, you might have to swim to the surface without it if you couldn't relocate it, or

Figure 3-41
In this confined-water training session, you'll use the skill of no-mask breathing to swim about 50 feet under water without your mask. Even with your mask off, be sure not to hold your breath.

you might have to get your buddy's attention to help you find it. In this session, you'll use the skill of no-mask breathing to swim about 50 feet under water without your mask.

Just like you did in the last session, avoid breathing through your nose so you don't inhale any water and choke. Remember that if you feel water in your nose, you can force it out by exhaling through your nose.

During your swim, open your eyes. Even without your mask, you'll be able to see shadows and objects, and tell which way you're headed. If you're wearing contact lenses, however, keep your eyes closed so you won't lose them. You can still complete the exercise by feeling your way on the bottom, or by having your buddy guide you. If your vision isn't that poor, you may want to take your contact lenses out for this session.

Neutral Buoyancy Under Water

By now you're aware of the importance of maintaining neutral buoyancy while diving so you can avoid touching the bottom, so you can relax and maneuver easily, and so you can prevent rapid, uncontrolled ascents and descents. In the last confined-water training session, you learned how to adjust your weight system so you're neutrally buoyant at the surface.

As you descend, you'll need to use your BCD to trim and fine-tune buoyancy. You may recall that this is because your buoyancy decreases as you descend, making it necessary to add air to your BCD. As you ascend, the air in your BCD expands, so you need to vent it to keep from having too much buoyancy and ascending too rapidly. When making changes to your buoyancy, whether adding or releasing air, do it *slowly*. Rapid changes make it difficult for you to control buoyancy and can lead to runaway ascents or descents.

To add air to your BCD, you may use either your low-pressure inflator or add it orally. To orally inflate your BCD under water, grasp your regulator in your right hand and the BCD inflator in your left. Take a breath and remove the regulator from your mouth. Blow this air into your BCD, operating the controls just like you did when orally inflating it at the surface. Put about two thirds of your breath into the BCD, saving enough to clear the regulator when you put it back in your mouth. Switch from the regulator to the BCD inflator until you've inflated the BCD sufficiently to attain neutral buoyancy.

If you use your low-pressure inflator, use it as you have

Figure 3-42
Orally inflating the BCD under water.

in the previous confined-water training, remembering to put air into the BCD in short bursts. Do not hold the button down continuously.

To release air from the BCD during ascent, hold the BCD deflator mechanism in one hand, raise it over your head and vent small amounts of air from time to time.

During this session, you'll be using the *fin pivot* method of achieving neutral buoyancy. This method involves 1) laying facedown on the bottom, 2) breathing slowly and deeply and 3) adding small amounts of air to your BCD until you reach the point where you slowly pivot upward on your fin tips as you inhale, and slowly pivot downward as you exhale. This means you're neutrally buoyant. Be sure you don't hold your breath at any time.

Maintaining neutral buoyancy with your BCD is easy with experience, though it may seem a little difficult at first.

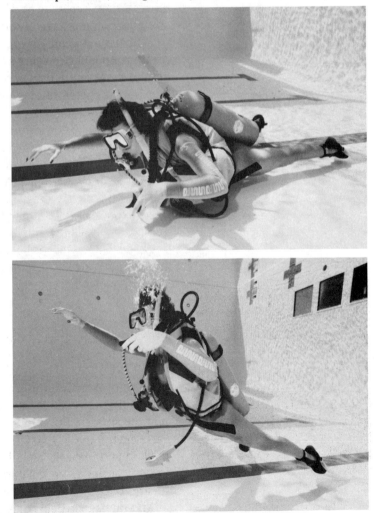

Figure 3-43
To check for neutral buoyancy, use the fin pivot. First, lie facedown on the bottom while breathing slowly and deeply. Next add small amounts of air to your BCD until . . .

Figure 3-44
. . . you pivot upward on your fin tips as you inhale and downward as you exhale.

Because water is so dense, movement occurs slowly. This means changes in your buoyancy will not have an immediate effect. When making changes to your buoyancy, add or release small amounts at a time and wait to see the effect before adding or releasing more.

Keep in mind that the volume of air in your BCD changes every time you change depth. In shallow water, where air expands and compresses the most rapidly, you'll find buoyancy control the most critical. Don't forget to adjust your buoyancy as you change depth, or you may find yourself floating away from the bottom unintentionally. If this should happen, exhale, swim downward, locate your BCD deflator and vent some air from it. If you're unable to do this and end up in a runaway ascent, assume a spread-eagle position to create resistance and slow your ascent, while breathing continuously and maintaining normal lung volume. With experience and by staying aware of your buoyancy, you should have few, if any, runaway ascents.

During a normal ascent, keep your hand on the deflator mechanism throughout the ascent, releasing small bursts of air periodically (as needed) to prevent excessive buoyancy. When you reach the surface, immediately inflate your BCD and establish positive buoyancy. Pay close attention to buoyancy control until you reach the point that you control it automatically.

Figure 3-45
During a normal ascent, keep your hand on the deflator mechanism throughout the ascent, releasing small bursts of air as needed to prevent excessive buoyancy.

Use of an Alternate Air Source

As you learned from the discussion on out-of-air options, the alternate air source is the preferred means of sharing air and one of the best solutions to the out-of-air problem.

In Module Two, you learned that an alternate air source may be 1) an alternate air source second stage, 2) an alternate inflator regulator or 3) a pony bottle. Regardless of which type you practice with during this confined-water training session, you must be able to locate, secure and breathe from an alternate air source supplied by a buddy.

The following procedures apply to the use of all three types of alternate air sources.

The alternate air source, as described in Module Two, should be located in the chest area — readily accessible — and secured so that it can easily be pulled free for use. Because an alternate air source may be attached in a number of different ways and mounted in different locations, this should be reviewed with your buddy prior to diving.

Depending on the alternate air source configuration, the donor (diver supplying air) may want to give the recipient (diver getting air) his alternate air source, or he may want to give the recipient the primary air source and switch to the alternate. Regardless, the procedure should be agreed upon by dive buddies before the dive.

If you're diving and require your buddy's alternate air source, get your buddy's attention and signal "out of air" and "share air." He should respond by swimming toward

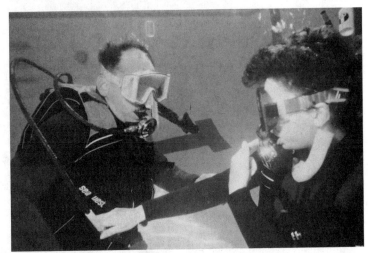

Figure 3-46
You should be able to locate and secure your buddy's alternate air source without his assistance.

you, offering you a second stage mouthpiece as he approaches. If you can't get your buddy's attention, you should locate and secure his alternate air source on your own and begin breathing.

Because there are many variations of alternate air sources, use caution when placing the regulator in your mouth. If you put it in upside down, you will have trouble clearing it and may inhale some water in attempting to use

Figure 3-47
Once you have the alternate air source
properly positioned, make physical and
eye contact with your buddy.

it. Once you have the alternate air source correctly positioned, make physical and eye contact with your buddy. The exact method for holding on to each other will depend on the configuration of the alternate air source, but in general you should try to hold on to your buddy's tank valve, arm or shoulder.

Figure 3-48
During ascent with an alternate air
source, maintain physical and eye
contact with your buddy while
breathing normally.

When you've made contact and are breathing comfortably, begin ascending. Continue eye and physical contact with your buddy while breathing normally. You and your buddy will each adjust your own buoyancy, and the rate of ascent will be controlled by the donor.

During this confined-water training session, your instructor will demonstrate the use of alternate air sources, and have you practice locating, securing and using one. You will do this both as a receiver and as a donor, while stationary and while swimming. You should practice this skill frequently, and every time you dive with a new buddy or encounter an unfamiliar alternate air source.

Free-Flow Regulator Breathing

Earlier in this module, you learned that it's possible to breathe from a free-flowing regulator. Refer to that information to refresh your memory on the technique and procedures.

During this skills development session, your instructor will have you practice breathing from a regulator while simulating a free flow. You simulate the free flow by holding in the purge button.

Remember to breathe without sealing your mouth on the regulator and to allow excess air to escape. Practice turning off your air after surfacing. If you can't reach your tank valve unless your remove the scuba unit, do so for practice. Although your buddy would normally turn the air off for you, learning to do it yourself builds self-reliance.

Figure 3-49
Remember to breath from a free-flowing regulator without sealing your mouth on it.

Controlled Emergency Swimming Ascent

You learned in the Knowledge Development portion of this module that the controlled emergency swimming ascent is one option if your air supply is lost at 30 to 40 feet or less, and your buddy is not close enough to assist with his alternate air source.

Emergency swimming ascents are interesting because you start with air in your lungs, exhale all the way to the surface and still have air in your lungs when you get there. This is due to air expanding in your lungs as you ascend. The potential hazard in this technique is a lung-expansion injury, but this is avoided by not holding your breath.

To make a controlled emergency swimming ascent, simply swim upward with all your equipment in place, including your regulator. Look up, reach up and come up. Rather than just exhaling, make a continuous *A-a-a-a-h-h-h* sound as you exhale during your ascent. By doing this, you exhale just the right amount of air so you don't hurt your lungs, but you don't exhale too much air either. The idea is to maintain a lung volume that is neither empty nor full.

During this session, you'll practice the controlled emergency swimming ascent first horizontally, then diagonally from the deeper area of the confined water. You will have enough air in your lungs to swim a long way horizontally

Figure 3-50
During this confined-water training session, you'll practice making controlled emergency swimming ascents both horizontally and vertically.

while exhaling continuously, but 30 feet is sufficient for training. Once you have practiced this exercise horizontally, you can imagine how easy it would be to make a controlled emergency swimming ascent vertically when assisted by air expanding in your BCD and lungs. After an actual controlled emergency swimming ascent, you don't feel out of breath — you still have air in your lungs.

Perhaps the greatest value of controlled emergency swimming ascent training is knowing you can do it. When you realize you can reach the surface without difficulty, even if you suddenly lose your air supply, you can relax and enjoy diving more.

Summary

You are now ready for the confined-water training session for Module Three. The new skills you will be practicing are:

1. No-mask Swimming
2. Neutral Buoyancy Under Water
3. Use of an Alternate Air Source
4. Free-flow Regulator Breathing
5. Controlled Emergency Swimming Ascent

General Open-Water Skills

At this point, you're ready to begin looking at some of the skills you'll be practicing in the actual diving environment — in open water. Depending on the location and scheduling of the course, you may make two open-water scuba dives before you go on to Module Four, or you may make all your open-water dives after completing all five modules.

During your open-water training, you'll be applying the skills you've learned during confined-water training, and you'll be learning some new skills that can only be learned in an actual open-water environment. These skills may include learning how to: 1) evaluate diving conditions, 2) put on your equipment before an actual dive, 3) make entries and exits through *mild* surf, 4) swim on the surface and 5) descend in open water. You will be using most of these skills on practically every open-water dive you make, so learning them now will make diving easier.

Evaluating Open-Water Diving Conditions

When you arrive at a dive site, you want to know whether the diving conditions are within your training and experience limitations. You should evaluate the conditions immediately upon arrival, *before* putting on your equipment. Your instructor will show you how to take into account considerations like weather, water temperature, bottom composition, waves, depth, local area hazards and anything else that has direct bearing on the dive.

In the section on dive planning, you learned that you

Figure 3-51
You should evaluate conditions immediately upon arrival at the dive site, before putting on your equipment.

167

should preplan your entry and exit points and procedures. This should be part of evaluating the dive site.

Decide whether you can make the dive safely. If you or your buddy don't feel confident about making the dive, check your alternate site to see if conditions are acceptable. If not, do something else that is enjoyable — diving in poor or potentially hazardous conditions isn't fun. You are learning to dive to have fun, not to expose yourself to unreasonable risks.

Suiting Up

From your experience during confined-water training and from the discussion on exposure suits, you've already learned a good deal about suiting up and avoiding overheating. In open-water training, you'll put this practice and knowledge to use.

Because you wear so much equipment in diving, putting it all on can create some problems if you don't handle the procedures properly. Improper suiting up can cause you to become somewhat frustrated, tired, breathless and overheated.

Ideally, you want to suit up so that you and your buddy finish simultaneously while staying cool and rested, ready to enter the water. To do this, be sure all your equipment has been checked, adjusted and packed properly before the dive. Take your time, and rest as needed. In hot weather,

Figure 3-52
You want to suit up so that you and your buddy finish simultaneously, while remaining cool and rested.

cool off in the water if you need to. Pace yourself with your buddy, but be as self-reliant and independent as possible, so you become familiar with your equipment.

As a suggestion, prepare and don your equipment in the following order:

1. Assemble your scuba unit and BCD. Prepare anything else that can be made ready without putting your exposure suit on, such as defogging your mask.

2. Don your exposure suit. If it is a wet suit, put on pants and boots first, then the jacket and hood.

3. Put on your BCD if it isn't part of the scuba unit.

4. Put on your weight belt. With some scuba units, you'll put your weight belt on after the unit.

5. Have your buddy help you put on your scuba unit.

6. Don your mask and snorkel, which should've been adjusted ahead of time.

7. Finally, put on your gloves and fins; fins should've been preadjusted.

8. Perform the Predive Safety Check as described in Module Two (Begin With Review And Friend) with your buddy. In some instances, it may be preferable to do this before donning your fins.

Suiting up may seem troublesome at first, until you get used to it. After one or two dives, you'll be more familiar with your equipment, and suiting up will become almost second nature.

Open-Water Entries

Entry techniques vary from place to place according to the diving environment. If a dive site requires entry techniques that are unfamiliar to you, always be sure to get an orientation to them so you can dive safely. If your open-water training includes dives from shore, your instructor will teach you the proper entry methods for the dive site.

The following practices are generally recommended for most scuba entries that require you to walk into the water from shore:

1. Have all your equipment in place before entering the water. Depending on the environment and conditions, you may have your fins on when you enter the water, or you may carry them in your hand until reaching water about waist to chest deep.

2. As a general rule, breathe from your regulator until you're floating in deeper water. This way, if you stumble,

169

you can still breathe, even if you end up with your face in the water. Once in deeper water, switch to your snorkel to conserve air if you have a surface swim before descending.

3. If you're walking in with your fins on, walk backward or sideways and shuffle your feet. This helps you find obstructions or holes, scares away bottom-dwelling animals that could sting if you stepped on one and helps minimize the chances of falling. In some environments, however, you may want to avoid shuffling your feet because it will disturb the visibility. Your instructor will teach you which is appropriate for your open-water training.

4. Swim as soon as the water is deep enough. Swimming is often easier than wading.

Figure 3-53
Enter the water with all your equipment in place and breathing through your regulator.

Surf Entries and Exits

Surf entries and exits require special training and shouldn't be attempted unless you have had that training. It is possible that you'll make entries and exits through mild surf as part of your open-water training. Here are a few simple general procedures.

Surf Entries — Before you enter the water, you want to watch the waves and note where they're breaking and how often. Do this during suiting up so you'll be familiar with the surf's pattern when you're ready to enter.

As you enter the water, breathe from your regulator. Back into the water, looking over your shoulder to watch where you're going and to see oncoming waves. Your buddy should be by your side, and if you're towing a float, it should be between you and the shore, so a wave can't push it into you.

Figure 3-54
When entering through surf, stop, hold your mask and lean against a wave as it meets you.

When a wave is about to meet you, hold your mask, stop, and lean into the wave as it hits you. Once the wave passes, move on again quickly. As soon as the water is deep enough, begin swimming steadily and move quickly until you clear the surf zone, then rejoin your buddy if you became separated during the entry. Be sure to keep a hand on your mask until outside the surf.

Surf Exits — When you're ready to leave the water through surf, stop outside the surf zone and watch the waves. Evaluate the situation and discuss it with your buddy.

Always save some air for exiting, because you will use your regulator as you pass through the surf. Wait until the

Figure 3-55
During your exit, avoid stopping in the surf zone. Swim in until you're in knee-deep water.

surf pattern reaches a lull, then swim toward shore as quickly as possible, keeping a hand on your mask and checking your buddy every few seconds. Swim steadily with a free hand extended ahead of you. Avoid stopping in the surf zone and swim until you're in knee-deep water. If

Figure 3-56
If the backrush is strong and you are tired, you may elect to swim all the way up the beach and crawl out on your hands and knees.

the backrush is strong and you are tired, you may elect to swim all the way up the beach and crawl out on your hands and knees.

Handle waves the same way you did while entering — by stopping, holding your mask firmly and leaning against it. When you stand up, walk backward and stay beside your buddy. If you have a surface float, push it ahead of you so it stays between you and the shore.

Surface Swimming

Swimming on the surface in open water is different than swimming on the surface in confined water. In open water, the visibility may be different, you may have longer distances to swim, and there may be currents or waves. By following a few simple recommendations, you can avoid overexertion and separation from your buddy during a surface swim.

1. Swim with your BCD about 50% inflated so you won't have to struggle to stay at the surface. Avoid overinflating the BCD, though, because it creates unnecessary drag.

2. Pace yourself. Swim at a steady, comfortable pace.

Figure 3-57
When swimming on the surface, avoid overexertion and streamline yourself as much as possible. Use your snorkel and keep your fins below the surface when kicking. Lift your head about every 30 seconds to check your location.

3. Streamline yourself as much as possible. Keep your arms at your sides.

4. Use your snorkel, breathing cautiously to avoid choking on water that may enter the snorkel due to small waves.

5. Keep your fins below the surface when kicking. Be sure to kick downward more than upward. Just like you did in your confined-water training sessions, you may wish to swim on your side or back if conditions allow.

6. Lift your head about every 30 seconds to check your location, direction and your buddy. Stay close to your buddy, maintaining physical contact if the visibility is poor. Keep an eye on a distant object as a location reference.

Descending in Open Water

You have already been practicing proper descents during confined-water training, but there are some points to remember in open water due to the greater depths and the bottom composition.

If you are weighted properly, you should be able to begin your descent by slowly deflating your BCD and exhaling. Make the entire descent feetfirst, so you maintain control and orientation, and keep contact with your buddy. Remember to equalize your air spaces early and often during the descent.

You want to maintain neutral buoyancy during the

Figure 3-58
For control and reference, use a line during descents.

173

descent — don't wait until you reach the bottom. Add small amounts of air during the descent so that when you reach the bottom, you can minimize kicking and stirring up the sediment.

For control and reference, use a line during descents. If you are descending from the anchor line of a boat, hold the line at arm's length so it won't strike you as the boat pitches up and down in the waves.

During all descents, you want to descend steadily and without effort, while maintaining neutral buoyancy so the descent can be stopped at any time. You also want to maintain buddy contact and your sense of direction.

Figure 3-59
After you've completed your first open-water training dive, chances are you'll say to yourself, "That was great! Let's do Dive 2!"

Open-Water Training Preview — Dives 1 - 3

It is almost time for your first open-water training dive. As you make your first dive in the actual diving environment, you'll be getting your first taste of what diving is all about, while learning and developing important skills. To help you have more fun on the dives, meet the performance requirements and avoid wasting time at the dive site, read the following performance requirements for Open-Water Training Dives 1, 2 and 3. A preview of Open-Water Training Dives 4 and 5 will be presented in Module Five.

The skills and procedures you'll practice and use in each dive are listed in the previews for each dive. The sequence, however, is at the discretion of your instructor. Before each dive, your instructor will conduct a pre-dive briefing, informing you of the sequence of the skills and procedures to be accomplished. Your instructor will also give you other important information, like communication signals, an environmental orientation, emergency procedures, safety rules, and so on.

During your first Open-Water Training Dive, you'll directly experience the differences between confined water and open water. You will demonstrate for your instructor your ability to correctly perform skills you learned in your confined-water training sessions. Before this first dive, you may feel some apprehension — that's normal. But don't worry: You'll only be performing skills you already know, and your instructor will be close at hand the entire time. Your instructor has confidence in your diving ability, and so should you. Chances are, once you've completed this dive, you'll say to yourself, "That was great! Let's do Dive 2!"

Open-Water Training Dive 1
Performance Requirements

After completing Open-Water Training Dive 1, you will be able to:

1. Descend in a controlled manner using a descent line or the sloping contour of the bottom to provide control and reference.

2. Achieve and maintain neutral buoyancy under water using a BCD low-pressure inflator.

3. Recover and clear a regulator at depth.

4. Clear a mask that has been only partially flooded.

5. In a stationary position, secure and breathe from an alternate air source supplied by another diver.

6. Tour under water for pleasure and experience.

Dive Overview

- Briefing, dive overview, environmental orientation and information on how to evaluate diving conditions
- Equipment preparation
- Suiting up (no scuba)
- Entry
- Predive acclimation
- Buoyancy check/adjust
- Exit
- Don tanks and weights
- Predive Safety Check
- Entry

- Buoyancy check
- Controlled descent
- Buoyancy control — fin pivot (low-pressure inflation)
- Regulator recovery and clear
- Clear partially flooded mask
- Alternate air source use — stationary
- Underwater tour for pleasure and experience
- Normal ascent
- Exit
- Debriefing and log dive

During Open-Water Training Dive 2, you'll be continuing your skill development in open water. You will feel more confident on this dive because the open-water environment has become more familiar.

Open-Water Training Dive 2
Performance Requirements

After completing Open-Water Training Dive 2, you will be able to:

1. Perform a free descent to a depth of 20-30 feet using a line only as a visual reference.

2. Achieve and maintain neutral buoyancy under water by means of orally inflating the BCD.

3. Clear a mask that has been completely flooded.

4. Ascend using an alternate air source provided by a buddy diver.

5. Perform a controlled emergency swimming ascent from a depth of 20 to 30 feet.

6. Tour under water for pleasure and experience.

7. Perform a cramp-release maneuver for yourself and your buddy at the surface in scuba equipment.

8. Tow a simulated tired buddy diver 25 yards at the surface in scuba equipment.

Dive Overview

- Briefing
- Equipment check
- Suiting up
- Entry
- Cramp removal (self and buddy)
- 25-yard tired-diver tow
- Free descent with reference
- Buoyancy control — fin pivot (oral inflation)
- Complete flooding and clearing of mask
- Underwater tour for pleasure and experience
- Alternate air source assisted ascent
- Controlled emergency swimming ascent
- Exit
- Debriefing and logging dive

Open-Water Training Dive 3 is a skin dive (no scuba) and isn't required for certification. This dive is included at the discretion of your instructor, based on logistical and environmental considerations. During this dive you'll practice skills designed for skin diving, to make you more adept at breath-hold diving in open water.

Open-Water Training Dive 3
Performance Requirements

After completing Open-Water Training Dive 3, you will be able to:

1. Perform a surface dive using skin-diving equipment, demonstrating proper descent and ascent techniques.

2. Clear a snorkel by the displacement method.

Dive Overview

- Briefing
- Equipment preparation
- Suiting up
- Equipment inspection
- Entry
- Buoyancy check
- Surface swim
- Surface dives and underwater swimming (buddies alternate)
- Displacement snorkel clear
- Exit
- Debriefing and logging dive

Four

- ☐ Accessory Diving Equipment
- ☐ Health for Diving
- ☐ Breathing Air at Depth
- ☐ Dive Tables Introduction
- ☐ Using the Recreational Dive Planner, (table version)
- ☐ Confined-Water Training Preview

Accessory Diving Equipment

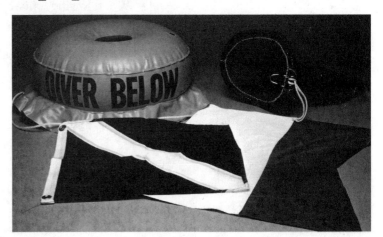

Figure 4-1

By now you've learned a great deal about recreational diving, including a lot about diving equipment. To this point in the course, you've focused on the major pieces of equipment every diver uses. In addition to the equipment discussed previously, there are a number of accessory items that contribute greatly to the enjoyment and safety of diving. You will learn here about some of the most commonly used accessories. As you take more diving courses and gain more experience, you'll learn about others.

Objectives

After reading this section on surface floats, you will be able to:

1. List five ways a diver may use a surface float.

2. Explain how to avoid entanglement in a line connected to a surface float.

Surface Floats

A surface float is any small float towed by a diver for purposes such as a resting, marking a dive site, assisting another diver, storing items, or supporting a dive flag (more about dive flags shortly). Surf mats, inner tubes, small rubber rafts and other floating materials are all common surface floats used by divers. Specially made canvas covers may be purchased to convert ordinary tire inner tubes into useful surface floats specifically for diving.

Depending on the dive site and the dive plan, a surface float may be anchored in one spot, or you may tow the float throughout the dive. In either case, you'll need a rope not

Figure 4-2
A surface float is used for resting, marking the dive site, assisting another diver and storing items.

less than 50 feet long for towing or anchoring. It is recommended that you use a reel or some device for storing excess line to avoid entanglement in slack rope loose in the water. When towing a float, always grasp the line and reel in your hand for safety. Never tie or fasten a float to yourself or your equipment.

Exercise 4-1

Surface Floats

1. Of the five ways a surface float can be used by a diver, check those listed here:
   ☐ a. Mark a dive site ☐ b. Support a dive flag ☐ c. Assist another diver

2. To avoid becoming tangled in a line attached to a surface float, it is recommended that you:
   ☐ a. Use a reel or some device for storing excess line. ☐ b. Attach the line directly to your BCD.

How did you do? *1. a, b, c* *2. a.*

Objectives

1. Explain why a dive flag
should be used on every dive.

2. State how close a diver
should stay to a dive flag and
how far boats, skiers and water-
craft should stay away if there
are no local laws governing
these distances.

Dive Flag

Places that are fun to dive are often fun for a lot of other
water sports, including boating and water skiing. Because it
will be nearly impossible for boaters to see you while you're
under water, for safety you need to make your presence
known by using a dive flag. The dive flag is an important
safety device used to warn boaters that divers are in the
area, and to be alert for them and stay clear. In some areas,
the use of a dive flag is required by law.

Depending on where and under what conditions you
dive, the appropriate dive flag is either a red rectangle with
a white diagonal stripe (Figure 4-3) or a blue-and-white
double-tailed pennant (Figure 4-4). Either flag must be large
enough to be visible from at least 100 yards. In some

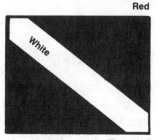
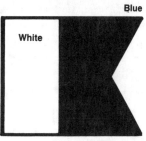

Figure 4-3
Sport diver flag.

Figure 4-4
International code flag.

instances you may be required to fly both flags, particularly
if you're diving from a boat.

When diving from a boat, place the dive flag on a mast,
radio antenna or other highly visible elevated location. If
you're diving from shore or have a long swim from the
boat, you'll need to fly the flag from a surface float. In this
case, your flag should have a wire to hold it in the extended
"flying" position and should be mounted on a staff at least
three feet high, so it can be seen in choppy water.

Local laws regulate how close you have to stay to your
flag, and how far boaters and skiers must stay away from
you. For areas where there are no laws stipulating these distances, the common rule of thumb is for you to stay within
50 feet of your flag and for boats to stay at least 100 to 200
feet away. Also, don't display the dive flag unless divers are
actually in the water. Your instructor will fill you in on local
dive flag laws.

Keep this note of caution regarding the use of dive flags
in mind: Sometimes a boater may not see or recognize the
purpose of a dive flag and may accidentally come much
closer to you and your flag than he should. For this reason,

always ascend cautiously, and if a boat sounds particularly loud and close, stay under water and deep enough to be safe until it clears the area. Remember, too, that you as a diver have an obligation to remain in the area where the flag is being displayed.

Exercise 4-2

Dive Flags

1. A dive flag should be used on every dive to: ☐ a. alert local officials of the fact that divers are in the area.
   ☐ b. warn boaters that divers are in the area and that they should stay clear.

2. Unless local laws state otherwise, divers should stay within _____ feet of the dive flag, whereas boaters and water-skiers should stay _____ feet away from the dive flag. ☐ a. 50, 100-200 ☐ b. 25, 50-100

How did you do? *1. b 2. a.*

Collecting Bags

Objectives

After reading this section on collecting bags, you will be able to:

1. Describe three features of a typical collecting bag and explain the bag's purpose.

Sooner or later, you'll find or catch some things while diving that you want to keep. Carrying several objects while trying to operate your equipment is a juggling act you won't enjoy, so you'll want a collecting bag (also referred to as a goodie bag, game bag or catch bag) to put them in.

Various types and sizes of collecting bags are available. The typical collecting bag is made of mesh nylon, so it

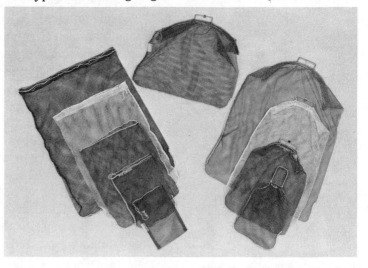

Figure 4-5
Collecting bags are available in a variety of sizes.

drains quickly, and a wire frame to hold the top open or closed. Most have a locking device to secure them in a closed position.

When you're using a collecting bag, keep in mind that

once it's full and heavy, it should be carried in one hand so it can be discarded easily. Do not attach it to yourself or your equipment.

Exercise 4-3

Collecting Bags

1. Check all appropriate responses. Collecting bags are:
   - ☐ a. made from mesh nylon, so they drain quickly. ☐ b. available in various sizes and types.
   - ☐ c. to be attached directly to your BCD while diving. ☐ d. used to help you carry several objects at once.

How did you do? *1. a, b, d.*

Objectives

After reading this section on underwater lights, you will be able to:

1. Explain two reasons for taking an underwater light on a dive during the daytime.

Underwater Lights 📖

Besides their obvious importance for special diving activities like night diving, underwater lights are useful for diving in broad daylight, too. You will find a compact underwater light useful for illuminating and restoring the color of natural objects at depth, as well as for looking into dark cracks and crevices.

An underwater light must be both watertight and pressure-proof; ordinary lights are ruined by submergence

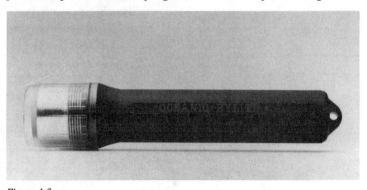

Figure 4-6
You will find a compact underwater light useful for illuminating and revealing the color of natural objects at depth, as well as for looking into dark cracks and crevices.

and can't be used. Underwater lights remain watertight by using an O-ring seal that you should inspect for wear periodically. Like most flashlights, always store underwater lights without their batteries, to prevent possible damage from battery leakage. Professional dive stores usually stock a wide array of underwater lights, varying in power source, size and brightness. Ask your PADI Instructor or Dive Center to help you select the best one for your needs.

Figure 4-7
Professional dive stores usually stock a wide array of underwater lights of varying size and brightness. Ask your PADI Instructor or Dive Center to help you select the best one for your needs.

Exercise 4-4

Underwater Lights

1. Underwater lights are only useful on night dives. ☐ True ☐ False

How did you do? *1. False. Underwater lights can be used on daytime dives to restore natural color at depth and to look into dark cracks and crevices.*

Objectives

After reading this section on underwater slates, you will be able to:

1. State two reasons for carrying an underwater slate on every dive.

Underwater Slate

In Module Two, you learned that hand signals and underwater slates are the two most common methods of communicating while diving. An underwater slate is an important communication tool, and it's also important for carrying general information like time and depth limits for the dive. Slates are compact, inexpensive and should be regarded as part of your standard equipment.

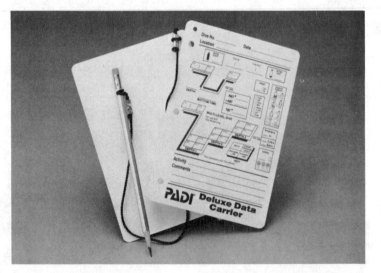

Figure 4-8
Slates are compact, inexpensive and should be regarded as part of your standard equipment.

Underwater slates are usually made of plastic and typically come with a pencil on a short cord (to prevent loss). Most slates are sized to fit in your BCD pocket, although some models are custom-tailored to fit on the back of instrument consoles or to strap onto your wrist. The PADI Data Carriers that come with The Wheel and PADI Deluxe Log Book are specialized slates you can take under water with you. Regardless of which slate you choose, be sure to secure it so it doesn't cause drag or pose an entanglement problem.

Exercise 4-5

Underwater Slates

1. Slates are an important underwater communication tool and are used to carry general information like time and depth limits for the dive. ☐ True ☐ False

How did you do? *1. True.*

Spare-parts Kit

Objectives

After reading this section on spare-parts kits, you will be able to:

1. Explain why a spare-parts kit should be taken on every dive trip.

2. Assemble a spare-parts kit for diving.

There's nothing quite so frustrating as having an entire day's diving ruined because you broke a fin strap and don't have a spare. By assembling a spare-parts kit and carrying it on every dive, you minimize the probability of missing dives from minor problems like a broken fin strap.

A spare-parts kit is simply a collection of various replacement items, stored in a rustproof container in your equipment bag. You can put a lot in your spare-parts kit, but here are few suggestions for starters:

1. Mask strap
2. Fin strap
3. O-rings
4. Silicone lubricant
5. Snorkel keeper
6. Cement for exposure suit repairs
7. Waterproof plastic tape
8. Quick-release buckle
9. Pocket knife
10. Pliers
11. Adjustable wrench
12. Screwdrivers

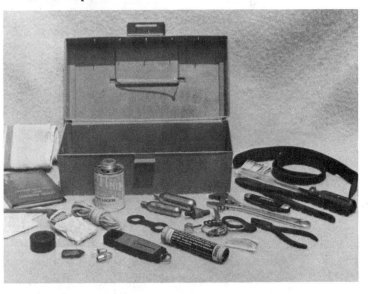

Figure 4-9
A spare-parts kit helps minimize the possibility of missing a dive because of minor problems like a broken fin strap.

Your instructor can suggest other items you should have in your spare-parts kits.

Exercise 4-6

Spare-Parts Kit

1. A spare-parts kit is not necessary if you take proper care of your equipment. ☐ True ☐ False

How did you do? *1. False. Even well-cared-for equipment can be broken unexpectedly. Carrying a spare-parts kit minimizes the probability of missing dives from minor problems like a broken fin strap.*

Objectives

After reading this section on log books, you will be able to:

1. State three reasons for using a log book.

Log Book

The certification you receive on successful completion of this course is an important credential signifying that you're a qualified scuba diver. Also important, however, is a log book.

While your certification card shows that you're qualified, it can't tell a divemaster or charter crew member how frequently you dive or what type of diving you've been doing. A detailed log book is the proof-of-experience documentation usually requested for additional diver training, and when diving at resorts or on boats.

Figure 4-10
A detailed log book is an important record of your diving history.

Log books provide an excellent means to remember your diving experiences, document your history as a diver and note details about a particular dive that may otherwise be forgotten. Make a habit of filling out your log book immediately after every dive, and having it signed for confirmation. You can choose from many log books, ranging from simple ones with room for a short dive description, to more complete ones with space to record training documentation, equipment purchases and maintenance, air use, dive site maps, personal information, and more. Some dive logs, such as the PADI Deluxe Diver's Log, have waterproof data carriers for jotting down notes during or immediately after a dive.

Your instructor or dive store can help you select a log book with the features you want.

Exercise 4-7

Log Books

1. Check all appropriate responses. A log book allows you to: ☐ a. remember your diving experiences. ☐ b. document your history as a diver. ☐ c. note details about a particular dive that may otherwise be forgotten. ☐ d. write notes to your buddy under water.

How did you do?   *1.* a, b, c.

Objectives

After reading this section on health for diving, you will be able to:

1. Name three substances that should not be used prior to diving.

2. State how often a diver should have a complete physical examination by a doctor.

3. Name two immunizations all divers should keep up-to-date.

4. Explain how to keep mentally sharp for diving.

5. Describe what effect menstruation has on diving.

6. Explain why pregnant women should not dive.

Health for Diving

From what you've learned in the previous three modules, you know that diving is a relaxing activity, if you dive correctly. You also realize, though, that there are times when strenuous activity may come into play. For this reason, you should have a level of health, fitness and conditioning sufficient to handle moderately strenuous activity. Being in good health will help ensure safe participation in diving.

General health recommendations regarding rest and diet apply to diving as well as everyday life. Never use alcohol, drugs or tobacco prior to diving. Alcohol and drugs — even in quantities that have minimal effect on the surface — can impair your judgment at depth, where their effects may be more intense. Also, alcohol before or immediately after a dive may increase your risk of decompression sickness (discussed later in this module). If you're taking a prescription drug, discuss its effects with your physician prior to diving. If in doubt, don't dive until you're no longer using the medication.

Smoking is undeniably detrimental to your health and should be avoided altogether. If you do smoke, abstain for several hours before diving because smoking significantly decreases the efficiency of your circulatory and respiratory systems.

Don't dive if you don't feel well, and, as you recall from

Figure 4-11
Regular exercise is an important part of maintaining good health for diving.

Module One, you never should dive with a cold. Doing so can cause ear and sinus squeeze or reverse blocks due to equalization difficulties. The use of medication to combat an ailment in order to dive is strongly discouraged. You should be in good health to dive.

Maintain a reasonable degree of physical fitness and have a complete physical examination when you first enter diving, and at least every two years thereafter. Ideally, you should be examined by a physician knowledgeable in diving medicine. Be sure to keep your immunizations current; this is especially important for your tetanus and typhoid immunizations. Eat a well-balanced diet and get proper rest. Maintain a regular exercise program.

Staying mentally sharp as well as physically sharp is an important part of being in shape for diving. Be an active diver to maintain your diving skills and continue your education so you can have fun while developing and improving new diving skills and knowledge (more about continuing education in Module Five). If possible, swim with your fins in a pool regularly. Practice the skills you learn in this course frequently. After a period of inactivity, refresh your diving skills with the PADI Scuba Review course.

If you are a woman, you have some special health considerations, including menstruation and pregnancy. As long as menstruation doesn't normally preclude your participation in other activities, there's no reason for it to keep you from diving either. However, since little is known about the effects diving may have on a developing fetus, so it's recommended that you discontinue diving while pregnant.

You need to feel well to dive well. Maintain good health, avoid harmful habits and keep yourself in good mental and physical shape for diving.

Exercise 4-8

Health for Diving

1. Check all appropriate responses. Prior to diving, never use: ☐ a. alcohol. ☐ b. tobacco. ☐ c. drugs.

2. As a diver, you should have a complete physical examination when you first enter diving and at least every _____ years after that. ☐ a. 2 ☐ b. 3 ☐ c. 5

3. It is especially important for all divers to maintain up-to-date immunizations against tetanus and typhoid.
   ☐ True ☐ False

4. To keep mentally sharp for diving, you should practice your skills regularly, continue your diving education and refresh you diving skills _____ after a period of diving inactivity.
   ☐ a. with a PADI Scuba Review course ☐ b. by reading a diving-related magazine

5. Women shouldn't dive during menstruation. ☐ True ☐ False

6. Pregnant women may dive only to 30 feet. ☐ True ☐ False

How did you do? *1.* a, b, c *2.* a *3.* True *4.* a *5.* False. As long as menstruation doesn't normally preclude a diver from other activities, there is no reason for it to keep her from diving. *6.* False. It is recommended that pregnant women avoid diving completely.

Breathing Air at Depth

From your experience in confined water and from what you have read in previous modules, you know that breathing air under water is different than breathing air at the surface. Besides the obvious effects, like increased breathing-air density, breathing air under pressure has some subtle effects, too. Fortunately, these effects are understood and predictable. By learning something about these effects and some guidelines to follow, you will easily be able to avoid problems associated with them.

Objectives

After reading this section on the air we breathe, you will be able to:

1. Name the two primary gases found in air.

The Air We Breathe

The compressed air in your scuba tank is essentially the same as the air you're breathing right now. It is mixture of nitrogen (approximately 79%) and oxygen (approximately 21%). Oxygen is used by your body to sustain life, and nitro-

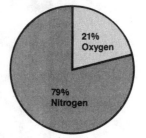

Figure 4-12
Air is a mixture of nitrogen (approximately 79%) and oxygen (approximately 21%).

gen is physiologically *inert* (not used by your body). While neither gas has adverse effects on you above water, both can produce difficulties when breathed under water at greater pressures.

Exercise 4-9

The Air we Breathe

1. Air is composed primarily of: ☐ a. oxygen and nitrogen. ☐ b. oxygen and carbon dioxide.

How did you do? *1.* a.

Objectives

After reading this section on contaminated air, you will be able to :

1. **State five possible symptoms of contaminated air.**

2. **Describe the treatment that should be given to a diver suspected of breathing contaminated air.**

3. **Explain how to prevent problems with contaminated air.**

Contaminated Air

Before discussing problems associated with the normal components of breathing air, it's important to look at problems that can arise from contaminates that aren't supposed to be in your air.

A compressor for filling scuba tanks must be set up and maintained correctly to avoid introducing contaminates such as carbon monoxide or oil vapor into your breathing air. Contaminated air generally tastes and smells bad, but it can also be odorless and tasteless. A diver breathing contaminated air may experience headaches, nausea, dizziness and even unconsciousness. A diver afflicted by contaminated air may have cherry-red lips and fingernail beds.

A person suffering from the effects of breathing contaminated air should be given lots of fresh air, and oxygen should be administered if available. In severe cases, mouth-to-mouth ventilation may be necessary. Medical attention is needed in all cases.

Fortunately, contaminated air is rare as long as you buy your air from reputable air sources, such as professional

Figure 4-13
Contaminated air is rare provided you buy your air from reputable air sources such as professional dive stores.

dive stores. These stores recognize the seriousness of contaminated air and have their air checked frequently to be sure of its quality.

Nevertheless, if you do find your air tastes or smells bad, regardless of your source, don't use it. If you feel ill or get a headache during a dive, end the dive immediately. If you suspect you may have contaminated air in your tank for any reason, save the air for analysis and don't dive with it.

To avoid contaminated air, be certain you have your tanks filled only with pure, dry, filtered compressed air from a reputable air station. Be aware, however, that you can experience contaminated air poisoning from breathing exhaust fumes aboard a boat, so be careful to stay where you get fresh air.

Exercise 4-10

Contaminated Air

1. Of the possible symptoms of breathing contaminated air, check those listed here:

   ☐ a. Euphoria ☐ b. Headaches ☐ c. Cherry-red lips and fingernail beds

2. A person suffering from the effects of breathing contaminated air should be given:

   ☐ a. lots of fresh air and oxygen if available. ☐ b. a brown paper bag to breathe into.

3. To prevent problems with contaminated air, you should have your tanks filled only with pure, dry, filtered compressed air from a reputable air station. ☐ True ☐ False

How did you do? *1. b, c* *2. a* *3. True.*

Objectives

After reading this section on oxygen, you will be able to:

1. State two ways divers prevent problems with oxygen.

Oxygen

Because you need oxygen to live, it may seem strange to learn that it can be toxic in high amounts and pressures. In fact, if you were to fill your scuba tank with pure oxygen instead of compressed air, you could experience oxygen problems in very shallow water. This is why you should never have your tank filled with anything except compressed air.

The oxygen in compressed air (which, as you learned, contains only 21% oxygen) can also be toxic, but not until you descend well past the recommended maximum limit for recreational diving, which is 100 feet. To prevent oxygen toxicity, never fill your tank with pure oxygen and never exceed the maximum recommended recreational depth limit.

Exercise 4-11

Oxygen

1. To prevent problems with oxygen toxicity, you should never fill your tank with pure oxygen and:

   ☐ a. never dive longer than 1 hour. ☐ b. never exceed the maximum recommended recreational depth limit.

How did you do? *1. b.*

Objectives

After reading this section on nitrogen narcosis, you will be able to:

1. State five symptoms of nitrogen narcosis.

2. Describe the action to be taken if nitrogen narcosis becomes a problem.

3. Explain how to prevent nitrogen narcosis.

Figure 4-14
The effects of nitrogen need to be considered on every dive.

Nitrogen Narcosis

Adverse effects from oxygen or contaminated air are rare in recreational diving, but the effects of nitrogen need to be considered on every dive.

While breathing air at depths approaching 100 feet, you can experience an effect called *nitrogen narcosis,* which is an anesthetic quality nitrogen has under pressure. The deeper you dive, the more pronounced this narcotic effect becomes.

A diver affected by nitrogen narcosis behaves as though he is intoxicated. He has impaired judgment and coordination, and may experience a feeling of false security and exhibit a lack of concern for safety. In short, he may behave foolishly. Also, he may feel anxious or uncomfortable. These effects can be disastrous as a result of poor decisions made by the diver.

Nitrogen narcosis affects individuals differently. You may be more or less susceptible than other divers. Also, the degree of susceptibility may vary from day to day and from dive to dive.

Nitrogen narcosis diminishes when you reach shallow water, with no aftereffects. If you begin to feel strange or intoxicated, immediately ascend to shallower depths to relieve the narcosis. It usually goes away quickly. If your buddy acts impaired, assist him to shallower water.

To prevent nitrogen narcosis, simply avoid deep dives.

Figure 4-15
If you begin to feel the effects of nitrogen narcosis, ascend to shallower depths to relieve its symptoms.

Nitrogen narcosis is not dangerous or harmful in itself, but the impaired judgment and loss of coordination it causes can be quite hazardous.

Exercise 4-12

Nitrogen Narcosis

1. Of the symptoms related to nitrogen narcosis, check those listed here:
   ☐ a. Impaired judgment and coordination ☐ b. Cherry-red lips and fingernail beds
   ☐ c. Lack of concern for safety

2. If you begin to feel the effects of nitrogen narcosis, you should:
   ☐ a. ascend to shallower depths. ☐ b. descend very slowly.

3. To prevent nitrogen narcosis: ☐ a. avoid deep dives ☐ b. descend very slowly.

How did you do? *1.* a, c *2.* a *3.* a.

Objectives

After reading this section on decompression sickness, you will be able to:

1. State the two primary factors that influence the absorption and elimination of nitrogen in a diver.

2. Name the condition that occurs when established depth and/or time limits have been exceeded, producing bubbles in the body during ascent.

3. List nine secondary factors that can influence the absorption and elimination of nitrogen from the body.

4. Identify eight signs and symptoms generally associated with less severe cases of decompression sickness.

5. State the necessary treatment for a diver suspected of having decompression sickness.

6. Outline the first aid procedure for assisting someone with decompression sickness.

7. Explain how to prevent decompression sickness.

Decompression Sickness 📖

In Modules One, Two and Three, you learned that there are limits to dive times and depths outside the obvious limits imposed by your air supply, cold or fatigue. These depth and time limits result from an effect of nitrogen other than nitrogen narcosis. This is the effect of nitrogen absorbed by the body while diving, and is perhaps one of the most significant effects of breathing air under pressure.

Figure 4-16
During a dive, increased pressure causes nitrogen from your breathing air to dissolve into your body tissues.

During every dive, the increased pressure causes nitrogen from your breathing air to dissolve into your body tissues. The amount your body absorbs on a given dive depends on how deep and how long your dive is, but the deeper you dive and the longer you stay, the more excess nitrogen your body absorbs.

When you ascend, decreasing the surrounding pressure, the nitrogen you absorbed begins to leave your body. This excess nitrogen must be slowly eliminated through respiration, because, unlike oxygen, your body doesn't use nitrogen. What goes in, must come out.

As long as the amount of excess nitrogen is kept within reasonable limits, your body can eliminate it without complication. Special tables have been developed that establish the limits necessary to keep nitrogen within acceptable bounds (these are discussed later in this chapter).

If, however, you should remain under water too long, the excess nitrogen will begin to form bubbles in your blood vessels and tissues when you ascend, much like when a bottle of soda is opened quickly. These bubbles cause a very serious medical condition called *decompression sickness* (DCS), sometimes referred to as "the bends."

Besides the time and depth of your dives, there are other factors that influence how your body absorbs and eliminates excess nitrogen that can contribute to developing DCS. These include fatigue, dehydration, vigorous exercise (before, during, or after the dive), cold, older age, illness, injuries, alcohol consumption before or after a dive, and being overweight. Also, an increase in altitude after diving (by flying or driving through mountains) can also contribute to getting decompression sickness. (Special procedures for flying after diving are discussed in Module Five.) Recreational divers should dive well within estab-

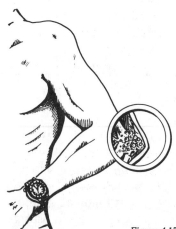

Figure 4-17
If you exceed safe nitrogen limits, bubbles will begin to form in your blood vessels and tissues when you ascend. This causes decompression sickness.

Figure 4-18
Special procedures must be followed for ascending to altitude after diving, such as flying or driving through mountains.

lished limits and use extra caution if any other influencing factors are involved.

Because bubbles can form in many different places in the body, the symptoms of decompression sickness can vary. Symptoms include: paralysis, shock, weakness, dizziness, numbness, tingling, difficulty breathing, and varying degrees of joint and limb pain. In the most severe cases, unconsciousness and death can result.

In recreational diving, decompression sickness may have symptoms that are more subtle. These can include a mild to moderate dull ache, usually *but not necessarily* in the joints. DCS can produce a mild to moderate tingling or numbness, usually, but not necessarily, in the limbs. Other common symptoms of DCS are weakness and prolonged fatigue. Decompression sickness symptoms can occur together or individually, and can occur anywhere in the body, and may be accompanied by a feeling of lightheadedness.

Symptoms of decompression sickness usually occur anywhere from 15 minutes to 12 hours after a dive, though they can occur later. Most symptoms come on gradually and persist, though they can be intermittent. Regardless of the severity of the symptoms, all cases of decompression sickness are to be considered serious. If a diver suspects he has symptoms of decompression sickness, or isn't sure, he should 1) discontinue diving, and 2) immediately seek medical attention and consult a diving physician. Some areas have special services available especially for diver emergencies.

Most cases of decompression sickness must be treated by repressurizing the afflicted diver in a recompression chamber. Under no circumstances should a diver suspected

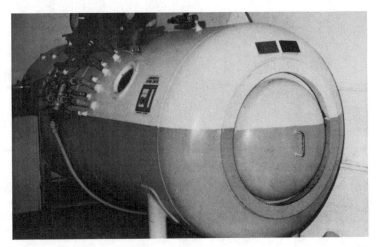

Figure 4-19
Most cases of decompression sickness must be treated by repressurizing the afflicted diver in a recompression chamber.

of having decompression sickness be put back under water. Once symptoms occur, treatment takes hours — much longer than the possible endurance of a diver, even if adequate air were available. Additionally, recompression often requires medical procedures and medication. Attempts to treat a diver under water may end with worsened symptoms and disastrous results.

If you are assisting a diver suspected of having decompression sickness, you must get the individual into medical care so he can be stabilized and transported to a recompression chamber. First aid for decompression sickness includes prevention or treatment of shock, administering oxygen and if necessary, CPR. If the diver is unconscious and breathing, lay him level on his left side, supporting his head and treat as described in Module Three, "The Unconscious Diver." The faster treatment begins, the less risk

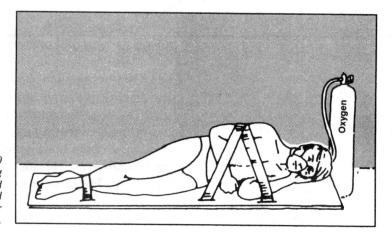

Figure 4-20
A diver suspected of having decompression sickness, should be placed on his left side with his head supported if he does not require CPR or mouth-to-mouth ventilation.

there is of permanent residual symptoms. (Note: Although decompression sickness is a serious medical condition, with proper treatment it is rarely fatal in recreational divers.)

Although decompression sickness is a serious condition, both painful and potentially life-threatening, it is avoided by properly following the established safe time and depth limits of *dive tables.* Additionally important is a slow, safe ascent rate with a stop for safety.

Exercise 4-13

Decompression Sickness

1. The two primary factors that influence the absorption and elimination of nitrogen in a diver are:

☐ a. depth and time limits. ☐ b. air supply and thermal regulation.

2. When established depth and/or time limits have been exceeded, producing _____ during ascent, the condition is known as decompression sickness.

☐ a. symptomatic bubbles in the body ☐ b. euphoria

3. Of the eight secondary factors that can influence the absorption and elimination of nitrogen from the body, check those listed here: ☐ a. Fatigue ☐ b. Alcohol consumption ☐ c. Cold ☐ d. Age

4. Of the six signs and symptoms associated with cases of decompression sickness, check those listed here:

☐ a. Numbness or tingling ☐ b. Bloodshot eyes ☐ c. Joint and limb pain

5. A diver suspected of having decompression sickness should: ☐ a. wait at least 6 hours before diving again.

☐ b. discontinue diving, immediately seek medical attention and consult a diving physician.

6. The first-aid procedures for assisting someone with decompression sickness are prevention and treatment for shock, administration of oxygen and, if necessary, CPR. ☐ True ☐ False

7. Decompression sickness can be prevented by properly following the established safe time and depth limits of dive tables. ☐ True ☐ False

How did you do? *1. a* *2. a* *3. a, b, c, d* *4. a, c* *5. b* *6. True* *7. True.*

Objectives

After reading this introduction on dive tables, you will be able to:

1. State the primary use of dive tables.

2. Explain why the maximum limits listed on dive tables should be avoided.

3. Define *repetitive dive*.

4. Explain what is meant by *no-decompression diving* and *decompression diving*.

5. Explain why a diver's body-nitrogen level is higher after a repetitive dive.

6. State one reason why the Recreational Dive Planner distributed by PADI is different from other dive tables.

7. Define *bottom time*.

8. Apply the eleven general rules when using the Recreational Dive Planner.

9. State the maximum depth limitation for all recreational diving.

Dive Tables Introduction 📖

As you just learned, your body has a higher-than-normal amount of nitrogen in it after a dive, and it can tolerate a certain level of excess nitrogen without developing decompression sickness. Dive tables are used to gauge how much excess nitrogen you have in your body, so you can determine your maximum safe time and depth limits. These limits can only be found through the use of dive tables, such as the *Recreational Dive Planner.*

Be aware that although dive tables give you maximum limits, you need to dive conservatively, avoiding the maximum

Figure 4-21

limits. This is especially true if any of the factors that contribute to decompression sickness (vigorous exercise, cold, older age, etc.) apply to your situation. Take extra precautions to not allow yourself to become dehydrated, for example, especially after several days of diving. *Because people differ in their susceptibility to decompression sickness, no dive table can guarantee that decompression sickness will never occur, even though you dive within the table limits. It is always wisest to plan dives well within table limits, especially if any contributing factors apply.*

Dive tables set maximum safe time and depth limits based not only on the amount of nitrogen you absorb during a dive, but also based on the amount of nitrogen you may have absorbed on previous dives. This is because it takes several hours after surfacing for all the excess nitrogen to leave your body. When using the Recreational Dive Planner to find your time and depth limits, if you don't plan to dive for at least six hours, this excess nitrogen is of little consequence. On the other hand, if you do plan to dive within six hours, you must take the extra nitrogen into consideration.

A dive made within six hours of another dive is called a *repetitive dive.* To more clearly understand how nitrogen from the first dive affects the repetitive dive, look at Figure 4-22. Before the first dive, your body's nitrogen level is normal (A). Upon surfacing, your nitrogen level is higher, though still within safe limits (B). After an hour at the surface, the excess nitrogen declines, but it hasn't had time to return to normal (C). After your repetitive dive, your nitrogen level has risen, and the extra nitrogen absorbed on the

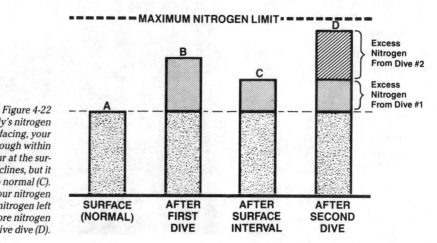

Figure 4-22
Before the first dive, your body's nitrogen level is normal (A). Upon surfacing, your nitrogen level is higher, though within safe limits (B). After an hour at the surface, the excess nitrogen declines, but it hasn't had time to return to normal (C). After your repetitive dive, your nitrogen level has risen to include the nitrogen left from the first dive, plus more nitrogen absorbed on the repetitive dive (D).

repetitive dive has been added to the excess nitrogen still in your body from the first dive (D). It is very important to take all the nitrogen in your body into account when determining safe time and depth limits.

These constantly changing and combining nitrogen levels are accounted for by proper use of the Recreational Dive Planner. The Recreational Dive Planner, distributed by PADI, simplifies dive planning and determining your depth and time limits. It is unique because it's the first dive table designed, tested and validated specifically for recreational diving, rather than commercial or military diving. The research and development of the Recreational Diver Planner involved the contributions of some of the foremost experts in the fields of diving physiology and diver education.

The Recreational Dive Planner was designed solely for *no-decompression* diving. No-decompression diving means that while staying within the limits of the tables, you may ascend directly to the surface at any time during the dive without significant risk of decompression sickness. Recreational diving is *always* planned as no-decompression diving.

Dive tables designed for commercial or military diving differ from the Recreational Dive Planner. Commercial or military divers generally stay at a given depth for times well beyond recreational time limits, so they use tables that were developed with *decompression* diving in mind. Decompression diving involves making a series of difficult and complex stops during ascent to avoid decompression sickness. Decompression diving requires significant surface support and emergency preparation, and lies beyond the scope of recreational diving because it can be quite hazardous. Using tables designed for decompression diving to plan no-decompression dives is safe, however recreational divers should never plan decompression dives.

Figure 4-23

General Rules for Using the Recreational Dive Planner

The Recreational Dive Planner comes in two different forms, the table version and The Wheel. Regardless of which version you use, there are several general rules you must follow. Apply the following rules anytime you use either version of the Recreational Dive Planner.

1. *Bottom time* is the total time in minutes from the beginning of descent until the beginning of final ascent to the surface or safety stop.

2. Any dive planned to 35 feet *or less* should be calculated as a dive to 35 feet.

3. Use the exact or next greater depth shown for the depths of all dives.

4. Use the exact or next greater time shown for the times of all dives.

5. Slowly ascend from all dives at a rate that does not exceed 60 feet per minute (one foot per second).

6. Always be conservative and avoid using the maximum limits provided.

7. When planning a dive in cold water, or under conditions that may be strenuous, plan the dive assuming the depth is 10 feet deeper than actual.

8. Plan repetitive dives so each successive dive is to a shallower depth. Never follow a dive with a deeper dive. Always plan your deepest dive first. Limit repetitive dives to 100 feet or shallower.

Figure 4-24

9. Limit all repetitive dives to 100 feet or shallower.

10. Limit your maximum depth to your training and experience level. As an Open Water Diver, limit your dives to a maximum depth of 60 feet. Divers with greater training and experience should generally limit themselves to a maximum depth of 100 feet. Divers with Deep Diver training and a reasonable objective may dive as deep as 130 feet. All

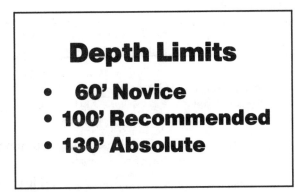

Depth Limits

- **60' Novice**
- **100' Recommended**
- **130' Absolute**

Figure 4-25

dives should be planned as no-decompression dives and no dive should ever exceed the maximum depth limitation for recreational scuba — 130'. Decompression diving is beyond the parameters of the Recreational Dive Planner.

11. Never exceed the limits of the Recreational Dive Planner and whenever possible avoid diving to the limits of the planner. 140 feet is for emergency purposes only, do not dive to this depth.

Be a S.A.F.E. Diver — **S**lowly **A**scend **F**rom **E**very Dive

You have learned the importance of helping your body adjust to increasing pressure during descent by equalizing your air spaces. During ascent, your body also needs time to adjust. And, you need time to be regulating your buoyancy, keeping track of your buddy and watching for overhead obstacles. It's important to ascend slowly — no faster than 1 foot per second (60 feet per minute), which is slower than you may realize.

As a new diver, you may find it a little difficult to judge your rate of ascent at first. Always start your ascent with plenty of air to allow a slow, leisurely trip to the surface. Preferably, ascend along a line or follow the contours of the bottom as you come up. This will give you a visual reference to help you gauge your speed. Use your depth gauge as you ascend to help you know how fast

you're going up, particularly when ascending without a visual reference. It should take you at least 10 seconds to ascend 10 feet — but don't worry about being exact, as long as you're not exceeding a foot per second. In fact, it's a good idea to come up *slower* than a foot per second, for extra safety.

Whenever possible, stop your ascent when you reach 15 feet, and wait three minutes before continuing your ascent — particularly after deep dives or dives close to the maximum time limit. This is called a *safety stop* (you'll learn more about safety stops in Module Five), which gives you an extra margin of safety.

Think of the 60-feet-per-minute rate of ascent as a speed limit. It's fine to go slower, but don't exceed it. Be a S.A.F.E. diver and **S**lowly **A**scend **F**rom **E**very dive.

Exercise 4-14

Dive Tables

1. Dive tables are primarily used: ☐ a. to gauge how much excess nitrogen you have in your body, so you can determine your maximum safe time and depth limits. ☐ b. to calculate your rate of air consumption for a dive at a given depth and time.

2. The maximum limits on dive tables should be avoided: ☐ a. so that you don't run out of air.
☐ b. at all times, especially when contributing factors (vigorous exercise, cold, older age, etc.) are present.

3. A repetitive dive is: ☐ a. a dive made within 10 minutes of another dive. ☐ b. a dive made within 6 hours of another dive.

4. No-decompression diving means: ☐ a. that you will never run out of air at depth. ☐ b. that while staying within the limits of the tables, you may ascend directly to the surface at any time during the dive without significant risk of decompression sickness.

5. After a repetitive dive, your nitrogen level has risen, and the extra nitrogen absorbed on the repetitive dive has been added to the excess nitrogen still in your body from the first dive. ☐ True ☐ False

6. The Recreational Dive Planners are different from other tables in that: ☐ a. they were designed for recreational, no-decompression diving. ☐ b. they were designed specifically for decompression diving.

7. Bottom time is calculated ☐ a. from the beginning of descent until you leave the bottom for a direct ascent to the surface. ☐ b. from the time you reach the bottom until you leave the bottom.

How did you do?   *1. a* *2. b* *3. a, b* *4. b* *5. True* *6. a* *7. a.*

NOTE: If you are learning to use The Wheel version of the Recreational Dive Planner, turn to the "Instructions for Use" booklet and read the first five sections, or watch PADI's wheel training video "Diving With The Wheel." When you have finished reading those sections and working the sample problems or watching the video, resume reading this manual at the "Confined-Water Training Preview" section of this module.

Using the Recreational Dive Planner (table version)

The Recreational Dive Planner (table version), is actually three tables linked together. Each of the three tables provides information you need for planning dives within safe nitrogen levels.

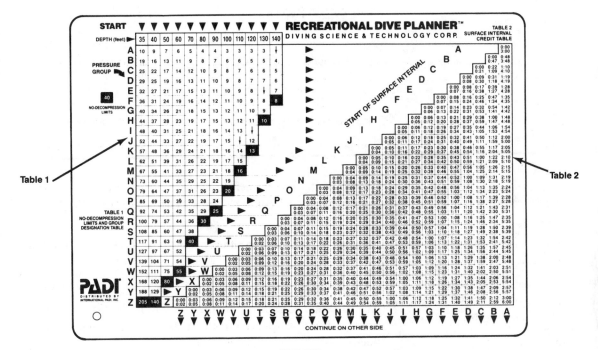

SIDE ONE

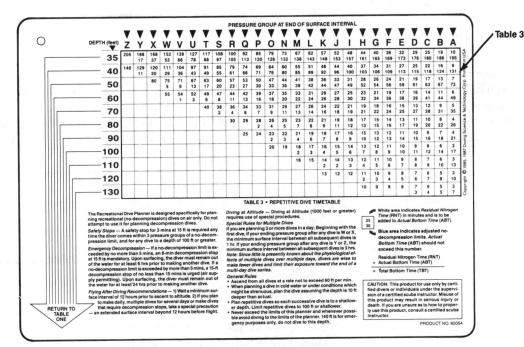

SIDE TWO

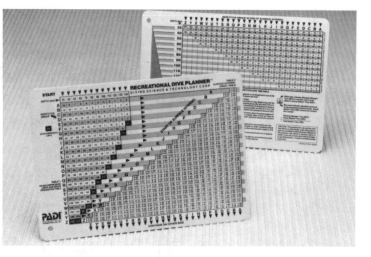

Figure 4-26
The Recreational Dive Planner (table version) is actually three tables linked together. Each table provides information you need for planning dives within safe nitrogen levels.

Objectives

After reading this section on Table 1, you will be able to:

1. Define *no-decompression limit* (NDL).

2. Find the NDL for any depths between 0 and 130 feet using the Recreational Dive Planner (table version).

3. Define *residual nitrogen*.

4. Define *pressure group*.

5. Find the pressure group for a certain dive depth and time using the Recreational Dive Planner (table version).

Table 1

When you begin planning your first dive of the day, you'll consult Table 1 of the Recreational Dive Planner (table version). In fact, if you're only planning to make one dive within a six hour period, Table 1 is the only table you'll need to use.

Table 1 has two purposes. It tells you the maximum amount of time you can stay at a certain depth on your first dive, and it tells you how much nitrogen you have in your body after a dive. The easiest way to learn how to use Table 1 is to follow an example.

Assume you plan to dive on a reef you know lies in 45 feet of water. How long can you safely stay at 45 feet? Enter Table 1 along the top *depth* row labeled *Start*. Note in Figure 4-27 that as you follow the depth line to the right, that depth (after the 35-foot column) increases in 10-foot increments, and 45 feet does not appear.

In the general rules you learned that you always use the exact or *next greater* depth, so in this example you will follow the depth row to the 50-foot column. All the numbers appearing below the depth row are in minutes, and at the bottom of the 50-foot column you will find the number 80 in a black box. All the times in the black boxes are maximum allowable times and referred to as *no-decompression limits* (NDLs). This means the maximum time for your dive to 45 feet (rounded up to 50) is 80 minutes. (Note: It is unlikely that you would spend an entire dive at exactly one depth. When using the Recreational Dive Planner (table version), for the purposes of calculation, you will use the deepest depth reached during the dive, regardless of how

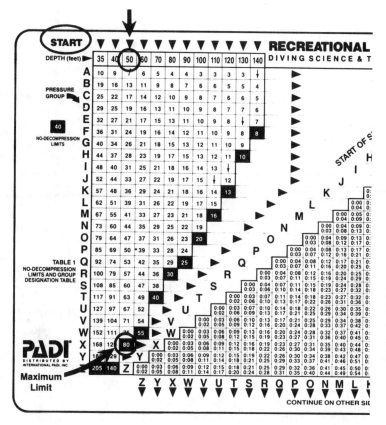

Figure 4-27
Table 1

long you actually remain at that depth.)

If you're planning only one dive, this is all the information you need. Your dive must not exceed 80 minutes. Similarly, you will note that a dive to 60 feet has an NDL of 55 minutes, and a dive to 40 feet has an NDL of 140 minutes.

On many occasions, you'll want to make more than one dive. As you just learned, that means you must account for the nitrogen you absorbed on the first dive when planning your next dive. The nitrogen left in your tissues after the first dive is called *residual nitrogen.* You will use Table 1 to tell you how much residual nitrogen you have in your body.

Continuing with the previous example, assume that you remained at 45 feet for 42 of the allowable 80 minutes. Follow the 50-foot column down until you find 42 minutes or the next greater time — in this case, 44 minutes. From 44 minutes, follow the horizontal row to the right to find the letter *N.* (See Figure 4-28, next page.) This letter is your *pressure group* (PG), and represents the amount of residual nitrogen left in your body after the dive. You will use your pressure group when you move into Table 2. Before moving to Table 2, complete a few sample problems to practice what you just learned.

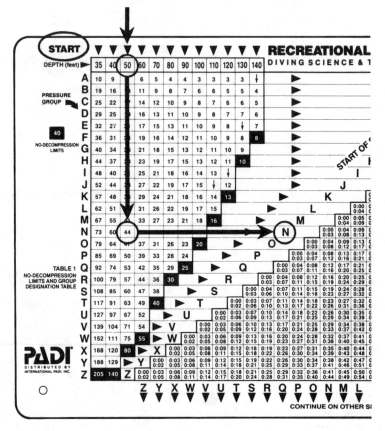

Figure 4-28
Using Table 1 to find your pressure group.

Sample Problems — Table 1

Solve these sample problems and check your answers against the answers given. Be sure your answers are correct before proceeding.

1. A dive to 43 feet for one hour yields what pressure group?
   a. Pressure group R.
   b. Pressure group Q.
   c. Pressure group S.
   d. Pressure group T.

Answer: c. Pressure group S.
43 feet doesn't appear on Table 1, so you must use the 50-foot column. Follow the 50-foot column down until you find 60 minutes (one hour). Next move horizontally along the row until you find pressure group S.

2. A dive to 28 feet for 70 minutes yields what pressure group?
   a. Pressure Group M.
   b. Pressure Group N.
   c. Pressure Group L.
   d. Pressure Group O.

Answer: b. Pressure group N.
28 feet does not appear on the top of Table 1, and any dive shallower than 35 feet should be planned as a 35-foot dive. Find 35 feet at the top of Table 1, move down the column until you find 70 minutes (one hour and ten minutes). 70 minutes is not on Table 1 under 35 feet, so you must use 73 minutes. From there, move horizontally until you locate pressure group N.

3. A dive to 60 feet for 40 minutes yields what pressure group?
   a. Pressure Group S.
   b. Pressure Group Q.
   c. Pressure Group R.
   d. Pressure Group P.

Answer: b. Pressure group Q.
Find 60 feet at the top of Table 1 and then follow the column down until you find 40 minutes. 40 does not appear, so you must use 42 minutes. Moving horizontally from 42 minutes, you find pressure group Q.

The Recreational Dive Planner, Table 1

1. A no-decompression limit is: ☐ a. the maximum allowable dive time for a dive to a specified depth.

   ☐ b. the maximum depth limit you can reach as a recreational diver.

2. Residual nitrogen is: ☐ a. the more-than-normal amount of nitrogen left in your tissues after a dive.

   ☐ b. the excess nitrogen that bubbles to cause decompression sickness.

3. A pressure group is: ☐ a. a letter that indicates how deep you went on the last dive.

   ☐ b. a letter that represents the amount of residual nitrogen in your body after a dive

How did you do? *1.* a *2.* a *3.* b.

Objectives

After reading this section on Table 2, you will be able to:

1. Define the term *surface interval* (SI).

2. Find the pressure group after a surface interval using Table 2 of the Recreational Dive Planner (table version).

Table 2

Remembering from the previous discussion on residual nitrogen, you know that as time goes by after a dive, residual nitrogen leaves your body. You will use Table 2 to determine how much residual nitrogen your body eliminates during a *surface interval* — that is, the time on the surface between two dives.

You enter Table 2 using the pressure group you found in Table 1. The numbers within the boxes in Table 2 are times expressed in hours and minutes. For example, 1:30 represents one hour and 30 minutes. Continuing the example of a 45-foot dive for 42 minutes, which yielded pressure group *N*, move into Table 2 horizontally from pressure group *N*. Assuming your surface interval has been one hour for this example, continue horizontally until you find the box where one hour falls on or between the two times listed (Figure 4-29). In this case, the box with the time interval list

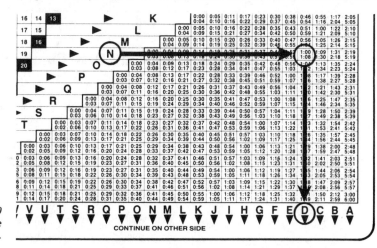

Figure 4-29
Using Table 2 to find your new pressure group after a surface interval.

ed as 1:00-1:08 is the one you are looking for. Now move downward vertically to the bottom of Table 2 until you find the new pressure group, in this example, pressure group D. That means in one hour, a diver with a pressure group of N loses enough residual nitrogen to move to pressure group D. With this new pressure group, you can proceed to Table 3 for planning your repetitive dive.

Sample Problems — Table 2

Solve the following sample problems and check your answers just like you did after reading the section on Table 1. Be sure your answers are correct before proceeding.

1. After a dive, Table 1 shows you are in pressure group J. What will your new pressure group be after a 32-minute surface interval?
   a. Pressure group E.
   b. Pressure group D.
   c. Pressure group F.
   d. Pressure group H.

Answer: a. Pressure group E.
Find pressure group J along the diagonal portion of Table 2. Moving inward horizontally, you will find the time interval of 0:32 - 0:40 (32 minutes through 40 minutes). 32 minutes falls within this interval. Next, move downward from this time interval box until finding new pressure group E at the bottom of Table 2.

2. A diver in pressure group P will be in what new pressure group after a 55-minute surface interval?
   a. Pressure group E.
   b. Pressure group A.
   c. Pressure group G.
   d. Pressure group F.

Answer: d. Pressure group F.
Find pressure group P along the diagonal portion of Table 2. Following the row horizontally inward from P, you will find the time interval of 0:52 - 0:59. 55 minutes falls within this interval. Now move downward vertically from this box until you find the new pressure group F at the bottom of Table 2.

3. A diver in pressure group I will be in what new pressure group after a surface interval of 4 hours?
   a. Pressure group Z.
   b. Pressure group B.
   c. Pressure group A.
   d. Pressure group C.

Answer: c. Pressure group A.
Find the pressure group I along the diagonal portion of Table 2 and follow the row in horizontally until you find the time interval 1:54 - 4:54. Four hours falls within this time interval. Next, move downward vertically until you find the new pressure group A at the bottom of Table 2.

Exercise 4-16

The Recreational Dive Planner, Table 2

1. A surface interval:
   ☐ a. must be longer than 12 hours.   ☐ b. is the time spent on the surface beetween two dives.

How did you do?   *1. b.*

Table 3

You will use Table 3 to find out how much residual nitrogen, expressed in minutes, you have remaining in your body pri-

Objectives

After reading this section on Table 3 of the Recreational Dive Planner (table version), you will be able to:

1. Define *residual nitrogen time (RNT)*.

2. Find residual nitrogen times on Table 3 of the Recreational Dive Planner (table version), for particular depths and pressure groups.

3. Define *adjusted no-decompression limit*.

4. Find adjusted no-decompression limit on Table 3 of the Recreational Dive Planner (table version), for particular depths and pressure groups.

or to entering the water for a repetitive dive. This amount is referred to as *residual nitrogen time (RNT)*. Essentially, Table 3 takes your pressure group and converts it into the time limit for your next dive.

Continuing with the same example, you were in pressure group *D* at the bottom of Table 2 after your surface interval of one hour. Flip the Recreational Dive Planner over and find pressure group *D* along the top row. Along the left side of Table 3, you will find the depths for the repetitive dive. For the sake of example, assume you plan your repetitive dive to 38 feet. Again, when the actual depth does not appear on the table, you must use the next greater depth, in this case, 40 feet. Locate 40 feet on the left side of Table 3 and follow the row horizontally to the right until you are under pressure group *D*. There you'll find two numbers: 25 in the white portion of the box and 115 in the blue portion (Figure 4-30).

25 is the RNT, which you'll use for returning to Table 1 after the repetitive dive (you'll learn more about this shortly), and 115 is the *adjusted no-decompression limit.*

The adjusted no-decompression limit is the maximum amount of time you can spend at that depth for the repetitive dive. In this example, because you are in pressure group *D* going to 38 feet (rounded to 40), you may stay under water no longer than 115 minutes. (Note: When the numbers contained in any box on Table 3 are added, the sum is the no-decompression limit contained in the black boxes in Table 1. The adjusted no-decompression limit is the result of subtracting the RNT from the NDL in Table 1.)

PRESSURE GROUP AT END OF SURFACE INTERVAL

Each cell below shows the residual nitrogen time (white) over the adjusted no-decompression limit (blue).

DEPTH (feet)	Z	Y	X	W	V	U	T	S	R	Q	P	O	N	M	L	K	J	I	H	G	F	E	D	C	B	A
35	205	188/17	168/37	152/53	139/66	127/78	117/88	108/97	100/105	92/113	85/120	79/126	73/132	67/138	62/143	57/148	52/153	48/157	44/161	40/165	36/169	32/173	29/176	25/180	19/186	10/195
40	140	129/11	120/20	111/29	104/36	97/43	91/49	85/55	79/61	74/66	69/71	64/76	60/80	55/85	51/89	48/92	44/96	40/100	37/103	34/106	31/109	27/113	25/115	22/118	16/124	9/131
50			80	75/5	71/9	67/13	63/17	60/20	57/23	53/27	50/30	47/33	44/36	41/39	38/42	36/44	33/47	31/49	28/52	26/54	23/56	21/59	19/61	17/63	13/67	7/73
60				55	54/1	52/3	49/6	47/8	44/11	42/13	39/16	37/18	35/20	33/22	31/24	29/26	27/28	25/30	23/32	21/34	19/36	18/37	16/39	14/41	11/44	6/49
70						40	38/2	36/4	34/6	33/7	31/9	29/11	27/13	26/14	24/16	22/18	21/19	19/21	18/22	16/24	15/25	13/27	12/28	9/31	7/33	5/35
80							30	29/2	28/3	26/4	25/5	23/7	22/8	21/9	19/11	18/12	17/13	15/15	14/16	13/17	11/19	10/20	8/22	6/24	5/25	4/26
90								25	24/1	23/2	22/3	21/4	19/6	18/7	17/8	16/9	15/10	13/12	12/13	11/14	10/15	9/16	7/18	6/19	5/20	4/21
100									20	19/1	18/2	17/3	16/4	15/5	14/6	13/7	12/8	11/9	10/10	9/11	8/12	7/13	6/14	5/15	4/16	3/17
110														16	15/2	14/2	13/3	12/4	11/5	10/6	9/7	8/8	7/9	6/10	5/...	3/13
120															13	12/2	12/3	11/4	10/5	9/6	8/7	7/8	6/...	5/...	4/...	3/10
130																10	9/3	8/4	8/5	7/7	6/...	5/...	4/...	3/...	...	...

TABLE 3 • REPETITIVE DIVE TIMETABLE

Figure 4-30
Using Table 3 to find your residual nitrogen time and your adjusted no-decompression limit.

Copyright © 1985, 1987 Diving Science & Technology Corp. Printed in USA

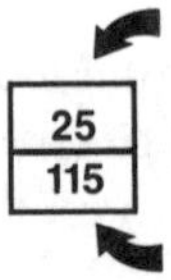

White area indicates *Residual Nitrogen Time* (RNT) in minutes and is to be added to *Actual Bottom Time* (ABT).

Blue area indicates adjusted no-decompression limit (ANDL). *Actual Bottom Time* (ABT) should not exceed this number.

Figure 4-31

Sample Problems — Table 3

Solve the following sample problems and check your answers against the answers given. Be sure your answers are correct before proceeding.

1. If you are in pressure group *K* after your surface interval, and you are planning a dive to 60 feet, what is your adjusted no-decompression limit?
   a. 24 minutes.
   b. 28 minutes.
   c. 29 minutes.
   d. 26 minutes.

Answer: d. 26 minutes.
On Table 3, find pressure group K along the top and the depth, 60 feet, along the left side. Follow the 60-foot row horizontally to the right until it intersects with the pressure group K column. There you find 29 in the top, white portion of the box and 26 in the bottom, blue portion. The adjusted no-decompression limit is the number in the bottom, blue portion: 26 minutes.

2. After a surface interval, you are in pressure group *P* and planning a dive to 50 feet. What is your adjusted no-decompression limit for this dive?
   a. 30 minutes.
   b. 27 minutes.
   c. 50 minutes.
   d. 33 minutes.

Answer: *a. 30 minutes.*
Locate pressure group *P* along the top row of Table 3. Next, find the depth, 50 feet, along the left side of Table 3. Intersect the *P* column and the 50-foot row to find the box containing 50 in the top, white

portion and 30 in the bottom, blue portion. The adjusted no-decompression limit is the bottom number: 30 minutes.

3. If you're in pressure group *M* after a surface interval, what is the residual nitrogen time if you're planning a repetitive dive to 60 feet?
   a. 35 minutes.
   b. 22 minutes.
   c. 33 minutes.
   d. 31 minutes.

Answer: c. 33 minutes.
On the top of Table 3, find pressure group M. On the left-hand side of Table 3, locate 60 feet. Intersect the 60-foot row and pressure group M column to find the box with numbers 33 in the top, white portion and 22 in the bottom, blue portion. The top number, 33 minutes, is the residual nitrogen time, or RNT.

4. Following a surface interval, you're in pressure group *T*. What would be your RNT for a repetitive dive planned to 50 feet?
   a. 63 minutes.
   b. 17 minutes.
   c. 67 minutes.
   d. 60 minutes.

Answer: a. 63 minutes.
On Table 3, find pressure group T at the top and the depth, 50 feet, on the left side. Intersect T and 50 to find the box containing 63 in the top, white portion and 17 in the bottom, blue portion. The RNT is the top number: 63 minutes.

Exercise 4-17

The Recreational Dive Planner, Table 3

1. Residual nitrogen time (RNT) is:

   ☐ a. the amount of residual nitrogen found in your body before you make your first dive of the day.

   ☐ b. the amount of residual nitrogn, expressed in minutes, you have remaining in your body prior to entering the water for a repetitive dive.

2. Adjusted no-decompression limit is:

☐ a. the maximum amount of time you can spend at a specified depth on a repetitive dive.

☐ b. the shorter-than-normal no-decompression limits you must follow until you become an experienced diver.

How did you do? *1.* b *2.* a.

Objectives

After reading this section on drawing dive profiles, you will be able to:

1. **Define the term *dive profile*.**

2. **Draw a complete three-dive profile, labeling all surface intervals, pressure groups, depths and bottom times.**

Drawing the Dive Profile

One way you can avoid confusion and make sure you don't miss any steps when using the dive tables is to graphically represent the dive as a drawing. This is called a *dive profile* (Figure 4-32).

Notice that there's a blank space for each piece of critical information. If you leave a space blank when drawing a dive profile, you've probably overlooked an important part of using the dive tables. The profile of the example you've been using is provided in Figure 4-33 for your reference. It's highly recommended that you make a habit of drawing a complete dive profile whenever you use the dive tables.

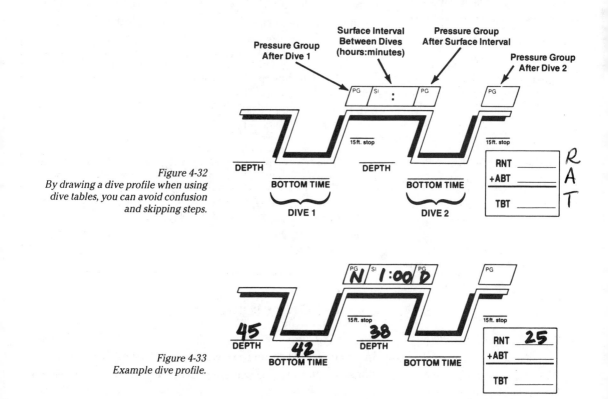

Figure 4-32
By drawing a dive profile when using dive tables, you can avoid confusion and skipping steps.

Figure 4-33
Example dive profile.

Exercise 4-18

Drawing the Dive Profile

1. A dive profile is a: ☐ a. method of calculating your bottom time. ☐ b. graphic representation of a dive.

How did you do? *1. b.*

Planning Multiple Repetitive Dives

If you only plan to make two dives — the first dive and one repetitive dive — then you've already learned what you need to know. If you want to make more than two dives, though, there's just one more short step you need to learn: How to get your new pressure group at the end of a repetitive dive.

You find your pressure group by using the RNT you found on Table 3 and the bottom time of your repetitive dive, on Table 1. Continuing with the previous example, suppose you stayed under water 50 minutes of the 115 adjusted no-decompression limit on the repetitive dive to 38 (rounded to 40) feet. Because this is the time you actually spent under water, it is called *actual bottom time (ABT)*.

During the actual bottom time of the repetitive dive, your body absorbed more nitrogen, but you also had residual nitrogen left from the first dive. To determine the pressure group for *all* the nitrogen in your body, add the Residual Nitrogen Time (RNT) to the Actual Bottom Time (ABT) to give you *Total Bottom Time* (TBT). In the example, you get 25 (RNT) + 50 (ABT) = 75 (TBT).

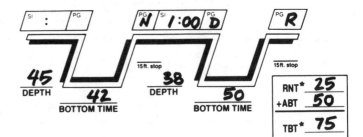

Figure 4-34
At the end of the dive profile, remember to add your residual nitrogen time to your actual bottom time to get your total bottom time.

Now all you have to do is use the total bottom time and the depth of the repetitive dive in Table 1 to find your new pressure group, just like you did at the end of the first dive. In the example, find 75 minutes in the 40-foot column. It doesn't appear, so you round up to 79 minutes, then move horizontally to find the new pressure group, *R*. You can now enter Table 2 with a new surface interval and proceed in the same sequence as before.

Figure 4-35
Use the total bottom time (TBT) to get your new pressure group after a repetitive dive.

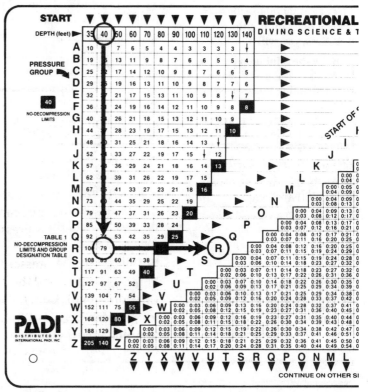

At the end of a repetitive dive, always remember that to get back to Table 1 and find your new pressure group, you must add the residual nitrogen time to your actual bottom time to find your total bottom time. *Forgetting to add RNT and ABT to get TBT is the single most common error made by divers learning to calculate multiple repetitive dives.* You may find it helpful to use this memory device: "Always find the RAT," as shown by Figure 4-36.

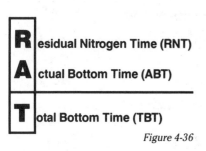

R esidual Nitrogen Time (RNT)

A ctual Bottom Time (ABT)

T otal Bottom Time (TBT)

Figure 4-36

Exercise 4-19

Planning Multiple Repetitive Dives

1. Actual bottom time (ABT) is: ☐ a. the amount of time you actually spent under water during a dive.

   ☐ b. the amount of time you actually spent under water added to the residual nitrogen time from your previous dive.

2. Total bottom time (TBT) is: ☐ a. the amount of time you actually spent under water during a dive.

   ☐ b. the amount of time you actually spent under water added to the residual nitrogen time from your previous dive.

How did you do? *1.* a *2.* b.

Objectives

After reading this section on special rules for multiple repetitive dives, you will be able to:

1. State the minimum surface intervals that must be made when planning three or more dives when:

    a. The ending pressure group after any dive is *W* or *X*.

    b.   The ending pressure group after any dive is *Y* or *Z*.

2. Apply the two special rules for repetitive diving.

Special Rules for Multiple Repetitive Dives

There are some special rules that apply when you plan to make 3 or more dives (the first and 2 repetitive) in a series of multiple repetitive dives. Making more than 3 dives in a series is common during diving vacations to a resort area or on a liveaboard dive boat.

If you're planning three or more dives, beginning with the first dive of the day, if your ending pressure group is *W* or *X*, the minimum surface interval between *all* subsequent dives is 1 hour. If your ending pressure group after any dive is *Y* or *Z*, the minimum surface interval between all subsequent dives is 3 hours.

Don't forget that a repetitive dive is always to the same or a lesser depth than the dive preceding. Make your deepest dive of the series first, and make progressively shallower dives as the series continues. Limit all repetitive dives to 100 feet or shallower.

Note: Since little is presently known about the physiological effects of multiple dives over multiple days, you are wise to make fewer dives and limit your exposure toward the end of a multi-day dive series.

Exercise 4-20

Special Rules for Multiple Repetitive Dives

1. If you are planning three or more dives in one day and your ending pressure group after the second dive is a *Y,* you should wait a minimum of _____ hour(s) between all subsequent dives. ☐ a. 1 ☐ b. 3

How did you do? *1.* b.

Summary

The intent and purpose of the Recreational Dive Planner is to make all dives no-decompression dives. Proper planning assures that all dives, single or repetitive, are within the no-decompression limits by controlling the length of the dive, the depth of the dive, and the surface interval between dives.

Use of the Recreational Dive Planner requires having and using an accurate depth gauge, an underwater timer, a slate and pencil, and the planner itself. You need to know the depth of each dive so you can determine the maximum time allowed, or you must limit your depth to a specific planned maximum depth.

Always consult the Recreational Dive Planner before

Sample Problems — Planning Multiple Repetitive Dives

Solve the following sample problems and check your answers against those given. Make sure your answers are correct before proceeding.

Indicate the final pressure group upon surfacing after the following series of dives. To avoid confusion, practice drawing the dive profile as you work the problems.

1. First dive: 50 ft/40 mins; surface interval: 1:00. Second dive: 40 ft/60 mins.
   a. Pressure group R.
   b. Pressure group P.
   c. Pressure group S.
   d. Pressure group T.

Answer: c. Pressure group S.
After the first dive to 50 feet for 40 minutes, your pressure group from Table 1 would be M (remember to use 41, since 40 minutes is not found on the table). On Table 2, begin at M and move horizontally to find the surface interval box that includes 60 minutes (1 hour) — that box is 0:56 - 1:04, making D your new pressure group. On Table 3, intersect D and 40 feet (the depth of the second dive) to 25 over 115. Add the top number, 25 minutes of residual nitrogen time to your actual bottom time of 60 minutes for a total bottom time of 85 minutes. Return to Table 1 and locate the 40-foot column, then follow it down until you find your total bottom time of 85 minutes. From there, move horizontally to locate your new pressure group, S.

2. First dive: 60 ft/30 mins; surface interval: 30 mins. Second dive: 50 ft/30 mins.
   a. Pressure group R.
   b. Pressure group P.
   c. Pressure group S.
   d. Pressure group T.

Answer: a. Pressure group R.
After the first dive to 60 feet for 30 minutes, your
pressure group is L on Table 1 (you use 31 minutes because 30 minutes is not found). On Table 2, follow horizontally from L to the surface interval box that includes 30 minutes: the 0:28 - 0:34 box. Move down vertically from there to find your new pressure group, G. On Table 3, intersect G and 50 feet (the depth of your second dive) to find the box containing 26 over 54. Add the 26 minutes of RNT to your 30-minute ABT (the time of your second dive) to get a TBT of 56 minutes. Return to Table 1 and locate the 50-foot column. Follow it down until you find 56 minutes, then proceed horizontally right to locate your new pressure group, R.

3. First dive: 55 ft/50 mins; surface interval: 24 mins. Second dive: 50 ft/30 mins.
   a. Pressure group W.
   b. Pressure group T.
   c. Pressure group X.
   d. Pressure group U.

Answer: c. Pressure group X.
After the first dive to 55 feet (must use 60) for 50 minutes (must use 52), your pressure group from Table 1 is U. On Table 2, begin at U and move in horizontally until you locate the box 24 minutes falls within, the 0:22 - 0:25 box. Move down vertically to find a new pressure group of O. On Table 3, intersect O and 50 feet to find an RNT of 47 (top number) and an adjusted no-decompression limit of 33 (bottom number). Add the 47 minutes RNT to your 30-minute ABT for a TBT of 77 minutes. Return to Table 1 and locate 50 feet at the top. Proceed down the column until you find 77 minutes (must use 80), then proceed horizontally to find your new pressure group X. Because you are in Group X, you must wait at least an hour between all subsequent repetitive dives.

each dive to be sure you know your no-decompression limit. Note the time on an underwater slate and carry it with you and also note the no-decompression limit for the next deep depth, in case you accidentally exceed your depth limit. Remember that your deepest dive is always first, and each successive dive is to an equal or shallower depth than the preceding dive. If residual nitrogen limits your dive time, consider making a shallower dive to permit more time.

The Wheel

As mentioned earlier, the other version of the Recreational Dive Planner is The Wheel. Both versions of the Recreational Dive Planner were researched, designed and tested specifically for recreational diving, but The Wheel uses a spiral format that gives you advantages in use and allowable bottom time.

There are two important differences between The Wheel and table formats. First, The Wheel's format is more precise and easier to use. This means you minimize unnecessary round-off penalties and, due to its design, the

Figure 4-37
The Wheel's spiral format has advantages in use and allowable bottom time compared to conventional table formats.

sometimes confusing concept of residual nitrogen time is eliminated.

The second important difference is that The Wheel allows *multilevel dives*. With table formats, the time limit of the dive is always determined by the deepest depth reached on the dive, regardless of how long you actually remain at that depth. With The Wheel, you can plan dives that give you more dive time as you move up to shallower depths, where your body absorbs nitrogen more slowly.

The Wheel offers you advantages in ease of use and

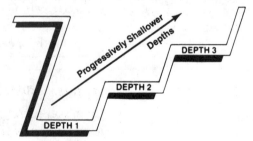

Figure 4-38
The Wheel permits multilevel dives, which gives you more time as you ascend to shallower depths.

allowable dive time. If you didn't learn to use The Wheel as part of this course, your PADI Instructor or Dive Center can give you more information about it.

Confined-Water Training Preview — Module Four

Figure 4-39
During this confined-water training session, you will learn some skin diving skills as well as scuba skills.

Until now, your confined-water training has focused exclusively on the use of scuba equipment. In this confined-water session, you'll learn some more scuba skills, but you'll also be learning some skin diving skills.

Although your primary interest in taking this class is to learn about scuba diving, you'll find skin diving useful and enjoyable, too. There may be times when you'd like to explore shallow water, and scuba equipment isn't available. You may want to skin dive to locate a scuba dive site without using your tank air.

Finally, some special diving activities, like underwater photography and spearfishing, require diving without scuba from time to time. Scuba sometimes scares shy fish, and in many areas, underwater hunting is not permitted with scuba.

The skin diving skills and scuba skills listed below are the skills you must successfully complete before moving onto Module Five. Read and become familiar with them, just like you have for the previous three modules.

Performance Requirements
Confined-Water Training Module Four

By the end of the confined-water training for Module Four, you will be able to:

1. Demonstrate the use of proper hyperventilation when skin diving.

2. Dive vertically headfirst from the surface in water too deep to stand up in (without excessive splashing or arm movement.)

3. Clear and breathe from a snorkel upon ascent

4. Using buoyancy control, hover motionless (without kicking or sculling) in the water for at least 30 seconds.

5. Buddy breathe sharing a single air source for a distance of at least 50 feet under water as both a donor and a receiver.

Hyperventilation

Since you don't use scuba equipment for skin diving, you must obviously hold your breath if you want to leave the surface. Most people have trouble comfortably holding their breath for more than a minute, especially when engaged in an activity that uses a lot of energy.

To hold your breath longer, you can use a technique called *hyperventilation* to temporarily suppress the stimulus to breathe. Intentional hyperventilation is nothing more than three or four deep, rapid breaths taken immediately before a breath-hold skin dive. After hyperventilating, it takes longer for you to feel the urge to breathe, so you can stay down longer.

Hyperventilation is valuable *only* if you limit it to a maximum of 3 or 4 breaths. Excessive hyperventilation — more than 3 or 4 breaths — can be dangerous. This is because excessive hyperventilation can suppress the stimulus to breathe so greatly that your body runs out of oxygen before you feel the urge to breathe. This would lead to sudden unconsciousness *without warning* and drowning. Do not hyperventilate excessively.

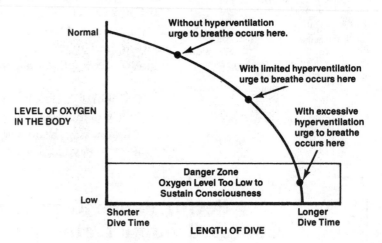

Figure 4-40
Excessive hyperventilation (more than 3 or 4 breaths) can cause unconsciousness without warning.

You can safely use hyperventilation limited to 3 or 4 deep, rapid breaths. Also, be sure to rest at least a minute or so between breath-hold dives so your body can return to its normal oxygen level. If you feel fatigued, dizzy or light-headed, stop diving and rest.

Unintentional hyperventilation can occur if you experience anxiety or stress, and would cause you to breathe rapidly and shallowly. This would lead to respiratory difficulty. By using proper diving techniques, you should normally avoid anxiety and stress, but if you find yourself breathing rapidly and shallowly, control your breathing to prevent difficulties. Force yourself to breathe slowly and deeply until you return to a relaxed state.

Surface Diving (skin diving)

Until now, all your descents have been made feetfirst, using scuba equipment. When you're wearing bulky scuba equipment and have an air supply so you can take your time, a feetfirst descent is generally the best. During skin diving, though, you don't have the bulk of scuba equipment, so you may choose to use a headfirst surface dive.

When executed correctly, a headfirst surface dive gets you under water and headed down quickly with minimum effort. To make a headfirst surface dive: deflate your BCD, hyperventilate not more than 3 or 4 times, take a large breath and hold it. Next, bend forward at your waist, thrusting your head and arms downward and simultaneously lifting your legs above the surface. The idea is to get your legs as high and straight as possible so their weight can drive your downward. Once your fins submerge, begin kicking toward the bottom, equalizing your ears and mask just like you do to descend using scuba. Use your fins, not your arms, to swim down.

Figure 4-41
To make a headfirst surface dive, first deflate your BCD, hyperventilate not more than 3 or 4 times and hold a large breath.

Figure 4-42
Next, from a facedown swimming position, bend forward at the waist, thrusting your head and arms downward . . .

Figure 4-43
. . . while simultaneously lifting your legs above the surface.

Figure 4-44
Once your fins are submerged, begin swimming toward the bottom.

While you are under water on a breath-hold dive, your buddy should remain at the surface, watching you. Always use this one-up, one-down, buddy technique while skin diving. That way, if you need assistance, your buddy can come to your aid with a fresh breath.

As you swim along under water, move slowly to conserve the oxygen in your body. If you relax and become interested in something, you'll be surprised how long you can comfortably stay under water.

When you feel the need to breathe, begin your ascent.

Figure 4-45
When you feel the urge to breathe, ascend with your hand over your head while looking up and rotating.

Place your hand over your head, look up and rotate so you can get a complete view of the surface as you come up. As you ascend, you'll be able to clear your snorkel using either the blast method or another method called the *displacement method.*

Displacement Snorkel Clearing

If you use a snorkel without a purge valve, the displacement method of clearing a snorkel is easier than the blast method. As you ascend properly from a skin dive, you will be looking at the surface with your head tilted back. In this position, the opening of your snorkel is actually lower than the mouthpiece. Keep your head tilted back throughout the ascent by continuing to look at the surface and exhale a small amount of air into your snorkel. As you ascend, this air will expand, forcing the water out of the snorkel's opening. Provided you keep looking at the surface, the snorkel

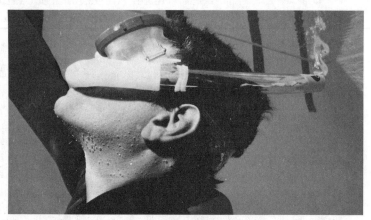

Figure 4-46
To clear the snorkel using the displacement method, look at the surface and exhale a small amount of air into the snorkel. This air will expand, forcing the water from the snorkel.

will remain free of water due to the trapped air inside.

When you reach the surface, begin exhaling and continue to exhale as you roll your head forward into the surface swimming position. The snorkel will be clear of water. Remember, however, to use airway control and take your first breath cautiously, in case a few drops of water remain.

Compared to the blast method, you'll find the displacement method both easier and less tiring when clearing a snorkel without a purge valve. For clearing your snorkel at the surface while scuba diving, you'll continue to use the blast method (because you're not making an ascent), but displacement clearing may quickly become your favorite method while skin diving.

After you've practiced snorkel clearing, your instructor will probably have you practice all your skin diving skills. Then you'll be ready to learn some more scuba diving skills.

Figure 4-47
When you reach the surface, begin exhaling and continue to exhale as you roll your head forward into the surface swimming position.

Entry

In your earlier confined-water training, you learned some entries appropriate to your local diving environment. This may have included the giant-stride entry and the controlled seated entry. In this session, your instructor will show you more entries appropriate to diving in your area. Remember that one reason area orientations are important is appropriate entry (and exit) techniques differ from one diving area to the next.

One entry you may learn in this session is the *sitting back-roll entry.* You'll find the sitting back-roll especially suitable for entering from a low, unstable platform such as a small boat or raft.

To accomplish a sitting back-roll entry, first make sure all your equipment is in place and that your SPG or other hoses are not snagged or hooked in the platform. Next, check the entry area to be sure it's clear. Sit on the edge of the platform with your BCD about half inflated and your

Figure 4-48
When making a sitting back-roll entry, make sure all your equipment is in place and that your SPG or other hoses are not snagged on another object.

Figure 4-49
Be sure to keep your legs tucked close to you during the entire entry so they don't strike the platform edge as you enter.

regulator in your mouth. Hold your mask firmly in place, and lean back, so you roll gently into the water. Keep your legs tucked close to you during the entire entry so they don't strike the platform edge as you go. You may feel momentary disorientation when you use the sitting back roll, but your buoyancy will immediately bring you to the surface for rapid reorientation.

Buoyancy Control (hovering)

To this point, you've been learning more and more about controlling your buoyancy while diving. Mastering buoy-

Figure 4-50
Hovering motionless in mid-water demonstrates complete buoyancy control.

ancy control will help you avoid stirring up the bottom, damaging aquatic life and wasting energy. In this confined-water training session, you'll learn to fine-tune your buoyancy and demonstrate complete control of it. You will do this by hovering motionless in mid-water.

First, descend to the bottom and adjust for neutral buoyancy. Once you are neutrally buoyant, push yourself gently off the bottom just a couple of feet. Then, *without holding your breath* use your lung volume to maintain a stationary position in mid-water. If you begin to rise, decrease your buoyancy by breathing with your lungs somewhat less full. If you begin to sink, increase your buoyancy by breathing with your lungs a little fuller. It's helpful to have a reference nearby, so look at a stationary object nearby and maintain your position in relation to it.

With a little practice, you'll find this skill easy to perform. After you have a little more experience diving, you'll begin subconsciously and automatically adjusting your buoyancy so you can remain off the bottom without effort.

Buddy Breathing

During academic training for Module Three, you learned about the options you have in the unlikely event you run out of air. During the confined-water training, you practiced two of these options: the controlled emergency swimming ascent and use of an alternate air source. A third option, called *buddy breathing,* requires you and your buddy to share a single second stage.

Buddy breathing is a less desirable option than the other two options simply because it is a more complex skill, which increases the possibility of error. If you remain close to your buddy and make certain you and your buddy are always equipped with an alternate air source, the need for buddy breathing is unlikely to arise. Nevertheless, if you should find yourself in need of air and without an alternate air source, then buddy breathing may help you solve your out-of-air problem.

Generally, buddy-breathing is an appropriate option when: 1) your buddy has no alternate air source, 2) you are close to your buddy, 3) you are too deep to make a controlled emergency swimming ascent (deeper than 40 feet) and 4) you have practiced buddy breathing with your buddy and feel confident both of you can make a safe, controlled buddy breathing ascent.

To initiate buddy breathing, swim to your buddy and

signal *out of air* and *share air.* Your buddy should respond by passing you his second stage and allowing you to take two breaths. Your buddy will not let go of the second stage, but will hold it by the hose near the mouthpiece so he doesn't cover the purge button. That way, you can use the purge button to clear the second stage if you need to.

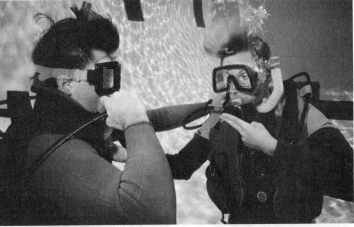

Figure 4-51
The first step in buddy breathing is to signal to your buddy that you are out of air and wish to share air.

Figure 4-52
Your buddy will respond by passing you his second stage and letting you take two breaths. You then return it to him.

As soon as you and your buddy begin buddy breathing, you and he should grasp each other face-to-face for stability. He will hold the second stage with his right hand and grasp your BCD or tank straps with his left. You should grasp him similarly with your right hand and guide the second stage to your mouth with your left.

After you take two breaths, allow your buddy to take the second stage back. Remember not to hold your breath and to make the *A-a-a-a-h-h-h* sound when the regulator isn't in your mouth. Your buddy will take two breaths and

221

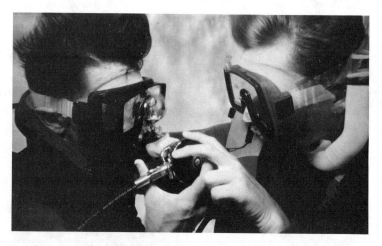

Figure 4-53
Make certain you do not hold your breath
while buddy breathing by making an
A-a-a-h-h-h sound when the regulator is
not in your mouth.

return it to you for two breaths. Continue the exchange back and forth until you and your buddy have a natural, relaxed rhythm established.

During a confined-water training session, your instructor may have you practice buddy breathing in a stationary position, and then swimming along the bottom to simulate an ascent while buddy breathing.

Summary

You are now ready for the confined-water training session for Module Four. The new skills you will be practicing are:

1. Hyperventilation
2. Surface Diving (skin diving)
3. Displacement Snorkel Clearing
4. Entry
5. Buoyancy Control (hovering)
6. Buddy Breathing

Five

☐ **Recreational Dive Planner Special Circumstances**

☐ **Finding Minimum Surface Interval on the Recreational Dive Planner (table version)**

☐ **Dive Tables Definitions Review**

☐ **Basic Compass Navigation**

☐ **Confined-Water Training Preview**

☐ **Open-Water Training Preview — Dives 4 and 5**

☐ **Continuing Education**

☐ **Epilogue**

☐ **Summary of Diving Safety Practices**

Recreational Dive Planner Special Circumstances

In Module Four you learned how to use the Recreational Dive Planner, (table version) or The Wheel, to find your time limits for a single dive, for repetitive dives and for multiple repetitive dives. In this module, you'll learn about special circumstances that apply to both versions of the Recreational Dive Planner: safety stops, emergency decompression stops, altitude limits, procedures for flying after diving and procedures for cold and strenuous conditions.

Objectives

After reading this section on safety stops, you will be able to:

1. State the depth and time of a safety stop.

2. Explain the purpose of a safety stop.

3. Describe the three recommended situations in which a safety stop should be made.

Figure 5-1
A safety stop at 15 feet for 3 minutes helps your body eliminate nitrogen slowly and gives you a moment to fine-tune your buoyancy before finishing your ascent.

Safety Stops

Although the Recreational Dive Planner is designed for no-decompression diving (which allows you to make a direct, continuous ascent to the surface), there are times when you'll want to make a *safety stop* for added conservatism and safety. A safety stop is a delay in ascent at 15 feet for 3 minutes. This delay assists your body in slowly eliminating excess nitrogen. It also gives you a moment to pause and fine tune your buoyancy before ascending through the final 15 feet.

The guideline for making a safety stop is simple: *You may make a safety stop at the end of any dive.* In fact, it's encouraged. However, always make a safety stop if:

1. your dive has been to 100 feet or deeper.

2. your pressure group at the end of the dive is within three pressure groups of the no-decompression limit.

3. You dive up to any limit on the Recreational Dive Planner.

Since bottom time is defined as the time from the beginning of your descent to the beginning of your final ascent to the surface (or the safety stop), the time of the safety stop doesn't need be added to the bottom time of the dive when using the Recreational Dive Planner.

Keep in mind that, although the safety stop should be a regular procedure for all your dives, it's an optional stop when circumstances such as very low air, assisting another diver or weather make stopping inappropriate.

Exercise 5-1

Safety Stop

1. A safety stop is a delay in ascent at _____ feet for _____ minutes. ☐ a. 15, 3 ☐ b. 10, 5

2. A safety stop is meant to: ☐ a. assist your body in slowly eliminating excess nitrogen. ☐ b. allow you to check your bottom time prior to completing your dive.

3. Check all appropriate responses. Always make a safety stop if:

   ☐ a. your dive has been to 100 feet or deeper. ☐ b. your dive was conducted in low-visibility water.

   ☐ c. your pressure group at the end of the dive is within three pressure groups of the no-decompression limit.

How did you do? *1.* a *2.* a *3.* a, c

Objectives

After reading this section on emergency decompression, you will be able to:

1. Explain what should be done if a no-decompression limit or an adjusted no-decompression limit is exceeded by *less* than 5 minutes.

2. Explain what should be done if a no-decompression limit or an adjusted no-decompression limit is exceeded by *more* than 5 minutes.

Emergency Decompression

As you've learned, recreational diving is no-decompression diving, and both versions of the Recreational Dive Planner were designed specifically for this type of diving. If you accidentally exceed the time limits of the Recreational Dive Planner, you need to know the procedure for an *emergency decompression* stop so you can make a safe ascent to the surface.

If you exceed a no-decompression limit or an adjusted no-decompression limit by no more than 5 minutes, slowly ascend at a rate not faster than 60 feet per minute to 15 feet and remain there for 8 minutes prior to surfacing. After reaching the surface, do not dive for at least 6 hours because you will have extremely high levels of residual nitrogen in your body.

If you exceed a no-decompression limit or an adjusted no-decompression limit by more than 5 minutes, a 15-foot stop for no less than 15 minutes is strongly urged, air supply permitting. Upon surfacing, you must remain out of the water at least 24 hours before diving again, due to the excess nitrogen in your body.

Emergency decompression stops differ from safety stops in that an emergency decompression stop 1) *must* be made or there is an excessive risk of decompression sickness, and 2) is an *emergency procedure only.* Remember, both versions of the Recreational Dive Planner were designed for *recreational* diving only. They should never be used in commercial/military diving situations in which decompression is likely or when a breathing gas other than air is used (neither situation falls within the scope of recreational diving).

Exercise 5-2

Emergency Decompression

1. If you accidentally exceed a no-decompression limit by less than 5 minutes, you should: ☐ a. slowly ascend to 15 feet, remain there for 8 minutes prior to surfacing and discontinue diving for 6 hours. ☐ b. ascend directly to the surface at a rate of 60 feet per minute.

2. If you accidentally exceed a no-decompression limit by more than 5 minutes, you should slowly ascend to 15 feet and remain there for no less than 15 minutes, air supply permitting. ☐ True ☐ False

How did you do? *1.* a *2. True.*

Objectives

After reading this section on altitude limits, flying after diving, and cold and strenuous conditions, you will be able to:

1. State the altitude (in feet) above which the Recreational Dive Planner should not be used unless special procedures are followed.

2. State the minimum surface interval, in hours, to be reasonably assured you remain symptom free from decompression sickness when flying in a commercial jet airliner after diving.

3. State the general guideline for determining when to fly in a commercial jet airliner after making daily, multiple dives for several days.

4. Explain the procedure you must follow when planning a dive in cold water or under strenuous conditions using the Recreational Dive Planner.

Altitude Limits, Flying After Diving, and Cold and Strenuous Conditions

Diving at Altitudes — In Module One, you learned about atmospheric pressure. You learned that as you ascend through the air, pressure decreases — just as pressure decreases as you ascend through water. The Recreational Dive Planner was designed for diving at sea level and may not be used at altitudes greater than 1000 feet. Above 1000 feet, special tables and procedures are required to account for the decreased atmospheric pressure. If you're interested in high-altitude diving, seek specialty training in this area.

Figure 5-2
When diving above 1000 feet of altitude, special dive tables and procedures are required.

Flying After Diving — The lowered atmospheric pressure at altitude must also be considered if you intend to fly after diving. The following are general guidelines for determining when to fly:

• A minimum surface interval of 12 hours is required to be reasonably assured you remain symptom free from decompression sickness upon ascent to altitude in a commercial jet airliner (altitude up to 8000 feet 2400 metres).

• If you plan to make daily, multiple dives for several days or make a dive requiring decompression, you should take special precautions and wait for an extended surface interval beyond 12 hours before flight. The greater the duration before flight, the less likely decompression sickness will occur.

There can never be a flying after diving rule that is guaranteed to prevent decompression sickness completely. The above represents the best estimate for a conservative, safe

Figure 5-3
Be sure to follow the proper procedures for flying after diving.

surface interval for the vast majority of divers. There will always be an occasional diver whose physiological makeup or special diving circumstances will result in decompression sickness. The responsibility for diving safety and proper behavior falls on you.

Since there are currently no recommendations for driving to altitude after diving, conservatism in this practice is prudent.

Cold and Strenuous Conditions — Cold or strenuous conditions may cause your body to have more excess nitrogen at the end of a dive than normally expected. When planning a dive in cold water or under conditions that may be more strenuous than usual, plan your dive as though the depth were 10 feet deeper than it actually is.

Figure 5-4
When planning a dive in cold water or under conditions that may be more strenuous than usual, plan your dive as though the depth is 10 feet deeper than it actually is.

Exercise 5-3

Altitude Limits, Flying After Diving, and Cold and Strenuous Conditions

1. The Recreational Dive Planner itself is not designed to be used at altitudes greater than _____ feet unless

Continue this exercise on page 229.

Dive Computers and Dive Planning

The use of electronic dive computers has become a popular approach to monitoring depth and time limits while diving. Although dive computers are expensive, they do offer some conveniences for many divers.

Most dive computers calculate multilevel diving. This increases dive time as the diver moves to shallower depths, where nitrogen absorption is slower. In addition, the dive computer often incorporates most of the required diving instruments into one compact package.

If you decide to purchase a dive computer, it's still important for you to have and use tables, such as the Recreational Dive Planner (table version or The Wheel). No dive computer is infallible. It can suffer from battery failure or damage from improper handling. If your computer fails and you've maintained a record of your dive profiles and the profiles fall within the no-decompression limits of your tables, you may still continue to dive using the tables. Otherwise, you must stay out of the water 12 to 24 hours (see the computer manufacturer's instructions).

When using a dive computer, keep these points in mind:

1. Each diver in a buddy team should have his own computer. You and your buddy should not attempt to share a single computer.

2. Different brands of computers have different time limits, and identical models can have slight individual variations. You and your buddy should follow the computer with the more conservative times.

3. If your computer malfunctions while diving, ascend immediately according to the instructions of the computer manufacturer.

4. Always back up your computer by calculating with tables.

Note: The Wheel comes closer to matching the dive profile followed by a computer than conventional tables. Also, if your computer were to fail and you were unable to use it for the remainder of a diving vacation, The Wheel would allow you to calculate dive times for multilevel profiles.

5. When diving in a group or from a charter boat, be sure to inform the divemaster that you're diving with a computer. This will make him aware that your time limits may differ from divers who are using conventional tables.

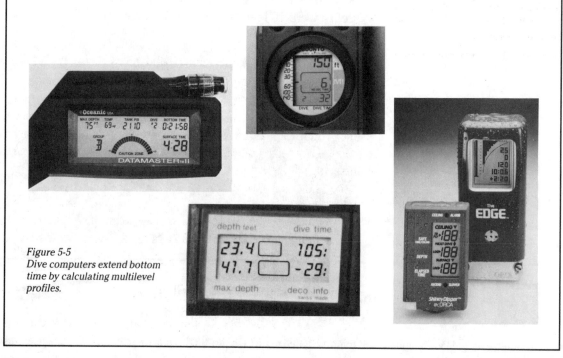

Figure 5-5
Dive computers extend bottom time by calculating multilevel profiles.

special procedures are followed. ☐ a. 1000 ☐ b. 8000

2. You made one shallow no-decompression dive in the morning. According to the flying after diving guidelines, what is the minimum time you should wait before you fly? ☐ a. 4 hours ☐ b. 12 hours

3. After making three dives per day over a five day vacation, how long should you wait after your last dive before flying in a commercial airliner? ☐ a. 12 hours ☐ b. An extended period beyond 12 hours (the longer the better)

4. In cold water or under strenuous conditions, plan your dive as though the depth is _____ feet deeper than actual:
   ☐ a. 15 ☐ b. 10

How did you do? *1. a 2. b 3. b. 4. b*

NOTE: If you've been using the Recreational Dive Planner (table version) for this course, continue reading into the next section on how to find your minimum surface interval.

If you're learning to use The Wheel, read section six in the *Instructions for Use* booklet on how to find your minimum surface interval. After you've read these sections, begin reading the section on Basic Compass Navigation.

Objectives

After reading this section on finding your minimum surface interval, you will be able to:

1. Find the minimum surface interval required to complete a series of no-decompression dives using the Recreational Dive Planner (table version).

Finding A Minimum Surface Interval on the Recreational Dive Planner (table version)

So far, you've learned to use the table version of the Recreational Dive Planner to plan your first dive, your surface interval and your second dive. Although you'll probably plan a lot of dives that way, there will also be times when you want to plan the times and the depths of both dives first, and then calculate the least amount of time (the minimum surface interval) that you must wait after the first dive to be able to make the second dive. This is a common planning technique on half-day boat trips, for example. By working through an example, you can get a clear idea of how to determine a minimum surface interval.

Suppose you're planning two dives — the first to 60 feet for 45 minutes, the second to 50 feet for one hour. How long does your surface interval need to be to be able to make the second no-decompression dive? Since you're looking for a minimum surface interval, you'll actually work the tables from both ends to find the answer in Table 2.

Begin by finding your pressure group at the end of the first dive. On Table 1 in the 60-foot column, you find that at the end

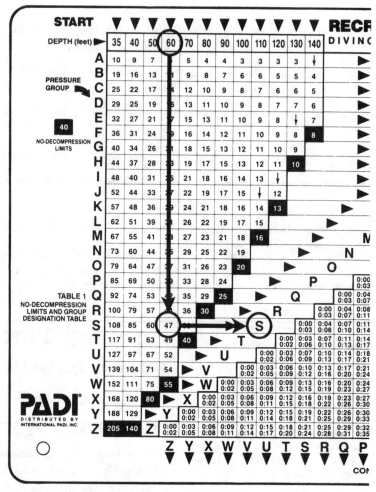

Figure 5-6
Your first step in determining your minimum surface interval is to use Table 1 to find your pressure group after the first planned dive. After 45 minutes at 60 feet, you are in pressure group S.

of a 45-minute dive, you will be in pressure group *S* (Figure 5-6). Record pressure group *S* on your dive profile (Figure 5-7).

Next, find the greatest pressure group that will allow you to make your second dive (50 feet for one hour). To find this pressure group, flip to Table 3 and find 50 feet on the left side. Follow the 50-foot row inward, from left to right, until you find the first adjusted no-decompression limit

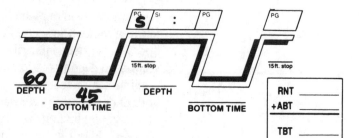

Figure 5-7
Put your first dive and pressure group on the dive profile.

(number in blue) that permits a dive of at least 60 minutes (one hour). You will find the number 61 in blue — the first adjusted no-decompression limit that is 60 minutes or greater. Now, move up the column from 61 minutes. You should

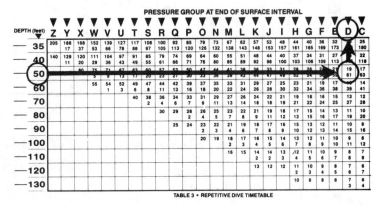

Figure 5-8
Next, go to Table 3, find 50 feet on the left and move to the right until you find the first adjusted no-decompression limit that permits a dive of at least 60 minutes. Follow the column upward to find pressure group D.

find pressure group *D* at the top of the column (Figure 5-8). You now know that to make a 60-minute dive to 50 feet, you must be at least a pressure group D diver after your surface interval. List this pressure group on your dive profile (Figure 5-9).

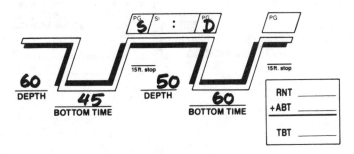

Figure 5-9
Your dive profile should now look like this.

Now use Table 2 to find out how long of a surface interval it will take for you to change from pressure group *S* (at the end of your first dive) to pressure group *D* (at the beginning of your second dive). Find pressure group *S* along the diagonal slope of Table 2 and pressure group *D* along the bottom. Move in from pressure group *S* and up from pressure group *D* until you find the box where they intersect. There you find 1:19 - 1:27 (see next page Figure 5-10). Since you're looking for the *minimum* surface interval, your answer is 1:19. You must wait at least one hour and 19 minutes between the two dives that you planned in this example.

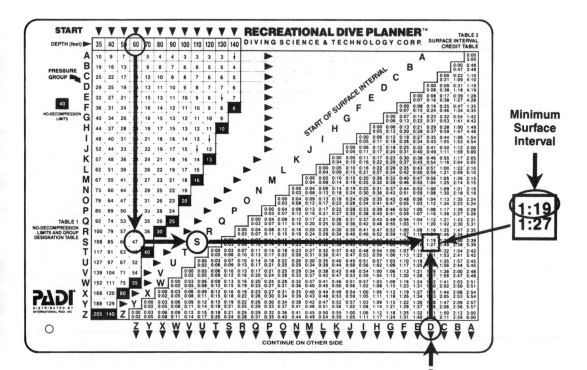

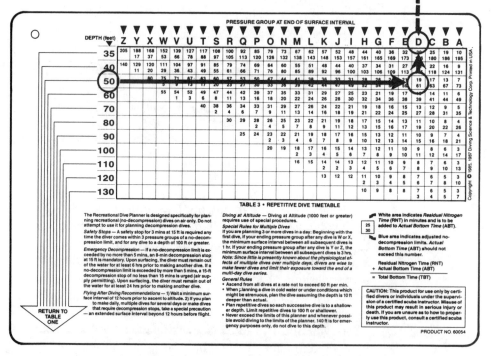

Figure 5-10
Finally, use Table 2 to determine how long it takes to go from pressure group S (found on Table 1 as the ending pressure group from the first dive) to pressure group D (found on Table 3 as the pressure group necessary to make the second dive). The shortest time shown is 1:19.

Sample Problems — Find Your Minimum Surface Interval

Find the minimum surface intervals required to complete the series of dives in the sample problems below, then check your answers against the answers given. Be sure your answers are correct before proceeding. Remember, drawing the dive profiles helps you avoid confusion.

1. First dive: 60 feet/40 mins. Second dive: 60 feet/40 mins. The minimum surface interval is:
   a. 1:42
   b. 1:21
   c. 1:12
   d. 1:20

Answer: b. 1:21.
Start with Table 1. After a dive to 60 feet for 40 minutes (40 minutes is not listed, so you must use 42), your pressure group is Q. Next go to Table 3. Find 60 feet on the left side and follow the row horizontally to the right until you find the first adjusted no-decompression limit (number in the bottom, blue portion of the box) that is 40 minutes or greater. The number you find is 41. Follow the column up to find pressure group C. Turn to Table 2 and find where pressure group Q on the diagonal intersects with pressure group C on the bottom. In that box, 1:21 - 1:42, 1 hour and 21 minutes is the minimum surface interval needed to make the two dives safely.

2. First dive: 50 feet/60 mins. Second dive: 40 feet/70 mins. The minimum surface interval is:
   a. 0:14
   b. 0:07
   c. 0:11
   d. 0:32

Answer: c. 0:11.
Start on Table 1. Under 50 feet find 60 minutes,

which puts you in pressure group S. Now turn to Table 3. Find the 40-foot row starting on the left side and follow it to the right until you find the first adjusted no-decompression limit in the bottom, blue portion of the box) that is 70 minutes or greater. The number you find is 71. Come up the column vertically until you find the pressure group P. Turn to Table 2 and find where pressure groups S and P intersect by following S from the diagonal slope horizontally and P from the bottom vertically. The interval you find is 0:11 - 0:14. Eleven minutes is the minimum surface interval required to make these two dives safely.

3. First dive: 60 feet/50 mins. Second dive: 50 feet/60 mins. The minimum surface interval is:
   a. 1:26
   b. 1:34
   c. 1:18
   d. 1:34

Answer a. 1:26.
Start on Table 1 and find 50 minutes in the 60-foot column (50 is not there, so you must use 52 minutes). This puts you in pressure group U. Go to Table 3 and find 50 feet on the left side. Follow the 50-foot row horizontally from left to right until you find the first adjusted no-decompression limit (the number in the bottom, blue portion of the box) that is 60 minutes or greater. You find 61 minutes and follow the column up vertically to find pressure group D. On Table 2, find pressure group U on the diagonal and pressure group D at the bottom and find the surface interval where they intersect. At the intersection you find 1:26 - 1:34, so 1 hour and 26 minutes is the minimum surface interval needed to make the two dives safely.

Dive Tables Definitions Review

The following terms have been defined in the previous material on using the Recreational Dive Planner. They are listed here for your convenience and quick reference.

Actual Bottom Time (ABT) — In repetitive diving, the total time actually spent under water (in minutes) from the beginning of descent until leaving the bottom for a direct continuous ascent to the surface or safety stop.

Adjusted No-Decompression Limit — The time limit for a repetitive dive, derived by subtracting the Residual Nitrogen Time from the No-Decompression Limit. Actual Bottom Time should never exceed the adjusted no-decompression limit.

Ascent Rate — The proper speed for ascending, which is no faster than 1 foot per second (60 feet per minute). A rate slower than 1 foot per second is acceptable, and appropriate.

Bottom Time — The time from the beginning of descent until the beginning a direct, continuous ascent to the surface or safety stop.

Decompression Diving — Diving in such a way that a complex and difficult series of stops is required prior to surfacing to avoid decompression sickness. In recreational diving (no-decompression diving), a decompression stop is considered an *emergency* procedure only, and is never an intentional part of the dive plan.

Dive Profile — A drawing of your dive plan, used to avoid confusion and omissions when using the dive tables.

Multilevel Diving — Planning profiles that credit the diver for slower nitrogen absorption as he moves to a shallower depth. This provides more dive time. Only The Wheel version of the Recreational Dive Planner can be used for multilevel diving.

No-Decompression Limit (NDL) — The maximum time that can be spent at a depth before decompression stops are required.

Pressure Group — A letter used on the Recreational Dive Planners to designate the amount of residual nitrogen in your body.

Repetitive Dive — Using the Recreational Dive Planner, a dive made within six hours of a previous dive.

Residual Nitrogen — The higher-than-normal amount of nitrogen remaining in your body after a dive.

Residual Nitrogen Time (RNT) — An amount of nitrogen, expressed in minutes (found on Table 3 by using a pressure group letter), that is added to the actual time of a dive to account for residual nitrogen from a previous dive.

Safety Stop — A stop made at 15 feet for 3 minutes at the end of a dive for additional safety. The safety stop is recommended after all dives (air supply and other considerations allowing), and required on those to 100 feet or greater, and those coming within 3 pressure groups of the no-decompression limit.

Surface Interval — The amount of time spent on the surface between two dives. It is usually recorded in hours:minutes (e.g. 3:25 — 3 hours, 25 minutes).

Total Bottom Time (TBT) — The sum of Residual Nitrogen Time and Actual Bottom Time after a repetitive dive, used on Table 1 to determine the pressure group.

Basic Compass Navigation

Objectives

After reading this section on compass navigation, you will be able to:

1. List two reasons for making a compass standard equipment for every dive.

2. Identify four features of a typical underwater compass.

3. Demonstrate proper hand and arm position when using a compass mounted on the wrist.

4. Demonstrate the proper method of holding a compass when it is mounted in an instrument console.

5. Set an underwater compass for a straight line from the beginning location to a predetermined destination.

6. Set an underwater compass for a reciprocal heading.

In Modules 1 through 4, you learned the importance of underwater navigation. Underwater navigation helps you know where you are, where you've been and where you're going. By carefully planning your dive pattern, you'll be able to surface close to your exit point. You won't have to fight surface currents and you'll have an adequate air supply for your exit.

Use of an underwater compass makes your underwater navigation both easier and more accurate. You will want to have a compass with you on every dive primarily 1) to help you find your dive site under water and 2) to help you find your exit point without surfacing.

Figure 5-11
Use of an underwater compass makes navigation both easier and more accurate.

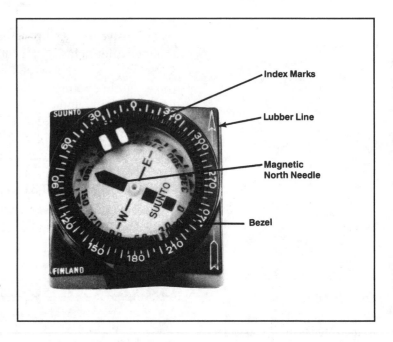

Index Marks

Lubber Line

Magnetic
North Needle

Bezel

Figure 5-12
Basic features of an underwater compass.

There are four basic features you'll find on most under-water compasses:

1. Lubber Line: The *lubber line* is stationary and indicates your direction of travel. It may be found in the center of your compass or just off to one side. Any time you are navigating with your compass, you will be swimming in the same direction as the lubber line.

2. Magnetic North Needle: In the center of the compass is a needle that rotates freely in the watertight capsule of the compass case. This is the *magnetic north needle*, sometimes simply called the *compass needle*, that always points to magnetic north. Because the needle always points to magnetic north, it creates an angle with the lubber line (your direction of travel), that, as you will see, allows you to maintain a straight line as you swim.

3. Bezel: Most underwater compasses come equipped with a rotating bezel. To set the compass, align the two small, parallel index marks on the bezel over the compass needle. These help you maintain a straight direction of travel.

4. Heading References: Many underwater compasses have numbers so you can record your heading (your direction of travel) in degrees of the compass. Others, however, have only general markings for north, south, east and west.

Before you begin actually navigating with a compass, you must hold it correctly. Align the lubber line with the center line of your body. If you wear your compass on your wrist,

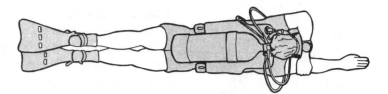

Figure 5-13
Proper positioning with a
wrist-mounted compass.

Figure 5-14
Proper positioning for using a
compass in a console.

lock your arms as in Figure 5-13. If your compass is in your console, hold it as in Figure 5-14. When using your compass, concentrate on keeping the lubber line aligned with your body. Otherwise, your navigation will be inaccurate, even if you use the compass correctly in all other respects.

To navigate a straight line, simply point the lubber line in the direction you want to go and align your body with the lubber line. Hold the compass level (to prevent the needle from locking in place) and allow the needle to "settle down." Next, turn the bezel so the index marks align over the compass needle. (For swimming in a straight line, you don't need to worry about degrees or north, south, east and west.)

Figure 5-15
To set the heading, point the lubber line in the desired direction, then align the index marks over the compass needle.

Now, all you have to do is swim in a straight line along the lubber line (your desired direction of travel) while keeping the compass level and the needle within the index marks. If the needle begins to leave the index marks, you're turning off course. Adjust your direction so the needle stays within the index marks. It helps if you realize that the compass needle never turns — it always points to magnetic

Figure 5-16
To set a reciprocal heading, simply turn
the index marks until they are exactly
opposite the original heading.

north. If the needle appears to have moved, it's you that has moved from the course.

To set the compass for a *reciprocal heading* (that is, to return in the direction you came from), first turn the bezel so the index marks are exactly opposite their original location on the compass face (Figure 5-16). Next, turn your body until the compass needle is within the index marks. You should now be facing in the direction you came from. You can return to your starting point simply by swimming like you did on the way out.

With a little practice, you'll find compass use both easy and useful. For diving in many environments, you'll use the compass to swim out, then set a reciprocal heading to return to the boat or shore at the end of the dive. Because the compass greatly improves navigation, its importance cannot be overemphasized. You can learn more about compass use in the Advanced Open Water Diver course and in specialty courses.

Figure 5-17
Because the compass greatly improves
navigation, its importance cannot be over-
emphasized. You can learn more about
compass use in the Advanced Open Water
Diver course and in specialty courses.

Exercise 5-4

Basic Compass Navigation

1. Check all appropriate responses. A compass should be used on every dive:

    ☐ a. so you and your buddy can split up under water and still find each other near the end of the dive.

    ☐ b. to help you find your dive site under water.   ☐ c. to help you find your exit point without surfacing.

2. On the illustration, identify the labeled feature every compass should have.

    ☐ a. Lubber-line ☐ b. Bezel ☐ c. Magnetic north needle

How did you do? *1.* b, c *2.* a.

Confined-Water Training Preview — Module Five

This is the last confined-water training session of the Open Water Diver course. As in the previous sessions, you'll be learning new skills and practicing ones you've already learned. Read about the skills you'll learn during this confined-water session and become familiar with them as you have done throughout the course. After you've finished this session, you'll be ready to complete your open-water training and become certified as a PADI Open Water Diver.

Performance Requirements
Confined-Water Training — Module Five

By the end of the confined-water training for Module Five, you will be able to:

1. Remove, replace, adjust and secure the scuba unit and weights at the surface with minimal assistance, in water too deep to stand up in.

2. Remove, replace, adjust and secure the scuba unit and weights under water on the bottom with minimal assistance, in water too deep to stand up in.

3. React appropriately to air depletion by giving the out-of-air signal, in water too deep to stand up in.

Weight Belt Handling

There may be occasions when you'll need to remove or replace your weight belt on the surface or under water. Your weight belt may have become tangled with other equipment, you may need to adjust it, or you may need to

Figure 5-18
When working with your weight belt, remember to hold the free end so the weights won't slide off.

Figure 5-19
If you intend to ditch your weight belt, pull it well away from your body before letting go to ensure that it is not caught in any equipment.

discard it in an emergency situation. When entering small boats or climbing onto a platform without a ladder, you typically remove your weight belt to hand up before you get out of the water.

To remove your weight belt, release the buckle with one hand and grasp the free end, pulling it clear of your body. If you intend to ditch the belt, hold it well away from your body to ensure that it is not caught on any equipment before letting go. If you're removing the belt to adjust it, keep it close to your body — holding it away tends to pull you over in the water. Keep in mind that once you release your weight belt, you will be buoyant and will probably begin ascending.

When working with your weight belt, remember to hold on to the free end (the end without the buckle) to keep weights from sliding off. If you're replacing it at the surface, breathe through your regulator so you can maneuver in the water without having to worry about flooding your snorkel. To replace the belt, you can use one of two methods.

To use the first method, position yourself horizontally, facing the surface. Hold the free end of the belt in your right hand. Place the free end with your right hand against your right hip and roll to the left so you're face down. Your weight belt should roll around your hips and fall into place across your waist. Lean forward slightly, and the belt will

Figure 5-20
You may find it easiest to replace your weight belt by rolling it into place.

slide into the small of your back. Check for twists, push any misadjusted weights into place and secure the buckle.

For the second method of donning your weight belt, hold both the free end and the buckle end in one hand so

Figure 5-21
Your BCD and mask may make it difficult to see your weight-belt buckle. Practice operating the buckle by feel, rather than by sight.

Figure 5-22
It's not unusual to remove you scuba unit when entering a boat. When diving from some boats, you may put the unit on when you enter the water, too.

Figure 5-23
The easiest way to remove the scuba unit under water is to swing it off like a sleeveless coat. Be sure to take it off your left arm first.

the belt forms a loop. Position the belt near your back and reach behind with your free hand, taking the belt so both hands have an end. Be sure that your right hand takes the free end and your left hand takes the buckled end so you have a right-hand release when you're done. Once you have an end in each hand, come to a horizontal face-down position so you can drape the belt across the small of your back while you adjust and buckle it.

With either method, you'll probably find that your mask and BCD interfere with seeing the buckle while you're trying to release or fasten it. Practice operating the buckle by touch, rather than by sight.

Removal and Replacement of Scuba Unit

There may be times when you'll want to remove and replace your scuba unit. Under water, your scuba unit may need adjustment or may be slightly entangled and need to be freed. On the surface, you may put your scuba unit on after entering the water and (as you may have already practiced) take it off before exiting. During this confined-water training session, you'll practice removing and replacing your scuba unit both at the surface and under water.

The procedure you follow will depend on the equipment configuration you're using. Under water, if you're using a jacket-style BCD, you may find it easiest to remove and replace your scuba unit like a sleeveless coat. First, be sure you have vented all the air from your BCD so it won't

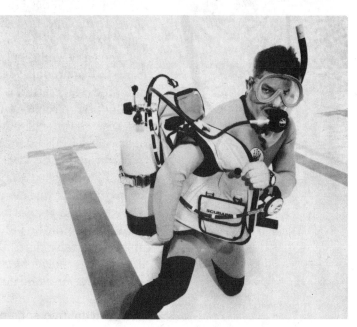

float away when you take it off. Release the waist strap. Then take your left arm out of the BCD, swing it behind you and take it off your right arm. Be sure to start with the *left* arm, or your regulator hose will be stretched — possibly pulling the mouthpiece out of your mouth. You should keep your regulator in your mouth at all times during this procedure.

Once the unit is off, you'll find it easy to handle because scuba tanks weigh very little in water. To replace the jacket-style BCD, hold it upright and be sure the straps are clear,

Figure 5-24
You can replace the unit like you're putting on a sleeveless coat, or . . .

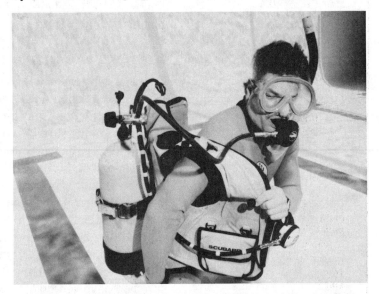

then put it on like a coat, starting with your *right* arm first. Once it's in place, fasten and adjust the waist strap and any other straps.

You can use the same removal method if you're using a front- or back-mounted BCD (if you're using a front-mounted BCD, be sure to disconnect your low-pressure inflator before removing the scuba unit). However, when you *replace* the scuba unit, you may find it easiest to lift it over your head. Lay the unit in front of you, with the valve toward you and the backpack facing up. Be sure any shoulder strap releases are fastened, then put your arms in the straps, up past your elbows. Keep the hose to your mouthpiece between your arms (if it is outside your arms, the mouthpiece may be pulled from your mouth as you don the unit). Next, raise the tank over your head and gently lower the tank into place. Finally, make sure all your hoses and straps are secure and clear before you fasten the waist strap.

Figure 5-25
. . . by lifting it over your head and lowering it into place.

You can follow the same procedure for removing and

Figure 5-26
At the surface, it helps to have
your buddy steady your scuba unit
as you get in and out of it.

Figure 5-27
Jacket-style and back-mounted BCDs are
easiest to get on and off at the surface
when they are only partially inflated.

Figure 5-28
One easy way to don a jacket-style BCD at
the surface is to sit on it, then slide into it.

replacing your scuba unit at the surface as you did under water. At the surface you can also use your BCD for flotation It often helps to have your buddy hold the tank steady and upright in the water while you get in and out of some units. Jacket-style and back-mounted BCDs are easiest to get on and off when they are only partially inflated.

For jacket-style BCDs, a popular donning technique is to sit on the slightly buoyant unit with the tank between your legs. The bottom of the tank should be in front of you, the valve behind you, and the jacket open beneath you. Put your arms into the jacket on each side of you, and then let yourself slip forward. This should cause the jacket to slide into place as you dip downward.

Your instructor will demonstrate the most appropriate methods for removing and replacing the scuba unit for your equipment configuration and diving environment.

Air-Depletion Exercise

Although you should never run out of air if you properly monitor your SPG, you should be able to recognize when your air feels low. When your air supply gets low, inhalation effort greatly increases, warning you to ascend.

To simulate low air, your instructor will move in front of you and slowly turn your air off as you breathe. You'll feel a

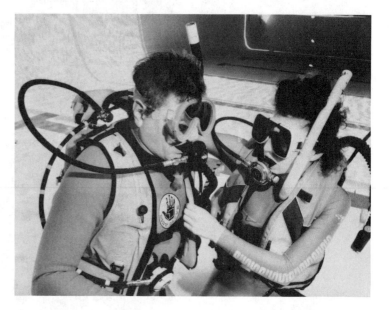

Figure 5-29
Your instructor will simulate low air by slowly turning your air off as you breathe.

gradual increase in breathing effort until you have great difficulty inhaling. At that point, signal out-of-air, and your

Figure 5-30
When you feel difficulty breathing, signal your instructor and he will immediately restore airflow.

instructor will immediately turn your air back on so you can resume normal breathing.

Naturally, an out-of-air situation is to be avoided by providing yourself with ample reserve air. You may need this air to retrieve a dropped object after surfacing, and to avoid damage that can result from water entering an empty scuba tank. Plan to surface with at least 300 psi in your tank. With proper planning, you should be able to make a slow, comfortable ascent, a 3-minute safety stop at 15 feet, and reach the surface with 300 psi. This is one of the marks of a good diver.

Summary

You are now ready for the confined-water training session for Module Five. The new skills you will be practicing are:

1. Weight-belt handling
2. Removal and replacement of scuba unit
3. Air-depletion exercise

Open Water Training Preview — Dives 4 and 5

Open Water Training Dives 4 and 5 mark the end of the Open Water Diver course, but the beginning of your enjoyment of the underwater world as a certified diver. These training dives will be fun, and like dives 1, 2 and 3, you will be practicing skills you learned during confined-water training, as well as some open-water skills.

This section introduces some of the procedures and skills you will be practicing in these two dives. Your instructor will decide on the sequence of the skills in each dive, based on your local diving environment. Before each dive, your instructor will inform you about the sequence and procedures for the dive, along with other important details such as communication signals, environmental orientation and emergency procedures.

Become familiar with the material listed in this section so your open-water training will go smoothly and enjoyably. Remember, you'll only be asked to perform skills you have already practiced and refined in your confined-water training sessions. After these dives, you'll be a PADI Open Water Diver.

Figure 5-31
Becoming a PADI Open Water Diver opens the door to a broad new world, and though you've learned a great deal so far, there is still much more to learn.

Open Water Training Dive 4
Performance Requirements

By completing Open Water Training Dive 4, you will be able to:

1. Perform a 50-yard surface snorkel swim in a straight line, keeping the head down and using a compass reference.

2. Clear water from the snorkel at the surface and resume breathing through the snorkel without removing the snorkel from the mouth.

3. Alternately breathe between snorkel and regulator at the surface without lifting the face from the water.

4. Perform a free descent to a depth of 20-30 feet with no visual reference.

5. Clear a mask that has been completely flooded.

6. Achieve and maintain neutral buoyancy under water.

7. Buddy breathe in a stationary position.

8. Perform a buddy-breathing ascent from a depth of 20-30 feet.

9. Tour under water for experience and pleasure under the instructor's direct or indirect supervision.

10. Remove and replace the scuba unit and weight belt at the surface, in water too deep to stand up in.

11. Demonstrate proper equipment care, dive logging and use of dive tables.

Dive Overview

- Briefing
- Equipment preparation
- Suiting up
- Entry
- 50-yard surface swim in a straight line with compass (Diver A out/ Diver B back)
- Snorkel/regulator exchange
- Free descent without reference
- Buoyancy control — Neutral buoyancy on bottom
- Clear flooded mask
- Buddy breathing (stationary)
- Buddy-breathing ascent
- Underwater tour for pleasure and experience
- Remove/replace scuba unit and weight belt at the surface
- Exit
- Debriefing and dive logging

Open Water Training Dive 5
Performance Requirements

By completing Open Water Training Dive 5, you will be able to:

1. Perform a free descent with no reference to a depth no greater than 60 feet.

2. Perform a navigation swim with a compass under water. Each diver navigates out and back.

3. Remove and replace the mask under water.

4. Achieve neutral buoyancy under water and hover in mid-water without swimming.

5. Tour under water for pleasure and experience.

6. Demonstrate proper equipment care, dive logging and use of dive tables.

Dive Overview

- Briefing
- Equipment preparation
- Suiting up
- Entry
- Free descent
- Underwater navigation with compass
- Remove/replace mask under water
- Neutral buoyancy — hovering
- Underwater tour for pleasure and experience
- Exit
- Debriefing and dive logging

Continuing Education

You're not far from being certified as a PADI Open Water Diver and by now, you've already begun to see the fun and adventure diving offers. As an Open Water Diver, you'll

Figure 5-32
The majority of the courses in the PADI Continuing Education program emphasize enjoyable learning in the actual diving environment. You'll not only be learning while diving, but making new friends, too.

have fun diving in conditions and environments similar to those you did your open-water training dives in.

Before long, you'll want to learn more about diving, meet more divers and participate in specialized diving activities. By becoming a PADI Open Water Diver, you've opened the door to a broad new world, and though you've learned a great deal so far, there is still much more to learn.

The PADI Continuing Education Program

Objectives

After reading this section on the PADI Continuing Education program, you will be able to:

1. State the purpose of the PADI Continuing Education program.

2. List three reasons why a diver should continue his education after he becomes certified as a PADI Open Water Diver.

The PADI Continuing Education program lets you participate in many new aspects of diving. Under the supervision of a professional PADI Instructor, you'll have fun as you develop specialized diving skills and knowledge.

The courses you'll take are even more fun than the Open Water Diver course. The majority of the courses in the PADI Continuing Education program emphasize enjoyable, practical learning in the actual diving environment while minimizing pool and classroom time. In most of the continuing education courses, you'll learn as you dive, explore new environments and make new friends.

Continuing education courses let you safely and confidently:

1. Participate in many fun, specialized diving activities,

Figure 5-33
Continuing education courses let you safely and confidently participate in specialized activities, such as diving at night, diving on shipwrecks, diving to deeper depths, taking underwater photographs and more.

such as diving at night, diving on shipwrecks, diving to deeper depths, taking underwater photographs and more.

2. Dive in conditions less ideal than those you are qualified for as an Open Water Diver.

3. Dive in a wider variety of aquatic environments.

Your next step: the PADI Advanced Open Water program.

Advanced Open Water Program

Following certification as an Open Water Diver, the Advanced Open Water program is your next step. With two options, it's one of the most fun and rewarding courses in the entire PADI System of continuing education!

The Advanced Open Water program continues your open water training, with minimal classroom and pool training. You'll want to enroll immediately after finishing your Open Water Diver course. Besides allowing you to dive more, it gives you additional skills and supervised experience. It also is a prerequisite for other PADI courses.

This program actually consists of two courses: the PADI Advanced Open Water Diver course and the PADI Advanced Plus course. Both courses develop your underwater skills and give you a taste of specialty diving activities, but the scope and duration of each varies to accommodate different interests.

In either course, you will make three "core" or required dives — a navigation, night and deep dive. You will also

Objectives

After reading this section on the Advanced Open Water Diver course, you will be able to:

1. State two reasons why the Advanced Open Water Diver course should be taken immediately following certification as an Open Water Diver.

2. Name the three "core" specialty diving experiences introduced in the Advanced Open Water program.

Night Diver

Deep Diver

Underwater Navigator

Figure 5-34
Your next step is the Advanced Open Water program. It will introduce you to the most popular special diving activities.

make "elective" dives that you choose with the guidance of your PADI Instructor. Elective dives include altitude, boat, drift, dry suit, multilevel, peak performance buoyancy, search and recovery, underwater naturalist, underwater photography and wreck dives. The number of elective dives you make depends upon you interest and whether you are taking the Advanced Open Water Diver or the Advanced Plus course.

Each dive of your Advanced program may count toward your certification in corresponding specialty courses at the discretion of your instructor.

Objectives

After reading this section on Discover Local Diving, you will be able to:

1. State the purpose of Discover Local Diving.

Discover Local Diving

In the Open Water Diver course, you've learned how important it is, regardless of your certification level, to get an orientation when you're going to dive in an unfamiliar location or participate in a new diving activity. The Discover Local Diving experience exists to provide you with a single, supervised open-water experience to a new diving area.

Discover Local Diving includes a briefing covering local

Figure 5-35
The PADI Discover Local Diving experience includes a briefing covering local conditions, hazards and points of interest.

conditions, hazards and points of interest, as well as an orientation to special procedures and techniques used in the area. During the dive, you'll be shown some of the interesting points, as well as the potential hazards to avoid. After the dive, there's a debriefing to discuss what you saw and the procedures you used. Discover Local Diving contains no specific skill evaluation other than a general assessment of your diving ability as it applies to the specific environment.

Objectives

After reading this section on PADI Scuba Review, you will be able to:

1. Explain when a diver should take a Scuba Review experience.

Figure 5-36
Scuba Review provides a quick, enjoyable way to update and improve your diving skills.

Figure 5-37
The Rescue Diver course refines your ability to prevent problems and develops the skills you need to respond to a diving emergency.

Scuba Review

If you go several months or longer without diving, you'll probably need to brush up on your diving skills and knowledge. The Scuba Review experience is quick, enjoyable and easy. It is designed to update and improve your knowledge and skills.

In Scuba Review, you update your knowledge by completing a self-study workbook and reviewing it with a PADI Instructor. Then you participate in a skills-review session in confined water, during which your instructor will assess and help you improve your diving skills. Upon successful completion of Scuba Review, your instructor will affix a decal to your certification card showing that you have refreshed your diving skills.

Rescue Diver Course

In the section on problem management in Module Three, you learned that the Rescue Diver course is an important

step in being prepared to deal with diving problems. Upon completion of the Advanced Open Water Diver course, you'll be qualified to take the Rescue Diver course.

As discussed in Module Three during the Rescue Diver course, you'll refine your ability to prevent problems and develop the specific skills you need to respond to a diving emergency. The PADI Rescue Diver course may be one of the most important and rewarding steps in your growth as a diver.

Medic First Aid

You also learned in Module Three about the importance of being qualified in CPR and first aid. Medic First Aid combines both of these disciplines into a single course, teaching

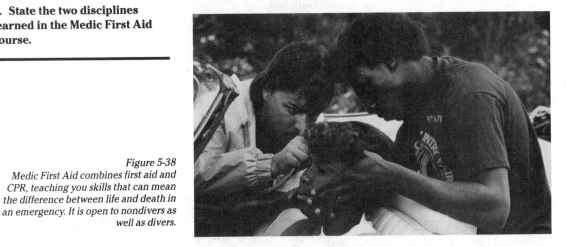

Figure 5-38
Medic First Aid combines first aid and CPR, teaching you skills that can mean the difference between life and death in an emergency. It is open to nondivers as well as divers.

you (at a layman's level) the same emergency techniques used by paramedics and doctors.

Medic First Aid teaches you the skills that can mean the difference between life and death. The Medic First Aid program is open to nondivers as well as divers, and is one course that can make a difference even when you're not diving.

Specialty Diver Courses

Some of the most fun in diving comes from taking PADI Specialty Diver courses. There is a wide variety of standard PADI Specialty Diver courses, as well as Distinctive Specialty courses your PADI Instructor or Dive Center may offer.

The most appropriate specialties for you to take in the near future are those that interest you the most. Here are the standard PADI Specialty Diver courses:

See *The Encyclopedia of Recreational Diving*

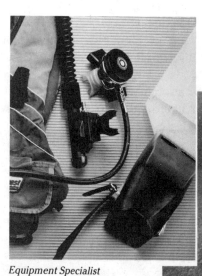

Equipment Specialist

Figure 5-39
*The most appropriate specialties to take
are those that interest you most.*

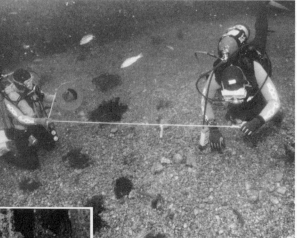

Search and Recovery Diver

Underwater Photographer

Wreck Diver

Underwater Photographer	Ice Diver
Night Diver	Cavern Diver
Deep Diver	Altitude Diver
Wreck Diver	Boat Diver
Equipment Specialist	Drift Diver
Search and Recovery Diver	Dry Suit Diver
Underwater Hunter	Multilevel Diver
Underwater Navigator	Underwater Naturalist
Research Diver	Peak Performance Buoyancy

Master Scuba Diver

As you learn more about diving and progress through the Continuing Education program, you will be able to attain the *PADI Master Scuba Diver* rating. This is the highest nonprofessional rating you can reach in recreational diving.

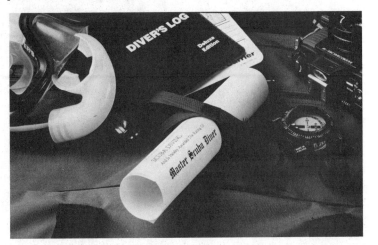

Figure 5-40
The PADI Master Scuba Diver rating is the highest nonprofessional rating in recreational diving. It is a mark of distinction that denotes high achievement.

This prestigious rating means you've developed skills and experience in a broad number of diving specialties and environments.

The PADI Master Scuba Diver rating is a mark of distinction that denotes high achievement. To qualify for this rating, you will need to either 1) become a PADI Advanced Open Water Diver, a PADI Rescue Diver and earn five PADI Specialty Diver ratings or 2) become a PADI Divemaster (the first level in becoming a professional) and earn five PADI Specialty Diver ratings.

Becoming a Professional

At some point, you may decide to make diving a profession. In this case, you'll want to look at the opportunities, recognition and satisfaction you can have as a PADI professional.

After becoming a PADI Rescue Diver, your next step is to become qualified as a PADI Divemaster. During the Divemaster course, you'll sharpen your diving skills to demonstration quality, gain a professional-level understanding of diving theory, learn how to organize and conduct diving activities, and learn how to supervise divers in training.

After becoming a Divemaster, your next step is to enroll in a PADI Assistant Instructor course or to enroll immediately in an Instructor Development Course (IDC —

Figure 5-41
Becoming a PADI Open Water Scuba
Instructor requires effort and commit-
ment, but if you're interested in diving as
a full- or part-time profession, every step
of the way is enjoyable and rewarding.

more about this later). The Assistant Instructor course gives you hands-on teaching experience with student divers under the direct supervision of a qualified PADI Instructor. The practical knowledge you gain as an Assistant Instructor will help you in becoming a full instructor.

Next, you attend a PADI Instructor Development Course (IDC). In this instructor-training course, you learn to teach people to scuba dive. After completing the IDC, you must pass a two-day Instructor Examination (IE) conducted by PADI Headquarters. Upon successful completion of the IE, you're certified as a qualified PADI Open Water Scuba Instructor.

Although it takes effort and commitment to become a PADI Open Water Scuba Instructor, every step of the way is enjoyable and rewarding when you are interested in making diving a full- or part-time profession.

Epilogue

By successfully completing the PADI Open Water Diver course, you have demonstrated your competence as a beginning diver. To help you remember some of the key points you've learned, review the safe diving practices outlined following this epilogue. You'll find the review organized into sections on diving preparation, pre-dive, diving and general diving safety practices.

As you begin diving and start into your Advanced Open Water Diver course, you'll discover that diving can be a life-long adventure, just as it has been for millions of diving enthusiasts. For many, diving has changed the course of their lives as their underwater experiences have shown them new worlds of adventure, fascination and beauty. May your diving opportunities bring you enjoyment, satisfaction, friendships and lasting memories.

Figure 5-42
For many, diving has changed the course of their lives as their underwater experiences have shown them new worlds of adventure, fascination and beauty.

Summary of Diving Safety Practices

The following summary of diving safety practices will help you remember important points of this course. Refer to this summary from time to time to refresh your memory on diving safety practices.

Preparation

1. Stay healthy and fit for diving. Eat right, exercise regularly and get adequate rest.

2. Have approval for diving from a physician who has given you a thorough medical examination and have one every two years.

3. Be recently trained in first aid and cardiopulmonary resuscitation (CPR). To acquire training in these areas, take the Medic First Aid course offered by PADI Instructors and Dive Centers.

4. Maintain your diving skills by diving as often as you can and continuing your diver education. Take the PADI Scuba Review experience after long periods of inactivity.

5. Get an orientation to new diving conditions, activities or areas. When planning a dive in a new, unfamiliar area, it is highly recommended that you participate in a Discover Local Diving experience. Remember that you should have special training for some activities.

6. Always have and use *all* the equipment needed for local diving conditions.

7. Have scuba equipment serviced annually. Have scuba tanks visually inspected regularly and pressure tested at required intervals. Maintain your equipment in good condition and inspect it before diving.

8. Only fill scuba tanks with pure, dry compressed air from reputable air stations.

Predive

1. Dive only when feeling well, both physically and mentally. Have a confident feeling about the dive. Be sure the dive and its activities are within your capabilities. Remember — diving is supposed to be fun. If you don't think it will be safe or fun, don't make the dive.

2. Know the dive site. Be familiar with the conditions and any possible hazards.

3. Check the weather forecast before leaving. Evaluate the diving conditions, those present and expected, and dive only when the conditions are as good or better than those you were trained in. Avoid diving when conditions are unfavorable.

4. Refrain from alcohol, smoking or dangerous drugs before or immediately after diving.

5. Plan your dives with your buddy. Agree on objectives, direction, and depth and time limits. Review underwater communications, emergency procedures and what to do if you become separated.

6. Always plan for no-decompression diving. Consult the Recreational Dive Planner and allow for a margin of safety. Avoid diving to the maximum time limits. Make your deepest dive of the day first. Know how to perform an emergency decompression stop, but avoid having to do so. Plan to make safety stops whenever possible. Be aware of the effects of flying after diving and diving at altitudes greater than 1000 feet.

7. Inspect both your and your buddy's equipment. Know how to operate each other's equipment. Always conduct the PADI Predive Safety Check: *Begin With Review And Friend.*

8. Be prepared for emergencies. Have local emergency contact information on hand, just in case.

Diving

1. Properly weight yourself for neutral buoyancy. Check your buoyancy at the surface and avoid being over-weighted.

2. Always wear a proper buoyancy control device (BCD). Use your buoyancy control device to regulate your buoyancy. Avoid contact with the bottom by being neutrally buoyant — for your benefit and the benefit of the aquatic environment. Inflate your BCD at the surface to provide ample positive buoyancy.

3. Display the dive flag and stay near it.

4. Begin dives against the current or take into consideration the effect the current will have during the dive. Plan your dive so you don't have to fight the current to reach your exit point.

5. Equalize pressure early and often during descents. If you feel discomfort in a body air space, ascend until the discomfort goes away, equalize, then continue the dive. If unable to equalize, abort the dive.

6. Remain with your buddy throughout the dive. Know how to reunite if you accidentally become separated.

7. Limit your depth to 60 feet or less. Remember that 60 feet is the recommended limit for new divers. Shallower diving conserves your air, increases your bottom time and helps reduce the risk of decompression sickness.

8. Treat spear guns as dangerous weapons. Never load them out of water and always unload them before leaving the water.

9. Avoid contact with unfamiliar aquatic plants and animals.

10. Be alert for possible problems and avoid them. Check your equipment frequently while under water, especially your gauges: depth gauge, timing device and submersible pressure gauge.

11. Exit the water with a minimum of 300 psi in your tank.

12. Pace yourself. Avoid overexertion and breathlessness. If you become breathless, stop, rest and recover before proceeding.

13. Breathe properly — slowly, deeply and continuously. Never hold your breath while scuba diving. Exhale slowly and continuously any time the regulator is not in your

mouth. Avoid excessive hyperventilation when skin (breath-hold) diving.

14. In an emergency, stop, think, get control and then take action. Act, don't react.

15. Ascend carefully and correctly. Reach up and look up during the ascent. Come up no faster than 60 feet per minute. Plan a 3-minute safety stop at 15 feet whenever possible. Listen for boats as you come up, and establish buoyancy as soon as you reach the surface. Be a S.A.F.E. Diver.

16. Stop diving when you're cold or tired. Don't overextend yourself.

17. Stick to your dive plan under water. Don't revise a dive plan under water.

General Diving Safety Practices

1. Be an active diver. Dive frequently to maintain your proficiency.

2. Build your experience and capabilities gradually under safe conditions.

3. Keep a log of your diving activities. This record of your training and experience is a valuable reference for future dives.

4. Don't lend your equipment to untrained persons. Never attempt to teach another person how to dive. Teaching diving requires a high degree of specialized training and skill. Leave instruction to trained professionals.

5. Continue your diving education. Remember that a good diver never stops learning.

Appendix

260   PADI Dive Planning Checklist

261   PADI Open Water Equipment Checklist

262   PADI Boat Diving Information Sheet

263   English-Metric Conversions

265   PADI Local Area Offices Worldwide

266   About PADI Dive Centres

267   ACE/Student Transcript Request

269   Divers Alert Network

 **DAN, Your Dive Safety Association**
FOR EMERGENCIES CALL
(919) 684-8111
24 hours   7 days a week

Further Reading*

Auerbach, P.S. (1987). *A Medical Guide To Hazardous Marine Life.* Progressive Printing Co., Inc.

PADI (1988). *The Encyclopedia of Recreational Diving.* International PADI, Inc.

Scarr, D. (1988). *Touch The Sea.* International PADI, Inc.

These books are available through a PADI Dive Center or PADI Instructor. For your FREE PADI Dive Center directory, write: PADI, 1251 East Dyer Road #100, Santa Ana, CA 92705-5605 USA

PADI DIVE PLANNING CHECKLIST

Advance Planning:

_____ Dive buddy(s) _____

_____ Date and time (Check tide tables) _____

_____ Dive objective _____

_____ Location_____

_____ Alternate location(s) _____

_____ Directions _____

_____

_____ Meeting place and time_____

_____ Any special or extra gear needed _____

_____ Pre-check of weather and water conditions

Preparation:

_____ Tank(s) filled	_____ Equipment packed
_____ Equipment inspected	_____ Fishing license current
_____ Equipment marked (ID)	_____ Transportation arranged
_____ Spare parts inventoried	_____ Obtain information on new location
_____ Weights adjusted	_____ Get local emergency contact information

Last Minute:

_____ Make sure you are healthy, rested, and nourished.

_____ Have a good, confident feeling about the dive.

_____ Check weather and water conditions.

_____ Make a final inventory of all needed items.

_____ Leave dive plan information with someone _not_ going (dive site, expected return time, what to do if you do not report back by agreed time, etc.).

_____ Pack food, snacks, drinks.

_____ Be sure you have: _____ Ticket _____ Money _____ Medications _____ Directions
_____ Swim Suit _____ Towel _____ Jacket _____ Sunglasses Other _____

Pre-Dive Planning

_____ Evaluate conditions, decide whether or not to dive.

_____ Locate and check nearest communications (telephone, radio).

_____ Select entry/exit points, alternates, methods.

_____ Discuss buddy system techniques.

_____ Agree on: _____ pattern or course for the dive.

_____ limits for the dive (depth, time, minimum air).

_____ emergency procedures.

Problems? Call_____or_____

PADI OPEN WATER EQUIPMENT CHECKLIST

Basic Equipment:
- ☐ Gear Bag
- ☐ Fins, Mask, Snorkel,
  Wet Suit:
  - ☐ Jacket
  - ☐ Pants
  - ☐ Vest
  - ☐ Hood
  - ☐ Boots
  - ☐ Gloves
- ☐ Weight Belt
- ☐ Buoyancy Control Device
- ☐ Tank (Filled)
- ☐ Backpack
- ☐ Regulator (with SPG & Alternate
- ☐ Compass   Air Source)
- ☐ Depth Gauge
- ☐ Knife
- ☐ Watch

Accessory Equipment:
- ☐ Float & Flag
- ☐ Thermometer
- ☐ Game Bag
- ☐ Abalone Iron
- ☐ Measuring Device
- ☐ Dive Light
- ☐ Slate and Pencil
- ☐ Marker Buoy
- ☐ Buddy Line
- ☐ Camera, Film
- ☐ Spear
- ☐ Lift Bag

Spare Equipment:
- ☐ Tanks
- ☐ Weights
- ☐ Straps
- ☐ O-Ring
- ☐ Tools
- ☐ CO_2 Cartridges
- ☐ Suit Cement
- ☐ Regulator HP Plug
- ☐ Bulbs, Batteries
- ☐ Nylon Line

Personal Items:
- ☐ Swimsuit
- ☐ Towel
- ☐ Jacket
- ☐ Extra Clothes
- ☐ Fishing License
- ☐ Tickets
- ☐ Money
- ☐ Certification Card
- ☐ Log Book
- ☐ Dive Tables
- ☐ Sunglasses
- ☐ Suntan Lotion
- ☐ Medications
- ☐ Toilet Articles
- ☐ Lunch, Thermos
- ☐ Ice Chest
- ☐ Fillet Knife
- ☐ Eating Utensils
- ☐ Sleeping Bag

PADI BOAT DIVING INFORMATION SHEET

Date of trip _____ Name of vessel _____

Landing _____ City _____

Directions _____

Destination _____ Cost _____

Departure time _____ Estimated return time _____

Items needed:

_____ Diving equipment	_____ Suntan lotion
_____ Gear bag	_____ Medication
_____ Extra tank	_____ Ticket
_____ Warm clothes	_____ Money
_____ Jacket	_____ Lunch, snacks
_____ Towel	_____ Drinks

Terminology:

Bow:	Front end of the boat
Stern:	Rear end of the boat
Port:	Left side of the boat when facing bow
Starboard:	Right side of the boat when facing bow
Bridge:	Wheelhouse, vessel control area
Leeward:	The downwind side, sheltered side
Windward:	Side facing into the wind; windy side
Galley:	Kitchen
Head:	Restroom

Instructions:

1. Double-check to be sure you have all required equipment and needed items.
2. Board vessel at least one half hour prior to departure time.
3. Ask crew where and how to stow your gear.
4. Place clothes, cameras, lunch, and all items to be kept dry, inside and all diving equipment outside, on the deck.
5. Wait in the stern area for pre-departure briefing.
6. Keep dockside rail clear during docking operations.
7. If susceptible to seasickness, take medication prior to departure.
8. If seasick, use the leeward rail, not the head.
9. Learn toilet operation and rules before using head.
10. Stay off the bow during anchoring operations.
11. Work out of your gear bag. No loose gear on deck.
12. Check out and check in with the divemaster for all dives.
13. Pack and stow all gear before return trip.
14. Be available for *visual* roll call before boat is moved.
15. Check to be sure nothing is left behind when disembarking.

Rules:

1. No trash or litter overboard. Use trash cans.
2. Bridge and engine room are off-limits.
3. Do not sit on the rails when underway.
4. Follow the instructions of the crew.

ENGLISH-METRIC CONVERSIONS

At some time or other, divers will find themselves struggling to convert cubic feet into cubic centimeters, or a similar conversion. The following figures will help you:

Length

1 inch	=	2.540 centimeters
1 foot	=	0.304 meters
1 yard	=	0.914 meters
1 fathom	=	1.828 meters or 6.0 feet
1 statute mile (5280 feet)	=	1.609 kilometers
1 nautical mile (6080 feet)	=	1.853 kilometers
1 centimeter	=	0.393 inches
1 meter	=	3.280 feet
1 meter	=	1.093 yards
1 meter	=	0.546 fathoms
1 kilometer	=	0.621 statute miles
1 kilometer	=	0.539 nautical miles

Capacity

1 cubic inch	=	16.378 cubic centimeters
1 cubic foot	=	0.028 cubic meters
1 cubic foot	=	28.317 liters
1 cubic yard	=	0.764 cubic meters
1 pint	=	0.568 liters
1 gallon	=	4.546 liters
1 cubic centimeter	=	0.061 cubic feet
1 cubic meter	=	35.314 cubic feet
1 cubic meter	=	1.308 cubic yards
1 liter (1000 cc)	=	0.035 cubic feet
1 liter	=	0.220 gallons
1 liter	=	1.760 pints

Weight

1 ounce	=	28.349 grams
1 pound	=	0.454 kilograms
1 long ton	=	1.016 metric tons
1 long ton	=	1.016 kilograms
1 kilogram	=	2.205 pounds
1 metric ton	=	0.984 long tons
1 metric ton	=	2,205 pounds

PRESSURE

1 pound per square inch	=	0.073 kilograms per square centimeter
1 kilogram per square centimeter	=	14.223 pounds per square inch
1 atmosphere	=	14.7 pounds per square inch
1 atmosphere	=	1.033 kilograms per square centimeter

ENGLISH-METRIC CONVERSIONS (CONTINUED)

WATER

1 cubic foot of fresh water weighs 62.5 pounds approx.
1 cubic foot of average salt water weighs 64 pounds approx.
1 gallon of water weighs 8 pounds approx.

TEMPERATURE

To convert degrees Fahrenheit to degrees Centigrade, deduct 32 and multiply by 5/9.
To convert degrees Centigrade to degrees Fahrenheit, multiply by 9/5 and add 32.

CONVERSIONS (APPROXIMATE)

Miles to kilometers .... multiply by 8/5
Kilometers to miles .... multiply by 5/8
Statute miles to nautical miles .... deduct 1/8
Nautical miles to statute miles .... add 1/7
Pounds per square inch (psi) to atmospheres .... divide by 14.7
Atmospheres or bars to kilos per square centimeter ..... nearly the same
Water depth (feet) to bars absolute .... divide by 33 and add 1 bar
Water depth (meters) to bars absolute .... divide by 10 and add 1 bar
Bars absolute to feet of water depth .... subtract 1 bar and multiply by 33
Bars absolute to meters of water depth .... subtract 1 bar and multiply by 10

WIND: DIRECTION, SPEED AND MEASUREMENT

Direction   Wind direction is always specified as the direction from which the wind blows. (A westerly wind blows from west to east.)

Speed   Wind speed is expressed in knots (nautical miles per hour) by mariners and airmen and in miles per hour by landsmen and coastal navigators.

Conversions	1 knot	=	1.7 feet per second approx.
		=	0.51 meters per second approx.
	1 mile per hour	=	1-1/2 feet per second approx.
		=	1.609 kilometers per hour approx.
	1 foot per second	=	2/3 miles per hour approx.
		=	0.3 meters per second approx.
	1 kilometer per hour	=	5/8 miles per hour approx.
	1 meter per second	=	3-1/3 feet per second approx.

PADI LOCAL AREA OFFICES WORLDWIDE

PADI International
1251 East Dyer Road #, Santa Ana, CA 92705-5605, U.S.A.
Phone: (714) 540-7234 • FAX: (714) 540-2609
PADI International services all countries not listed below under Local Area Offices.

PADI Australia
PO Box 713 Willoughby
New South Wales 2068, Australia
Phone: 61-2-417-2800, FAX: 61-2-417-1434
PADI Australia services: Australia, Fiji, Papua New Guinea, Solomon Islands and Vanuatu

PADI Canada
#3-10114 McDonald Park Road, RR#3
Sidney, B.C., Canada V8L 3X9
Phone: (604) 656-7234, FAX #(604) 656-6221
PADI Canada services: Canada

PADI Europe
Oberwilerstrasse 3
CH-8442 Hettlingen, Switzerland
Phone: 41-52-392727, FAX: 41-52-391887
PADI Europe services: Austria, Belguim, France, Israel, Italy, Lietchenstein, Luxembourg, Republic of Maldives, Monaco, Netherlands, Portugal, Spain, Switzerland, Germany and all republics of former Yugoslavia

PADI Japan
1-20-1 Ebisu-Minami
Shibuya-ku, Tokyo 150, Japan
Phone: 813-57211731, FAX: 813-57211735
PADI Japan services: Japan including Okinawa

PADI New Zealand
NZUA Commercial, Ltd.
Corner of Shaw and Collins Streets, Morningside, P.O. Box 875
Auckland, New Zealand
Phone: 64-9-8495456, FAX: 64-9-8497051
PADI New Zealand services: New Zealand, Cook Islands, New Caledonia, Niue, Tonga, American and Western Samoa and French Polynesia

PADI Norway
Waldemar Thranesgt. 84 B OPPG.C
0175 Oslo 1, Norway
Phone: 47-22-380259/47-22-380281, FAX: 47-22-380301,
PADI Norway services: Norway and Denmark

PADI Sweden
Gullbergs Strandgata 36D
411 04 Goteborg, Sweden
Phone: 46-31-159800, FAX: 46-31-153200
PADI Sweden services: Sweden and Finland

WHAT IS A PADI DIVE CENTER?

Besides offering the finest in dive instruction, your PADI Dive Center provides first-class sales and service. Whether you need dive equipment, dive travel arrangements or any number of recreational dive services, your PADI Dive Center is the place to go, PADI Dive Centers have different designation. The following explains what they offer and how they differ.

What is a PADI Dive Center? A PADI Dive Center is a dive store and training facility that is a member of the largest dive retail association in the world — the PADI Retail Association. There are more than 2500 PADI Dive Centers worldwide.

What distinguishes a PADI Dive Center from other dive stores? For a dive store to qualify as a PADI Dive Center, it must be a full-service facility, providing diver education, equipment sales and maintenance, travel, and other related services. PADI certification programs must be taught by certified PADI Instructors. The store must offer quality, tested compressed air for scuba tanks, along with a full line of dive rentals to meet your diving needs.

What is a 5 Star Dive Center? Select retailers who have achieved excellence in scuba training, sales and service may qualify as PADI 5 Star Dive Centers. To attain this prestigious rating, 5 Star Dive Centers must meet the highest standards of educational proficiency and business conduct, reach out to its community with regularly scheduled and publicized dive activities and organize special programs that benefit the public. Raising money for the Muscular Dystrophy Association and organizing environmental cleanups to improve local beaches are examples of the kinds of activities PADI 5 Star Dive Centers have conducted.

A PADI 5 Star Instructor Development Center is a Dive Center that has met the additional requirements necessary to be able to train PADI Instructors. A 5 Star Instructor Development Center must have a PADI Course Director on staff. The PADI Course Director is the highest rated instructor in the PADI System and is able to conduct the PADI Instructor Development Course, prerequisite training for the PADI Instructor Examination.

See your yellow pages for the PADI Dive Center nearest you. For a free complete listing of PADI Dive Centers, write to PADI, 1251 East Dyer Road #100, Santa Ana, CA 92705-5605 USA

Receive College Credit for PADI Diver-Training Courses

The American Council on Education (ACE) recommends college credit for certain PADI scuba diver courses. ACE represents all colleges and universities before the U.S. federal government and as such is the unified voice of higher education. ACE evaluates educational courses according to established college-level criteria and recommends college credit for those that measure up to these standards.

The ACE credit recommendations for PADI courses may help you in receiving college credit at an American university or college – *even if the courses aren't conducted on a university or college campus.* Courses offered through PADI Dive Centers, Resorts and other locations qualify.

Take a Course – Use the Credit
A university or college may use the ACE credit recommendations in a variety of ways. The institution may apply the credit to your major replacing a required course. They may also use the credit as a general elective to possibly waive a prerequisite course.

College Credit at No Extra Charge
Universities and colleges that accept ACE credit recommendations for PADI courses typically handle them like transfer credit. Transfer credit is often awarded without an additional fee. This may save you tuition fees while at the same time allowing you to possibly meet graduation requirements.

How Much College Credit Can I Earn?
ACE has set forth the following college credit recommendations for PADI Courses:

Course	Semester Credit Hours	Division*	Instructional Area
Open Water Diver	1	Lower	Recreation/Physical Education
Night Diver	1	Lower	Recreation/Physical Education
Advanced Open Water Diver and Advanced Plus	1	Lower	Recreation/Physical Education
Deep Diver	1	Lower	Recreation/Physical Education
Rescue Diver	1	Lower	Recreation/Physical Education
Divemaster	2	Lower	Recreation/Physical Education
IDC	2	Upper	Recreation/Physical Education or Education
Course Director Training Course	3	Upper	Recreation/Physical Education or Education

*Lower - Typically Freshman/Sophomore Level; Upper - Typically Junior/Senior Level

Ordering an Official PADI Transcript
To secure credit for a PADI course at a college or university you need an official transcript as proof of course completion. *Colleges and universities will not accept certification cards or wall certificates as proof of course completion.* PADI will send your transcript directly to you or the college or university you are currently attending or planning to attend. It is recommended that you also order a transcript for your own records. To order an official transcript, complete the application on the next page and enclose the indicated processing fee.

PADI Student Transcript Request

Mail This Request To:
Office of Academic Transcripts
PADI International, Inc.
1251 E. Dyer Rd. #100, Santa Ana, CA 92705-5605

Personal Information – (Please Type or Print Clearly)

Student Name _____

Student Mailing Address _____

City _____ State/Province _____

Country _____ Zip Code _____

Phone (____) _____ FAX (____) _____

Birth Date _____ Sex ☐ M ☐ F Social Security Number _____ _____ _____

Transcript Mailing Information

☐ Self Mail _____ transcript(s) to address indicated in Personal Information section.

☐ College or University – One transcript will be sent to the institution listed below.

Name of Institution _____

Address _____

City _____ State/Province _____

Country_____ Zip Code_____

Note: If you need transcripts sent to more than two institutions, please include the addresses on an additional sheet of paper. All transcripts sent to a college or university are addressed to the Registrar's Office.

Transcript Fee

Please include $15 for the first transcript and $5 for each additional transcript ordered.

Payment Method

☐ I am requesting _____ transcript(s) at $15 for the first and $5 for each additional.

Total Enclosed $ _____

Check (Must be payable to PADI International in U.S. Dollars and drawn on a U.S. Bank.)

☐ MasterCard ☐ VISA Card No. _____ _____ _____ _____

Expiration Date _____

Cardholder Name (please print) _____

Authorized Signature _____

Verification of Certification — Please Read Carefully

For **each** recognized PADI course you want to have listed on your transcript, you must submit proof of course completion by one of the two following methods: 1) include this form with either a PIC envelope or Divemaster Application, OR 2) attach a clear photocopy of the **front** and **back** of your certification card(s) or validation card(s) to this form.

Index

A

actual bottom time   211
adjusted no-decompression limit   207
Advanced Open Water Diver program   248
air   187 - 189
air-depletion exercise   244 - 245
airway control   78
alcohol   185
allergies   16 - 17
alternate air source   44, 90 - 93, 154, 162 - 165
alternate inflator regulator   91 - 92
altitude   226
aquatic life   128 - 131
ascent rate   198 - 199
ascents   67
assisting another diver   152 - 153
atmosphere, as pressure reference   10

B

backpacks   41 - 42
BCD (see buoyancy control device)
bends (see decompression sickness)
boat diving   144 - 148
body air spaces   13 - 19
body suits   80
boots   86
bottom composition   126 - 127
bottom time   197
breathing   18, 20, 75 - 78
breathing, effects of air at depth   187 - 195
buddy breathing   155, 220 - 222
buddy system   47 - 48, 105 - 107
buoyancy   6 - 7
buoyacy control   219 - 220
buoyancy control device   32 - 34, 53, 55, 59 - 60
buoyant emergency ascent   155

C

certification   3, 5
choking on water   150
cold conditions   227
colds   16 - 17
collecting bag   180 - 181
color   71
communications   101 - 105

compass   98 - 99, 235 - 238
computers   100
consoles (see instrument consoles)
contaminated air   188 - 189
Continuing Education program   247 - 248
controlled emergency swimming ascent   154, 165 - 166
controlled seated entry   109 - 110
CPR   149
cramp removal   116 - 117
currents   124 - 126, 135 - 138, 147

D

dead-air spaces   75 - 76
decompression diving   197, 225 - 226
decompression sickness   191 - 195
deep-water exit   118
density, air   10 - 12, 20
density, water   69
depth gauge   98
descents   66 - 67, 173 - 174
Discover Local Diving   249 - 250
displacement snorkel clearing   218
dive computers   228
dive flag   179 - 180
dive planning   141 - 143
dive profile   209 - 210
dive table definitions   233 - 235
dive tables   195 - 215
diver emergency services   149
diving instruments   97 - 101
diving safety practices, summary   255 - 258
donning equipment   54 - 58
drugs   185
dry suits   81

E

ear plugs   17
ears   13 - 17
emergency contact information   149
emergency decompression   225 - 226
entanglement   130 - 131, 156
entries   109 - 110, 169 - 170, 219
equalization   14 - 17, 65 - 66
equipment bag   95 - 96
equipment disassembly   68
equipment identification   47
equipment inspection   58
evaluating conditions   167 - 168

exits   67 - 68, 118, 147, 171 - 172
exposure suit accessories   85 - 87
exposure suits   79 - 84

F

fin pivot   161 - 162
fins   29 - 31, 58, 64
first aid   149
fish and game laws   130
floats   178
flutter kick   54
flying after diving   226 - 227
free-flowing regulator   155 - 156, 165
freshwater environments   132 - 133

G

gaining attention under water   104
gear bag (see equipment bag)
giant stride entry   110 - 111
gloves   86

H

hand signals   102 - 103
health for diving   185 - 186
hearing   72
heat, loss in water   72 - 73
hoods   85
hovering   219 - 220
hydrostatic test   40
hyperventilation   215 - 216

I

injuries, aquatic animal   129 - 130
instrument consoles   99 - 100
integrated instruments   100

K

knife   95

L

left-side-down, head supported position   194
lights   181 - 182
log book   184 - 185
longshore current   137
low-pressure inflator   33, 93 - 94

lung overpressurization   18
lungs   14

M

magnification, effect of water   70 - 71
mask   17, 22 - 25, 57
mask clearing   63 - 64
mask replacement under water   114 - 115
mask, breathing without   113 - 114
Master Scuba Diver rating   253
Medic First Aid   149, 251
medical statement   3
menstruation   186
minimum surface interval   229 - 233
modified tired-swimmer carry   117
motion   74
multilevel dives   214, 228
multiple repetitive dives   210 - 212

N

navigation   235 - 238
negative buoyancy   6 - 7
neoprene   82 - 83
neutral buoyancy   6 - 7, 65, 160 - 161, 219 - 220
nitrogen narcosis   190
no-decompression diving   197
no-decompression limit   202
no-mask breathing   113 - 114
no-mask swimming   159 - 160

O

ocean diving   135 - 139
offshore currents   135
overexertion   77, 154
overhead environments   134
overheating   87
oxygen   189

P

PADI   3
panic   151 - 152
plankton bloom   123
pony bottle   92
positive buoyancy   6 - 7
pre-dive safety drill   108 - 109
pregnancy   186
pressure   8 - 9

pressure group   203
pressure, effects on diver   13 - 19
pressure/volume/density relationships   10 - 12
problem management   148 - 158
purge valve   23, 63 - 64

Q

quick release, weight system   88

R

recall   105
recompression chamber   193 - 194
Recreational Dive Planner   195 - 215, 223 - 235
red tides   123
regulator clearing   60 - 61
regulator recovery   62 - 63
regulators   42 - 46, 50 - 53
repetitive diving   196 - 197, 210 - 212, 226
Rescue Diver course   149, 250 - 251
residual nitrogen   203
residual nitrogen time   207
respiration   75 - 78
reverse block   19
rip current   138
running out of air   154

S

safety practices, summary   255 - 258
safety stop   224
saltwater environments   133 - 134
scuba equipment assembly   50 - 53
Scuba Review   250
scuba unit removal and replacement   241 - 243
seasickness   145 - 146
shivering   73
sinuses   13 - 17
sitting back-roll entry   219
skin diving   215 - 218
slates   182, 213
smoking   185
snorkel   26 - 29
snorkel breathing   112
snorkel clearing   112, 218
snorkel/regulator exchanges   113
sound   72
spare-parts kit   183 - 184
Specialty Diver courses   251 - 252
squeeze   13 - 14

streamlining   74
strenuous conditions   227
submersible pressure gauge   46 - 47, 50 - 53, 99
suiting up   168 - 169
sunlight   132
surf   136, 170 - 172
surface dive   217 - 218
surface floats (see floats)
surface interval   205
surface swimming   172 - 173
surge   137

T

tank valve tow   117
tank valves   37 - 41
tanks   35 - 41, 50 - 53
teeth   14, 19
temperature, water   121 - 122
terms, boating   145
thermocline   121 - 122
thermometer   99
tides   140
timepieces   97 - 98
tired-diver tow   117
total bottom time   211

U

unconscious diver   157 - 158
undertow   137
upwelling   138 - 139

V

visibility   123 - 124
vision   70 - 71
vision correction   24
volume, air   10 - 12

W

waves   135 - 138
weight belt   54, 56, 88 - 90
weight belt handling   239 - 241
weight systems   88 - 90
weighting, proper   115 - 116
wet suit   54, 80
Wheel, The   214 - 215, 228